Magical Meals Made Easy

Magical Meals Made Easy

404 family favorites

Four Fantastic Foods
to Get Dinner on the Table FAST!

GIBBS
SMITH

This bindup edition published by Rodale Inc. in 2011 for Gibbs Smith, Publisher,
includes *101 Ways with Canned Soup, 101 Ways with Mac 'n' Cheese,
101 Ways with Meatballs*, and *101 Ways with Canned Biscuits*.

Casa Di Bertacchi® and Farm Rich® are registered trademarks of Rich Products Corporation.

Text © 2007, 2008, 2009, 2011 by Toni Patrick, Donna Kelly, and Stephanie Ashcraft

Photographs © 2011 by Rodale Inc.

Printed in the United States of America
Rodale Inc. makes every effort to use acid-free ∞, recycled paper ♺.

Book design by Christina Gaugler

Library of Congress Cataloging-in-Publication Data is on file with the publisher.

ISBN-13   978–1–4236–0672–7 hardcover

2   4   6   8   10   9   7   5   3   1   hardcover

For more information, contact Gibbs Smith at 800-835-4993 or
www.gibbs-smith.com.

GIBBS
SMITH

Contents

INTRODUCTION vii

CHAPTER 1: 101 Ways with Canned Soup 1

CHAPTER 2: 101 Ways with Mac 'n' Cheese 85

CHAPTER 3: 101 Ways with Meatballs 153

CHAPTER 4: 101 Ways with Canned Biscuits 229

INDEX 304

Introduction

What can you do with a box of macaroni and cheese, a can of soup, refrigerated biscuits, and frozen meatballs? Prepare 404 family favorite recipes at a moment's notice. Sure to please the whole family, these recipes are the answer to "What's for dinner?" When time is of the essence, but a home-cooked meal is desired, *Magical Meals Made Easy* comes to the rescue.

Keeping these four common ingredients—canned soup, macaroni and cheese, refrigerated biscuits, and frozen meatballs—in your pantry, fridge, or freezer arms you to prepare a slew of dishes (101 each to be exact!) such as soups, salads, casseroles, stews, burgers, chilis, pastas, breads, pies, cookies, and cakes. When choosing your meal, select one of these four key ingredients, then see what other ingredients you have on hand (or what you're in the mood for). Flip through the pages of *Magical Meals Made Easy* to find the perfect recipe. Another way to choose: Go to the mini table of contents at the beginning of each chapter, where you'll find a listing of recipes by category.

Any brand will work in these recipes, whether top name, off-brand, or generic. So go with the one you typically buy. Or, feel free to vary some of the recipes. Reach for classic mac and cheese with elbow pasta, or change it up with shells, spirals, or even whole wheat pasta. Many soups can be used interchangeably, particularly cream of mushroom, cream of celery, cream of broccoli, and cream of chicken. Watching your sodium or fat intake? No problem. The reduced fat or sodium variations work beautifully, too. Meatballs come in a variety of flavors. Original (sometimes called home style), Italian, Swedish, and cheese are the most common ones. Try them all and pick your favorite. When it comes to biscuits, select a package that's closest in size to the one called for in the ingredient list. Should you need regular biscuits and only have the extra-large ones, cut them in half or in quarters.

Become a kitchen magician by turning these four ordinary, quick products into extraordinary family dishes. Your friends and family will think you spent hours preparing a meal that tastes as though you did. Enjoy!

CHAPTER 1

101 Ways with

Canned Soup

Appetizers

Sour Cream Meatballs 3 • Salsa Nacho Cheese 3 • Baked Pepperoni Dip 4 •
Creamy Chicken Dip 4 • Pork Chili Dip 5 • Beefy Bean Dip 5 • World's Easiest
Cheese Fondue 6 • Savory Sun-Dried Tomato Cheesecake 7 • New England
Clam Dip 8 • Bean and Bacon Fondue 8 • Zesty Roast Beef Bites 9

Side Dishes

Decadent Spinach Casserole 10 • French Onion Mushroom Rice 10 • Squash
Cornbread Casserole 11 • Midwest Veggie Casserole 12 • Easy Cauliflower
Casserole 12 • Grilled Potatoes, Mushrooms, and Onion 13 • Vegetable Custard
Cups 14 • Souper Scalloped Potatoes 15 • World's Best Baked Beans 16 • Caesar
Veggie Bake 17 • Cheesy Baked Corn Pudding 18 • Creamy Baked Risotto
Primavera 19 • Classic Green Bean Bake 20

Soups & Stews

Sizzling Rice Soup 21 • Dinner Stew in a Pumpkin 22 • Wedding Soup 23 •
Chicken Enchilada Soup 24 • Creamy Corn Chowder 25 • Autumn Mushroom
Soup 25 • Bacon Red Potato Chowder 26 • Easy Clam Chowder 26 • Cheesy
Sausage Soup 27 • Pork Stew 27 • Oyster and Shrimp Soup 28 • Taco Stew 28

Poultry & Seafood

Weeknight Bistro Chicken 29 • Chicken Durango 30 • Southwest Chicken Polenta
Stacks 31 • Chile Verde Chicken Enchiladas 32 • Chicken and Broccoli Cups 33 •
Hot Turkey Salad 34 • Company's Coming Chicken 35 • Chicken Curry in a
Hurry 36 • Creamy Italian Chicken 37 • Chicken Fettuccine 37 • Parmesan Chicken

and Rice Bake 38 • Creamy Chicken Spaghetti 39 • Cornbread Chicken 40 • Chicken Cordon Bleu Bake 40 • Cajun Jambalaya 41 • Seafood Gumbo Casserole 41 • Maryland Crab Cakes 42

Beef & Pork

Souper Tamale Pie 43 • Broccoli Beef Stir-Fry 44 • Unstuffed Cabbage 45 • Corn Chip Casserole 46 • Effortless Beef and Mushrooms 46 • Tater Tot Gumbo Casserole 47 • Wrapped-Up Pot Roast 47 • Creamy Tender Cube Steaks 48 • Main Dish Bread Pudding 49 • Saucy Pork Chops 50 • Pork Chops and Potatoes 50 • Shredded Barbecue Pork Sandwiches 51 • Slow-Cooked Potatoes and Sausage 51 • Beef and Bean Burritos 52 • Polynesian Pork and Rice 53

Family Favorites

Specialty Sauces 54 • Winter Chili 56 • Upside-Down Pizza Casserole 57 • Classic Tuna Noodle Casserole 58 • Do-It-Yourself Quesadillas 59 • Sloppy Joes 60 • Debbie's Mushroom Burgers 60 • Yummy Meatballs 61 • Easy Chicken Potpie 61 • Hamburger Vegetable Pie 62 • Chile Relleno Casserole 63 • Harvest Veggie Stuffing Casserole 64 • Potluck Potatoes 65 • Never-Fail Veggie Soufflé 65 • Creamy Pasta Primavera 66 • Florentine Lasagna Rolls 67 • Cheesy Stuffed Mushrooms 68 • Family Favorite Meat Loaf 69

Breakfast or Brunch

Canadian Bacon and Egg English Muffins 70 • Spinach and Sausage Breakfast Casserole 71 • Breakfast Pizzas 72 • Baked Hash Brown and Ham Casserole 73 • Cheesy Egg and Sausage Casserole 74 • Mix 'n' Match Quiche 75 • Baked Brunch Enchiladas 76 • Ham and Asparagus Rolls 77

Baked Goods

Tomato Soup Cake 78 • Cheesy Mexicali Cornbread 79 • Savory Mushroom Muffins 80 • Baked Potato Biscuits 81 • No-Knead French Onion Bread 82 • Sweet Potato Pies 83 • Chocolate Zucchini Cake 84

Appetizers

Sour Cream Meatballs

5 pounds fully cooked frozen Italian meatballs, thawed

1 can (10.5 ounces) cream of onion soup, condensed

1 can (10.5 ounces) cream of mushroom soup, condensed

2 teaspoons minced garlic

¾ cup water

1 container (16 ounces) sour cream

Place meatballs in a greased 5- to 7-quart slow cooker.

In a bowl, combine soups, garlic, and water. Pour soup mixture evenly over meatballs. Cover and cook on low heat for 3–4 hours until heated. Stir in sour cream during the last 30 minutes of cooking. Serve hot with toothpicks. MAKES 20 SERVINGS.

Salsa Nacho Cheese

1 pound ground beef, browned and drained

1 jar (16 ounces) chunky salsa

1 can (10.5 ounces) tomato soup, condensed

2 pounds Velveeta cheese, cubed

Combine all ingredients in a greased 3½- to 5-quart slow cooker. Cook on high heat, stirring occasionally, for 1 hour or until cheese melts. Reduce heat to low or warm until ready to serve. Serve with tortilla chips. MAKES 15 SERVINGS.

Baked Pepperoni Dip

½ pound pepperoni, cubed

1 can (10.5 ounces) cream of celery soup, condensed*

1 package (8 ounces) cream cheese, softened

Preheat oven to 350 degrees.

In a greased 8 x 8-inch baking pan, combine pepperoni, soup, and cream cheese. Bake 25 minutes, or until light brown and bubbly. Serve with toasted baguette slices, mini bagel halves, or breadsticks. MAKES 6–8 SERVINGS.

*Cream of chicken or cream of mushroom soup can be substituted.

Creamy Chicken Dip

1 can (10–12.5 ounces) chunk chicken, drained and shredded

1 can (14.5 ounces) diced tomatoes with green chiles, with liquid

1 package (8 ounces) cream cheese, softened

1 can (10.5 ounces) cream of chicken soup, condensed

1 can (10.75 ounces) nacho cheese soup, condensed

Combine all ingredients in a medium saucepan. Cook 20 minutes over medium heat, stirring constantly until bubbly. Serve with tortilla chips, French bread cubes, toasted baguette slices, or crackers. MAKES 10–12 SERVINGS.

COOKING TIP

Using canned soup as a convenience item is a smart way to make delicious and almost effortless meals quickly. Soups come in a wide variety, including health-conscious and international recipes.

Pork Chili Dip

½ pound cooked ham, finely chopped

8 ounces Velveeta Mexican cheese, cubed

1 can (10 ounces) diced tomatoes with green chiles, with liquid

1 can (10.5 ounces) cream of mushroom soup, condensed

1 can (4.25 ounces) chopped black olives, drained

1 can (15 ounces) chili

Combine all ingredients in a 3-quart saucepan. Cook over medium heat, stirring slowly until cheese is completely melted. Serve with tortilla chips or strips. MAKES 10–12 SERVINGS.

VARIATION: *This can also be made in a greased slow cooker over high heat. Once cheese is melted, reduce heat to low to serve.*

CHEESY VARIATION: *Add an extra 8 ounces Velveeta Mexican cheese.*

Beefy Bean Dip

1 pound ground beef, browned and drained

1 can (10.75 ounces) nacho cheese soup, condensed

1 can (16 ounces) refried beans

1 jar (16 ounces) hot salsa

1 can (4 ounces) diced green chiles

½ pound Velveeta cheese, cubed

In a 3- to 4-quart saucepan, combine cooked beef, soup, beans, salsa, chiles, and cheese. Cook over medium heat, stirring every once in a while until melted and bubbly. Serve with tortilla chips or strips. MAKES 10–12 SERVINGS.

VARIATION: *For a hotter version, use jalapeño peppers in place of green chiles.*

World's Easiest Cheese Fondue

2 cans (10.75 ounces each) cheddar cheese soup, condensed

1 can (12 ounces) evaporated milk

1 teaspoon Worcestershire sauce

1 teaspoon dry mustard

½ cup white grape juice

8 ounces Swiss or Havarti cheese, grated

1 tablespoon flour

8 to 10 cups cubed lightly steamed vegetables*

1 loaf French bread, cut into cubes

In a medium saucepan, mix together soup, milk, Worcestershire sauce, dry mustard, and grape juice. Bring to a simmer over medium heat. Toss cheese with flour and then stir into pan; turn off heat. Pour into a fondue pot for serving. Serve warm with vegetables and bread for dipping. MAKES 6–8 SERVINGS.

*Try using broccoli, cauliflower, zucchini, potatoes, and squash.

COOKING TIP

This book is designed to keep the number of ingredients to a minimum. Generally, the fewer the ingredients, the more important it is to use better-quality ingredients. Check soup labels to make sure they have the quality and quantity of ingredients that will work with your recipes.

Savory Sun-Dried Tomato Cheesecake

1½ cups crushed club crackers

¼ cup butter, melted

¼ cup grated Parmesan cheese

2 packages (8 ounces each) cream cheese, softened

1 can (10.75 ounces) cream of onion soup, condensed

½ cup sour cream

1 tablespoon lemon juice

4 large eggs

1 jar (8 ounces) sun-dried tomatoes in oil, drained

Preheat oven to 350 degrees.

In a bowl, mix together cracker crumbs, butter, and Parmesan cheese. Spread mixture in the bottom of a 9-inch springform pan.

In a separate bowl, mix cream cheese, soup, sour cream, lemon juice, and eggs with a mixer on medium-high speed. Finely mince tomatoes and add while mixing. Pour mixture on top of crust and bake 45–50 minutes, or until center is nearly set and top is lightly browned. Turn off oven and let sit 15 minutes before removing. Remove from oven and remove sides of pan. Bring to room temperature before serving. Spread on thin toasted slices of bagels or French bread to serve. MAKES 10–12 SERVINGS.

SAVORY PESTO CHEESECAKE VARIATION: *Replace sun-dried tomatoes with 1 jar (6 ounces) pesto.*

SAVORY SMOKED SALMON CHEESECAKE VARIATION: *Replace soup with cream of shrimp soup. Replace sun-dried tomatoes with 1 package (6 ounces) Nova Scotia–style smoked salmon, finely minced.*

New England Clam Dip

1 package (8 ounces) cream cheese, softened

1 can (15 ounces) New England clam chowder, condensed

1 teaspoon Worcestershire sauce

1 teaspoon grated horseradish or more, to taste

1 teaspoon white pepper

3 green onions, thinly sliced with tops included

2 cans (6 ounces each) minced clams, well drained

Stir together all ingredients until well blended and then pour into a small serving bowl. Refrigerate 2 hours or more. Serve chilled with chips. MAKES 2½ CUPS.

Bean and Bacon Fondue

2 cans (11.5 ounces each) bean with bacon soup, condensed

1 envelope taco seasoning

½ cup salsa

1 cup sour cream

½ cup grated cheddar cheese

In a 2-quart saucepan, combine soup, taco seasoning, and salsa. Cook over medium heat until bubbly. Stir in sour cream and cheese. Cook an additional 2–3 minutes until hot. Serve with lightly toasted tortilla triangles, French bread cubes, and tortilla chips. MAKES 6–8 SERVINGS.

Zesty Roast Beef Bites

8 ounces cream cheese, softened

½ can (10.75 ounces) cream of onion soup, condensed

1 tablespoon grated horseradish or more, to taste

16 ounces cooked deli roast beef, sliced ⅛ inch thick

In a food processor, mix cream cheese, soup, and horseradish until well blended. Spread a thick layer of this mixture on each slice of roast beef. Roll up widthwise. Chill in refrigerator 1–2 hours, or until cream cheese mixture is firm. Remove and slice into ½-inch-thick slices. Place on a serving plate so that cut spiral side is showing. MAKES ABOUT 30 BITES.

COOKING TIP

For recipes that call for minced garlic, prepared jarred garlic may be used.

Side Dishes

Decadent Spinach Casserole

½ medium onion, chopped

1 tablespoon olive oil

1 can (10.5 ounces) cream of celery soup, condensed

1 square (3 ounces) cream cheese, softened

2 packages (10 ounces each) chopped frozen spinach, thawed and drained

⅓ cup real crumbled bacon bits or pieces*

½ cup crushed seasoned croutons

Preheat oven to 350 degrees.

Sauté onion in olive oil. Stir soup and cream cheese into onion until cream cheese melts. Stir in spinach and bacon. Pour into a greased 1- to 1½-quart casserole dish. Sprinkle croutons over top. Bake 35–40 minutes, or until bubbly. MAKES 6 SERVINGS.

*4–5 slices bacon can be cooked and crumbled instead of using bacon bits.

French Onion Mushroom Rice

1 cup uncooked long-grain rice

¼ cup butter, melted

1 can (10.5 ounces) French onion soup, condensed

1 can (10.5 ounces) beef broth

1 teaspoon minced garlic

1 can (4 ounces) sliced mushrooms, drained

Preheat oven to 350 degrees.

In a bowl, combine rice and butter. Stir in soup, broth, garlic, and mushrooms. Spread rice mixture into a greased 8 × 8-inch pan. Cover with foil and then bake 60 minutes. MAKES 4 SERVINGS.

Squash Cornbread Casserole

1 box (8.5 ounces) corn muffin mix

2 to 3 medium yellow summer squash, peeled and cubed

¼ cup butter

1 can (10.5 ounces) cream of chicken soup, condensed

1 cup sour cream

1 tablespoon sugar

1 green bell pepper, chopped

1 medium onion, chopped

salt and pepper, to taste

Follow directions on the mix to make cornbread. Bake in a greased 8 × 8-inch pan according to directions. Preheat oven to 375 degrees. Boil squash in water until tender; drain.

In a large bowl, combine cooked squash and remaining ingredients. Crumble cornbread and stir it into squash mixture. Place mixture in a 2-quart casserole dish. Bake about 35–40 minutes, or until golden brown. MAKES 6 SERVINGS.

COOKING TIP

Cream of chicken, cream of onion, cream of mushroom, and cream of celery condensed soups can be used interchangeably in most recipes.

Midwest Veggie Casserole

- 1 can (11 ounces) white shoepeg corn, drained
- 1 can (14.5 ounces) French-cut green beans, drained
- 1 can (5 ounces) water chestnuts, drained and chopped
- ½ medium onion, chopped
- 1 can (10.5 ounces) cream of celery soup, condensed
- 1 cup sour cream
- 1 cup grated cheddar cheese
- 35 round snack crackers, crushed

Preheat oven to 350 degrees.

In a greased 9 × 9-inch pan, layer corn, green beans, water chestnuts, and onion.

In a bowl, combine soup and sour cream. Spread mixture over layered vegetables. Sprinkle cheese and then crackers over top. Bake 30–35 minutes, or until bubbly. MAKES 6–8 SERVINGS.

Easy Cauliflower Casserole

- 1 head cauliflower, washed and cut into florets
- 1 can (10.5 ounces) cream of chicken soup, condensed*
- ⅓ cup mayonnaise
- 1 teaspoon Worcestershire sauce
- 1 cup grated cheddar cheese
- ½ cup crushed seasoned croutons

Preheat oven to 350 degrees.

In a saucepan, boil cauliflower until tender. Drain and place in a greased 2-quart casserole dish. Stir in soup, mayonnaise, Worcestershire, and cheese. Sprinkle croutons over top and then bake 30 minutes. MAKES 6 SERVINGS.

*Condensed cheddar cheese soup can be substituted.

Grilled Potatoes, Mushrooms, and Onion

6 medium potatoes, thinly sliced

salt and pepper, to taste

1 can (10.5 ounces) cream of mushroom soup, condensed

1 package (6 ounces) sliced fresh mushrooms

1 medium onion, thinly sliced

¼ cup butter, cut into small cubes

2 teaspoons Italian seasoning

1 teaspoon minced garlic

Preheat an outdoor grill.

Place a large, heavy duty aluminum foil strip, big enough to hold all the ingredients, shiny side up on the counter. Lightly spray foil with vegetable oil. Place potatoes evenly over the center of the foil, leaving room around all the edges. Salt and pepper to taste. Spread soup over potatoes. Layer mushrooms and onion over soup layer. Place butter over and around the vegetables. Sprinkle seasonings over top. Fold foil over or top with another layer of aluminum foil. Seal edges by folding. Grill over medium heat on top rack for 50–60 minutes or until vegetables are tender. MAKES 6–8 SERVINGS.

COOKING TIP

Generally, use canned soups that would be good enough to eat alone and are made with only water or milk added.

Vegetable Custard Cups

1 can (10.75 ounces) cream of celery soup, condensed

3 large eggs

¼ teaspoon nutmeg

½ teaspoon white pepper

2 cups finely diced lightly steamed vegetables*

2 cups grated Monterey Jack cheese

2 tablespoons grated Parmesan cheese

Preheat oven to 350 degrees.

Process all ingredients in a food processor or blender. Pour mixture into six 1-cup custard baking cups that have been sprayed with nonstick cooking spray. Set cups in a 9 × 13-inch baking pan and fill pan with hot water until level is halfway up the sides of the cups. Bake 40–45 minutes, or until set in center and lightly brown on top. Let sit 5 minutes before serving. MAKES 6 SERVINGS.

*Try using any combination of broccoli, cauliflower, spinach, mushrooms, squash, and onions.

COOKING TIP

The first time you try baking a recipe, check the food 3–5 minutes before its minimum cooking time ends. Each oven heats differently, so cooking times can vary.

Souper Scalloped Potatoes

½ cup thinly sliced celery

½ cup diced onion

2 cans (10.75 ounces each) cheddar cheese soup, condensed

1 can (12 ounces) evaporated milk

8 cups peeled and thinly sliced russet potatoes

1 cup grated cheddar cheese

Preheat oven to 350 degrees.

In a bowl, mix together celery, onion, soup, and evaporated milk. Layer in a 9 × 13-inch pan in the following order: half the soup mixture, half the potato slices, and half the cheese; repeat layers. Cover with foil and bake 50 minutes. Uncover and bake another 20–30 minutes, or until cooked through, bubbly, and golden brown on top. MAKES 6–8 SERVINGS.

CELERY VARIATION: *Replace soup with cream of celery soup. Mix 1 teaspoon celery salt into soup. Replace cheddar cheese with Swiss or Havarti cheese.*

SOUTHWEST VARIATION: *Replace soup with southwest pepper jack soup. Replace celery with 1 can (4 ounces) diced mild green chiles. Replace cheddar cheese with pepper jack cheese.*

World's Best Baked Beans

4 strips bacon, diced

1 yellow onion, diced

1 green bell pepper, diced

1 red bell pepper, diced

1 can (10.75 ounces) tomato soup, condensed

2 tablespoons mustard

1 teaspoon liquid smoke

¼ cup brown sugar

1 can (16 ounces) white beans, drained

1 can (16 ounces) pinto beans, drained

2 cans (16 ounces each) baked beans, with liquid

Preheat oven to 350 degrees.

In a frying pan, cook bacon pieces over medium-high heat until crisp. Add onion and bell peppers and cook another 2–3 minutes, or until limp. Drain oil and then transfer mixture to a 3- to 4-quart casserole dish. Add remaining ingredients and mix well. Bake about 1 hour, or until cooked in center and bubbly around edges. MAKES 10–12 SERVINGS.

Caesar Veggie Bake

2 bags (16 ounces each) frozen broccoli, carrots, and cauliflower

1 can (10.75 ounces) cream of celery soup, condensed

1 can (10.75 ounces) cream of onion soup, condensed

1 container (8 ounces) garlic-and-herb-flavored cream cheese, softened

½ cup grated Parmesan cheese

1 bag (6 ounces) garlic or Caesar flavored croutons, crushed

Preheat oven to 350 degrees.

Cook veggies until just tender according to package directions.

In a large bowl, stir together soups, cream cheese, and Parmesan cheese and then mix with cooked vegetables. Spread in a 2-quart casserole dish and sprinkle croutons over top. Bake 25–30 minutes, or until browned and bubbling. MAKES 6–8 SERVINGS.

COOKING TIP

The sodium content of soups varies, so use salt carefully in recipes, adding only a little at a time and tasting as you go. If watching sodium, reach for the low-sodium version of the soup called for in recipes.

Cheesy Baked Corn Pudding

1 can (10.75 ounces) cream of celery soup, condensed

½ cup milk

½ cup sour cream

3 large eggs

2 cups fresh or thawed frozen corn

½ cup cornmeal

1 cup grated white cheese*

¼ cup grated Parmesan cheese

3 tablespoons thinly sliced green onion

Preheat oven to 350 degrees.

In a food processor or blender, blend soup, milk, sour cream, and eggs until smooth. Pour into an 8 × 8-inch baking pan that has been sprayed with nonstick cooking spray. Stir in corn, cornmeal, cheese, and onion. Bake 40–45 minutes, or until firm in center and lightly brown on top. MAKES 4–6 SERVINGS.

*Any mild firm white cheese works well here such as mozzarella, Monterey Jack, provolone, Havarti, or Baby Swiss.

COOKING TIP

For an emergency dinner, try creating sauces using undiluted cans of condensed soups with fresh herbs, spices, and a few finely minced onions or garlic cloves to add flavor. Use sauces to flavor cooked meats, vegetables, and/or pastas.

Creamy Baked
Risotto Primavera

- 1 can (10.75 ounces) cream of asparagus soup, condensed
- 1½ cups water
- 1 can (12 ounces) evaporated milk
- ¼ cup grated Parmesan cheese
- 1 teaspoon salt
- 1 cup diced asparagus
- ½ cup diced bell pepper, any color
- 1 cup uncooked risotto rice*
- 2 tablespoons dried basil or parsley flakes

Preheat oven to 400 degrees.

In a bowl, stir together all ingredients. Pour into a 2½-quart casserole dish. Cover and bake 30 minutes and then uncover and stir. Bake uncovered another 10 minutes. Remove from oven and let stand 10 minutes before serving. Garnish with additional parsley or basil flakes, if desired. MAKES 6–8 SERVINGS.

*Do not rinse risotto before using in recipe. This will destroy the starch, and risotto will not be creamy.

GARLIC MUSHROOM VARIATION: *Replace asparagus soup with cream of mushroom and roasted garlic soup. Replace asparagus with diced button mushrooms. Replace bell peppers with diced yellow onion.*

Classic Green Bean Bake

4 cups fresh green beans*

1 can (10.75 ounces) cream of mushroom soup, condensed

½ cup milk

1 tablespoon soy sauce

1 can (3.5 ounces) french-fried onions, divided

Preheat oven to 350 degrees.

Cut ends from green beans. Steam or microwave green beans to tender-crisp stage, about 3 minutes. In a 2-quart casserole dish, mix soup, milk, soy sauce, beans, and half the onions. Bake 25–30 minutes, or until bubbly on sides and cooked through. Remove from oven, stir, and then sprinkle remaining onions over top. Bake for another 10–12 minutes, or until onions are browned. MAKES 4–6 SERVINGS.

*Frozen and thawed green beans can be substituted for a quicker version.

MEDITERRANEAN-STYLE VARIATION: *Omit the soy sauce and onions. Add 1 teaspoon Italian seasoning and ¼ cup grated Parmesan cheese. Top with sliced tomatoes and ½ cup grated mozzarella cheese.*

SOUTHWEST-STYLE VARIATION: *Omit soy sauce, milk, and onions. Replace soup with southwest pepper jack soup. Add ½ cup salsa. Top with ½ cup grated cheddar cheese and 1 cup crushed corn chips.*

ASIAN-STYLE VARIATION: *Omit the onions. Add 1 can (4 ounces) sliced water chestnuts, chopped. Top with 1 cup crunchy chow mein noodles.*

Soups & Stews

Sizzling Rice Soup

2 cups cooked white rice

2 cans (26 ounces each) chicken and rice soup, condensed

8 cups water

½ pound cooked deli tiny cocktail shrimp

1 cup thinly sliced green onions

1 can (8 ounces) sliced water chestnuts, drained and chopped

1 cup frozen peas or frozen pea pods, chopped

2 cups thinly sliced celery

¼ cup soy sauce

2 tablespoons peanut oil

Preheat oven to 300 degrees.

Spread rice onto a large jellyroll pan sprayed with nonstick cooking spray. Bake 60 minutes, stirring occasionally to break up any clumps. About 10 minutes before rice is done baking, place all remaining ingredients except peanut oil in a large stockpot. Bring to a boil and then simmer for 10 minutes. Ladle soup into serving bowls and place on table.

In a large frying pan or wok, heat peanut oil. Remove rice from oven and immediately cook in wok for 3–5 minutes over medium-high heat, stirring constantly until rice is lightly brown and puffed. Add about ¼ cup rice to each serving bowl. Enjoy the sizzle—it will only last a few seconds, but will be a showstopper! MAKES 8 SERVINGS.

Dinner Stew in a Pumpkin

1 medium whole pumpkin, about 8 to 10 pounds

3 large potatoes, peeled

1 yellow onion

4 stalks celery

3 carrots, peeled

3 boneless, skinless chicken breasts, cooked

2 tablespoons butter

1 can (26 ounces) cream of chicken soup, condensed

8 ounces sliced mushrooms

1 tablespoon garlic powder

1 tablespoon seasoned salt

1 tablespoon Worcestershire sauce

Preheat oven to 350 degrees.

Cut the top off the pumpkin so that the lid can still sit on top. Clean out the seeds and slime; place pumpkin on a baking sheet. Dice all vegetables and chicken to uniform sized ½-inch cubes.

In a large frying pan, cook potatoes in butter about 3 minutes over medium-high heat. Stir in onion, celery, and carrots and cook another 5 minutes, stirring occasionally, until all vegetables are cooked through to firm stage. Mix in chicken, soup, mushrooms, garlic powder, salt, and Worcestershire sauce. Pour this mixture into pumpkin and place top back on pumpkin. Place in oven on lowest rack and bake 1 hour. Remove top and bake another 20–30 minutes, or until mixture inside is bubbling. Place whole pumpkin on table as a centerpiece. Serve in large flat bowls. When serving, scoop out some of the pumpkin meat with the stew mixture. MAKES 8–10 SERVINGS.

Wedding Soup

1 **pound ground turkey**

2 **large eggs**

¼ **cup seasoned breadcrumbs**

¼ **cup grated Parmesan cheese**

2 **cans (26 ounces each) chicken and rice soup, condensed**

6 **cups water**

1 **box (10 ounces) frozen chopped spinach**

In a medium mixing bowl, mix together turkey, eggs, breadcrumbs, and cheese. Form mixture into small balls the size of marbles.

In a large pot, bring soup, water, and spinach to a boil. Meanwhile, sauté meatballs in a frying pan sprayed with nonstick cooking spray, stirring often until well browned. Add browned meatballs to soup mixture and simmer for about 5 minutes. Serve hot with additional cheese sprinkled on top as a garnish, if desired. MAKES 8–10 SERVINGS.

Chicken Enchilada Soup

½ cup thinly sliced green onion

1 cup cooked diced chicken

2 tablespoons butter

1 can (10.75 ounces) chicken chile verde soup, condensed

1 can (20 ounces) red enchilada sauce

1 can (14 ounces) chicken broth

1 teaspoon chili powder

1 teaspoon cumin

1 cup sour cream

1 cup grated cheddar cheese

4 corn tortillas

Sauté onion and chicken in butter in a large saucepan over medium-high heat until onion is limp and chicken is lightly browned. Stir in soup, enchilada sauce, broth, and spices. Bring to a simmer. Stir in sour cream and cheese. Simmer a few minutes more until cheese is melted. Remove from heat. Cut tortillas into very thin, matchstick-size strips. Stir tortilla strips into soup just before serving. MAKES 4–6 SERVINGS.

FOOD FACT

On average, Americans purchase 80 cans of Campbell's soups every second of every day of the year, or 290,520 cans per hour.

Creamy Corn Chowder

2 tablespoons butter

½ cup thinly sliced green onion

½ cup diced cooked ham

2 cups fresh or thawed frozen corn

2 cans (10.75 ounces each) cream of potato soup, condensed

2 cups milk

½ teaspoon pepper

½ cup sour cream

Heat butter in a large soup pot over medium-high heat. Add onion and sauté until limp, about 2 minutes, stirring frequently. Add remaining ingredients except sour cream and simmer for 15–20 minutes, stirring occasionally. Remove from heat and stir in sour cream; serve warm. MAKES 6–8 SERVINGS.

Autumn Mushroom Soup

6 ounces sliced fresh mushrooms

½ tablespoon minced garlic

¼ cup butter or margarine

2 cans (10.75 ounces each) cream of mushroom soup, condensed

1 cup half-and-half

1 cup milk

1 teaspoon dried rosemary, crushed

½ teaspoon paprika

In a 2-quart saucepan, sauté mushrooms and garlic in butter until tender. Stir in soup, half-and-half, milk, rosemary, and paprika. Cook over medium-low heat without boiling until hot. Serve in bread bowls. MAKES 4 SERVINGS.

CREAMY VARIATION: *Before serving, blend soup in batches in a blender or food processor.*

Bacon Red Potato Chowder

  8 slices bacon, cut into 1-inch pieces

  2 cups cubed new red potatoes

  ½ medium onion, chopped

  1 cup sour cream

1¼ cups milk

  1 can (10.5 ounces) cream of chicken soup, condensed

  1 can (11 ounces) Green Giant Mexicorn, drained

  ½ teaspoon pepper

  ½ teaspoon crushed thyme

In a 3-quart saucepan, cook bacon over medium heat for 5 minutes; add potatoes and onion. Continue cooking, stirring occasionally, until potatoes are tender, about 15–20 minutes. Add remaining ingredients. Reduce heat to medium-low and continue cooking, stirring constantly, until heated through, about 10–15 minutes. MAKES 6–8 SERVINGS.

Easy Clam Chowder

  1 can (14.5 ounces) diced potatoes, drained

  1 can (10.5 ounces) cream of celery soup, condensed

  1 can (10.75 ounces) cream of potato soup, condensed

  1 can (6.5 ounces) minced clams, with liquid

  ¼ cup dried minced onion

2½ cups half-and-half

  1 teaspoon pepper

In a 3-quart pan, combine all ingredients. Simmer over medium heat without boiling, stirring occasionally until hot and onions are reconstituted. MAKES 6–8 SERVINGS.

Cheesy Sausage Soup

　1　pound sage-flavored ground sausage

　1　small onion, diced

　1　package (8.8 ounces) precooked long-grain and wild rice

　2　cans (10.75 ounces each) cream of potato soup, condensed

1¼　cups milk

　1　can (12 ounces) evaporated milk

　2　cups grated cheddar cheese

In a frying pan, brown sausage and onion together until meat is crumbly and cooked; drain if necessary.

In a 4-quart pot, combine sausage and onion with rice, soup, milk, and evaporated milk. Cook over medium heat until warm. Slowly stir in cheese and continue to cook over medium heat until cheese is melted. MAKES 6–8 SERVINGS.

Pork Stew

1½　pounds pork stew meat, cubed*

　2　cans (10.75 ounces each) golden mushroom soup, condensed

　1　medium onion, chopped

25　baby carrots, cut into thirds

　6　ounces sliced fresh mushrooms

In a greased 4- to 5½-quart slow cooker, combine all ingredients. Cover and cook on high heat for 3–4 hours or on low heat for 6–8 hours. MAKES 8–10 SERVINGS.

*Venison or beef stew meat can be used in place of pork.

Oyster and Shrimp Soup

1 can (10.75 ounces) cream of shrimp soup, condensed

1 can (10.5 ounces) cream of potato soup, condensed

1 can (10.75 ounces) oyster stew, condensed

1 cup small shrimp, cooked and peeled

2 cups half-and-half

½ cup milk

1 teaspoon thyme or rosemary

½ teaspoon pepper

Combine all ingredients in a 3- to 4-quart saucepan. Stirring constantly, simmer over medium heat for 20 minutes until heated through. Serve with French bread and oyster crackers. MAKES 6–8 SERVINGS.

Taco Stew

1 pound ground beef, browned and drained

1 envelope taco seasoning

1 can (10.75 ounces) tomato soup, condensed

1 can (15.25 ounces) black beans, rinsed and drained

4 cups water

½ medium onion, chopped

4 carrots, chopped

3 potatoes, peeled and cubed

1 can (15.25 ounces) kernel corn, with liquid

Combine all ingredients in a 4- to 6-quart pot. Bring to a boil. Reduce heat and simmer an additional 35–45 minutes, or until vegetables are done. MAKES 6–8 SERVINGS.

Poultry & Seafood

Weeknight Bistro Chicken

- 4 boneless, skinless chicken breasts
- 3 tablespoons peanut or canola oil
- 1 can (14 ounces) diced tomatoes, undrained
- 1 can (10.75 ounces) French onion soup, condensed
- 1 can (10.75 ounces) golden mushroom soup, condensed
- 2 tablespoons minced garlic
- 2 cups grated Swiss or Havarti cheese
- 8 cups cooked rice or egg noodles

Lay chicken breasts flat on a cutting board. With a large flat knife parallel to the cutting surface, cut each chicken breast in half, forming two large flat planks. Sauté chicken planks in batches in a large frying pan in oil over medium-high heat until browned, about 2 minutes on each side. Place browned chicken in a 4- to 6-quart slow cooker.

In a bowl, mix together remaining ingredients except cheese and noodles and pour into slow cooker, moving chicken planks so that sauce is evenly distributed throughout. Cook on high heat for 3–4 hours or low heat for 6–8 hours. Remove chicken to an ovenproof serving platter. Sprinkle with cheese. Broil in oven for 2–3 minutes, or until cheese is bubbling and lightly browned. Mash sauce with a potato masher until there are no large chunks. Use sauce to top rice or noodles. MAKES 4–6 SERVINGS.

Chicken Durango

3 tablespoons butter

3 boneless, skinless chicken breasts

1 large yellow onion, julienned

1 green bell pepper, julienned

1 red bell pepper, julienned

1 can (10.75 ounces) chicken chile verde soup, condensed*

½ cup water

½ cup sour cream

8 cups hot cooked regular or Spanish rice

Heat butter in a large frying pan or wok. Thinly slice chicken breasts and sauté over medium-high heat until chicken turns white. Add onion and bell peppers and cook until onion is translucent, about 3 minutes.

In a bowl, mix together soup, water, and sour cream. Pour into the pan with the chicken and simmer about 2 minutes. Serve over rice. MAKES 6–8 SERVINGS.

*Cream of chicken soup can be substituted.

COOKING TIP

One-dish meals make dinnertime a breeze. To make cleanup easier, spray baking pans with nonstick cooking spray before adding ingredients.

Southwest Chicken Polenta Stacks

3 boneless, skinless chicken breasts, diced

2 tablespoons canola oil

1 green bell pepper, diced

1 large onion, diced

2 cans (10.75 ounces each) Southwest pepper jack soup, condensed

2 tubes (18 ounces each) ready-to-eat polenta

4 cups grated pepper jack cheese

1 red bell pepper, diced

In a medium frying pan, sauté chicken in oil over medium-high heat until lightly browned. Add green bell pepper and onion. Sauté for 2–3 minutes, or until onion is limp. Stir in soup and reduce heat to low. Slice polenta into ½-inch-thick slices and arrange on a large serving platter. Microwave 2 minutes until heated through. Spoon chicken mixture onto polenta slices. Sprinkle cheese and then red bell pepper on top. Serve warm, two or three stacks per person. MAKES 6–8 SERVINGS.

Chile Verde Chicken Enchiladas

18 corn tortillas

3 tablespoons butter

1 rotisserie chicken, about 4 to 5 pounds

1 can (14 ounces) green or red enchilada sauce

1 can (10.75 ounces) chicken chile verde soup, condensed*

16 ounces Monterey Jack cheese, grated

½ cup thinly sliced green onion

Preheat oven to 375 degrees.

In a frying pan, sauté each tortilla over medium-high heat in a little of the butter until cooked through but not crisp, about 1 minute on each side. Remove meat from chicken and shred with two forks.

In a small mixing bowl, mix together enchilada sauce and soup. Pour 1 cup of sauce in the bottom of a 9 × 13-inch pan. Roll about ⅓ cup cheese, ¼ cup shredded chicken, and 1 teaspoon green onion in each tortilla. Place each roll in pan, seam side down. Pour remaining sauce over top of rolls and sprinkle remaining cheese on top. Bake 25–30 minutes, or until cooked through and bubbling. MAKES 8 SERVINGS.

*Cream of chicken soup can be substituted.

CHEESE ENCHILADA VARIATION: *Instead of chicken use a total of 32 ounces Monterey Jack cheese, grated. Replace soup with southwest pepper jack cheese soup.*

Chicken and Broccoli Cups

3 boneless, skinless chicken breasts, cooked and diced

1 can (10.75 ounces) broccoli cheddar soup, condensed

2 cups chopped, lightly steamed broccoli

1 carrot, peeled and grated

1 tablespoon Dijon mustard

1 teaspoon garlic powder

½ teaspoon white pepper

1 box (17 ounces) frozen puff pastry, thawed

½ cup grated Parmesan cheese

Preheat oven to 350 degrees.

In a large bowl, mix together the first 7 ingredients and set aside. Lay both pastry sheets on a nonstick surface. Cut each pastry sheet into 4 squares, forming a total of 8 squares. Press the pastry squares into large muffin tins or individual ramekins that have been sprayed with nonstick cooking spray. Fill each pastry cup with chicken mixture. Bake 25–30 minutes, or until bubbly and golden brown. Remove from oven and sprinkle Parmesan cheese over each cup. MAKES 8 SERVINGS.

FOOD FACT

The best-selling Campbell's soup of all time is tomato soup (they've been selling this variety since 1897).

Hot Turkey Salad

2 cans (10.75 ounces each) cream of celery soup, condensed

1 cup regular or light sour cream

2 tablespoons lemon juice

1 teaspoon salt

1 teaspoon white pepper

6 cups ½-inch cubed cooked turkey

2 cups finely diced celery

½ cup thinly sliced green onion

6 hard-boiled eggs, divided

¾ cup sliced toasted almonds, divided

Preheat oven to 350 degrees.

In a 3-quart casserole dish, stir together soup, sour cream, lemon juice, salt, and pepper. Stir in turkey, celery, and onion. Peel and slice eggs. Stir half the eggs and ½ cup almonds into chicken mixture. Sprinkle remaining eggs and almonds on top. Bake 40–50 minutes, or until cooked through and bubbly; serve warm. MAKES 6–8 SERVINGS.

Company's Coming Chicken

 2 tablespoons canola oil

10 skinless chicken thighs (about 5 pounds)

 2 teaspoons garlic powder

 2 cans (10.75 ounces each) golden mushroom soup, condensed

 2 tablespoons balsamic vinegar

 1 cup light sour cream

 2 cups thinly sliced button mushrooms

Preheat oven to 350 degrees.

In a large frying pan, heat oil to medium-high heat. Sauté chicken in batches for about 5 minutes on each side until well browned. Sprinkle garlic powder on cooked chicken. Mix together soup, vinegar, and sour cream. Spread ½ cup on bottom of a 9 × 13-inch pan. Place chicken in pan, completely filling pan. Sprinkle mushrooms evenly on top. Spread remaining soup mixture over top, completely covering top and sealing edges. Bake 60–70 minutes, or until well browned on top. Serve using excess sauce over cooked rice, noodles, or diced red potatoes, if desired. MAKES 4–6 SERVINGS.

Chicken Curry in a Hurry

2 pounds chicken breasts (about 4 breasts)

4 tablespoons extra virgin olive oil, divided

1 medium yellow onion, diced

2 cans (10.75 ounces each) cream of celery soup, condensed

1 can (14 ounces) coconut milk, shaken

1 tablespoon mild curry powder or curry paste

1 teaspoon ginger

1 teaspoon garlic powder

1 teaspoon salt

1 cup frozen tiny peas

½ cup roasted cashews, diced

8 cups cooked rice

Slice chicken into ¼-inch-thick slices, each about an inch long. Heat 2 tablespoons oil in a wok or large frying pan. Sauté chicken over medium-high heat until lightly browned, about 8–10 minutes. Remove chicken and add remaining oil and onion, sautéing about 3 minutes or until onion is translucent.

In a bowl, mix together soup, coconut milk, curry, and spices. Add soup mixture to wok and bring to a simmer, stirring constantly. Stir chicken back in and then add peas and cashews; turn off heat. Serve over rice. MAKES 6–8 SERVINGS.

Creamy Italian Chicken

4 boneless, skinless chicken breasts

1 envelope Italian salad dressing mix

¼ cup water

1 package (8 ounces) cream cheese, softened

1 can (10.75 ounces) cream of chicken soup, condensed

Preheat oven to 350 degrees.

Place chicken breasts on the bottom of a greased 9 × 13-inch pan. Combine salad dressing mix and water; spread evenly over chicken. Combine cream cheese and soup; spread evenly over chicken. Cover pan with foil and then bake 40 minutes. MAKES 4 SERVINGS.

Chicken Fettuccine

2 boneless, skinless chicken breasts, cubed

1 tablespoon minced garlic

½ medium onion, chopped

2 tablespoons olive oil

2 teaspoons Italian seasoning

1 can (10.5 ounces) cream of mushroom soup, condensed

½ cup milk

½ cup grated Parmesan cheese

1 bag (16 ounces) fettuccine pasta

In a large frying pan, sauté chicken, garlic, and onion in hot oil until chicken is no longer pink. Sprinkle seasoning over chicken. Stir in soup, milk, and cheese. Simmer over low heat 10–15 minutes. While sauce simmers, cook pasta according to package directions and drain. Serve sauce over hot cooked pasta. MAKES 3–4 SERVINGS.

Parmesan Chicken and Rice Bake

1   **pound boneless, skinless chicken breasts, cut into small pieces**

1   **tablespoon olive oil**

    salt and pepper, to taste

1   **can (10.5 ounces) cream of chicken soup, condensed**

1⅔   **cups milk**

½   **cup grated Parmesan cheese**

½   **teaspoon Italian seasoning**

1   **large tomato, diced**

2   **cups uncooked instant rice**

In a frying pan, sauté chicken in hot oil until lightly browned. Season with salt and pepper. While chicken cooks, combine soup, milk, cheese, and seasoning in a 2-quart saucepan. Heat until it starts to bubble. Stir in tomato and instant rice. Cover and cook over low heat for 5 minutes, or until rice is done. Serve chicken over individual servings of rice. MAKES 4 SERVINGS.

FOOD FACT

Americans buy 92 million gallons of soup in January.

Creamy Chicken Spaghetti

1 can (28 ounces) diced tomatoes seasoned with basil, garlic, and oregano, with liquid

1 medium onion, chopped

½ teaspoon minced garlic

1 package (16 ounces) spaghetti

1 can (10.5 ounces) cream of chicken soup, condensed

1 can (12.5 ounces) white chicken, with broth

1 tablespoon Worcestershire sauce

1 can (10.5 ounces) cream of mushroom soup, condensed

1 cup grated medium cheddar cheese

Preheat oven to 350 degrees. In a 2½- to 3-quart saucepan, combine tomatoes, onion, and garlic. Simmer over medium heat until onion is tender.

Cook spaghetti according to package directions. Stir cream of chicken soup, chicken, and Worcestershire sauce into tomato mixture. Simmer over low heat until spaghetti is done. Drain spaghetti and place in a greased 9 × 13-inch pan. Spoon hot chicken mixture over spaghetti noodles. Spread cream of mushroom soup over top. Sprinkle cheese over soup. Bake 15–20 minutes, or until bubbly. MAKES 6–8 SERVINGS.

Cornbread Chicken

1 (2.25-pound) lemon pepper rotisserie cooked whole chicken
1 bag (16 ounces) frozen mixed vegetables, thawed and drained
1 can (10.5 ounces) cream of chicken soup, condensed
1 can (10.5 ounces) cream of celery soup, condensed
½ teaspoon pepper
1 box (8.5 ounces) corn muffin mix

Preheat oven to 350 degrees. Shred cooked chicken meat.

In a bowl, combine chicken, vegetables, soups, and pepper. Spread chicken mixture into a greased 9 × 13-inch pan. Prepare muffin mix batter according to package directions. Pour batter evenly over chicken layer. Bake 30–35 minutes, or until golden brown and bubbly. MAKES 6–8 SERVINGS.

Chicken Cordon Bleu Bake

5 to 6 boneless, skinless chicken breasts, cubed
1 can (10.5 ounces) cream of celery soup, condensed
1 can (10.5 ounces) cream of chicken soup, condensed
½ pound cubed ham steak
8 ounces Swiss cheese, grated

Preheat oven to 375 degrees.

Place raw cubed chicken in a greased 9 × 13-inch pan. Spread soups over chicken. Layer ham and cheese over soup. Bake 40–50 minutes, or until chicken is done. MAKES 6–8 SERVINGS.

Cajun Jambalaya

½ red bell pepper, diced

½ green bell pepper, diced

1 box (8 ounces) frozen sliced okra

2 cups uncooked rice

1 can (10.75 ounces) French onion soup, condensed

3 cups water

1 teaspoon salt or more, to taste

¼ cup Louisiana-style cayenne pepper hot sauce (optional)

1 cup cooked chopped sausage, bacon, or ham

½ pound cooked cocktail shrimp

1 box (10 ounces) frozen peas

Combine bell peppers, okra, rice, soup, water, salt, and hot sauce in a wok or large frying pan. Cover and simmer 20–25 minutes, or until all liquid is absorbed and rice is cooked. Add meat, shrimp, and peas; heat through and serve hot. MAKES 6–8 SERVINGS.

Seafood Gumbo Casserole

2 cans (10.75 ounces each) chicken gumbo soup, condensed

2 cups water

1 teaspoon gumbo filé or Cajun seasoning

1 teaspoon garlic powder

1 bag (16 ounces) frozen okra, onions, and tomatoes

1 cup uncooked rice

½ cup diced ham

1 bag (16 ounces) frozen cooked cocktail shrimp

Preheat oven to 350 degrees.

Stir together all ingredients in a 2½- to 3-quart casserole dish. Bake 60 minutes. Remove from oven and stir before serving to fluff rice. MAKES 6–8 SERVINGS.

Maryland Crab Cakes

1 can (10.75 ounces) cream of shrimp soup, condensed

1 large egg

32 ounces fresh crabmeat*

½ cup minced green onion

2 tablespoons dried dill

2 tablespoons parsley

1 teaspoon Old Bay seasoning

1 cup toasted breadcrumbs

¼ cup peanut oil

In a medium mixing bowl, blend soup and egg with a fork until smooth. Stir in remaining ingredients, except oil, until blended. Make patties about 4 inches in diameter and 1½ inches thick. Chill patties in refrigerator for at least 30 minutes, or overnight. Heat oil in a medium frying pan to medium heat. Sauté patties, a few at a time, with pan covered for about 5 minutes on each side. Patties should be well browned. MAKES 12–15 PATTIES.

NOTE: *If patties don't stick together well after forming, return mixture to bowl and add more breadcrumbs as needed.*

*Crabmeat may be replaced with an equal amount of imitation crabmeat, but it must first be finely diced.

Beef & Pork

Souper Tamale Pie

1 pound lean ground beef

1 bunch green onions, thinly sliced (about 1 cup)

2 cans (15 ounces each) ready-to-serve steak fajita soup

1 can (6 ounces) tomato paste

2 cups frozen corn, thawed

1 can (4 ounces) sliced black olives

1 tablespoon chipotle chili powder or more, to taste

3 cups grated cheddar cheese, divided

1 large egg, lightly beaten with a fork

1 cup milk

2 tablespoons canola oil

¾ cup cornmeal

¾ cup flour

1 tablespoon baking powder

Preheat oven to 400 degrees.

In a frying pan, brown the ground beef; drain oil and place in a 3- to 4-quart casserole dish. Stir onions, soup, tomato paste, corn, olives, chili powder, and 2½ cups cheese into the cooked beef.

In a medium mixing bowl, stir egg, milk, and oil together. Mix dry ingredients together and stir into egg mixture. Pour on top of mixture in casserole. Bake 20–25 minutes, or until cornbread topping is cooked through in the middle and lightly browned on top. Remove from oven and sprinkle remaining cheese on top; serve warm. MAKES 8–10 SERVINGS.

VARIATION: *Replace ground beef with ground turkey or chicken. Replace soup with chicken fajita or chicken tortilla soup.*

Broccoli Beef Stir-Fry

16 ounces top round or sirloin steak

1 tablespoon minced garlic

1 tablespoon ginger

4 tablespoons cornstarch, divided

2 tablespoons soy sauce

2 tablespoons peanut oil

4 cups diced fresh broccoli

½ red bell pepper, sliced in thin strips

1 can (10.75 ounces) French onion soup, condensed

8 cups hot cooked rice

Slice beef in very thin strips and place in a small mixing bowl. Stir garlic, ginger, 2 tablespoons cornstarch, and soy sauce into beef. Let sit on counter at room temperature for 20 minutes to marinate. Heat oil in a large frying pan or wok. Sauté beef for about 2 minutes, stirring occasionally. Add broccoli and bell pepper and cook another 2 minutes, stirring occasionally. Drain a little of the broth from the soup into a small bowl and mix remaining cornstarch into broth. Add cornstarch mixture and remainder of soup to pan. Stir and cook another 3–5 minutes, or until sauce has thickened slightly. Serve immediately over hot rice. MAKES 6–8 SERVINGS.

Unstuffed Cabbage

1 small cabbage, shredded

2 pounds lean ground beef

1 large yellow onion, diced

1 tablespoon minced garlic

2 teaspoons seasoned salt

1 can (26 ounces) tomato soup, condensed

1 tablespoon Worcestershire sauce

2 tablespoons brown sugar

2 cups cooked rice

Preheat oven to 375 degrees.

In a large stockpot, bring about 2 quarts water to a boil. Turn off heat and add cabbage. Let stand 10 minutes to soften and then drain.

In a large frying pan or wok, cook the ground beef over medium-high heat until it is no longer pink, about 5 minutes, stirring frequently to break up clumps. Add onion, garlic, and salt to beef. Cook another 2–3 minutes, or until onion is limp. Stir in soup, Worcestershire sauce, and brown sugar.

In a 4-quart casserole dish, layer one-third of the cabbage, 1 cup rice, and half of the meat mixture; repeat layers and top with remaining cabbage. Cover and bake 45 minutes. Uncover and bake another 15 minutes. MAKES 8–10 SERVINGS.

Corn Chip Casserole

1 pound ground beef

1 can (10 ounces) tomatoes and green chiles, with liquid

1 can (10.5 ounces) cream of mushroom soup, condensed

1 can (15 ounces) black beans, rinsed and drained

3½ to 4 cups Fritos corn chips

1¾ cups grated cheddar cheese

Preheat oven to 350 degrees.

In a frying pan, brown ground beef until no longer pink; drain if necessary. Stir in tomatoes, soup, and beans. Simmer over low heat for 10 minutes. Lay chips in bottom of a 9 × 13-inch pan. Spoon beef mixture over chips and bake 15–20 minutes. Sprinkle cheese over top and bake 5 minutes more.

MAKES 6–8 SERVINGS.

Effortless Beef and Mushrooms

2 pounds stew meat

2 cans (10.5 ounces each) cream of mushroom soup, condensed

½ cup ginger ale

1 envelope dry onion soup mix

1 can (4 ounces) mushrooms, drained

Preheat oven to 300 degrees.

Combine all ingredients in a greased 2-quart casserole dish and cover. Bake 2½–3 hours. Serve over hot cooked rice, egg noodles, or mashed potatoes.

MAKES 4–6 SERVINGS.

Tater Tot Gumbo Casserole

- 1 pound ground beef
- 1 medium onion, chopped
- 1 bag (16 ounces) frozen green beans, thawed
- 1 can (10.75 ounces) chicken gumbo soup, condensed
- 1 can (10.5 ounces) chicken rice soup, condensed
- 1 can (10.5 ounces) cream of mushroom soup, condensed
- 1 bag (32 ounces) tater tots

Preheat oven to 350 degrees.

In a frying pan, brown ground beef and onion over medium heat until no longer pink; drain if necessary. Spread beef mixture evenly in a greased 9 × 13-inch pan. Layer green beans over top.

In a small bowl, combine the soups and pour over green beans. Top with tater tots and bake 45–60 minutes, or until tater tots are crisp. MAKES 6–8 SERVINGS.

Wrapped-Up Pot Roast

- 1 (3- to 3½-pound) boneless pot roast
- 1 can (10.5 ounces) cream of mushroom soup, condensed
- 1 envelope dry onion soup mix
- ¼ cup Worcestershire sauce
- 2 teaspoons minced garlic

Preheat oven to 300 degrees. Place a 30-inch-long piece of foil in the bottom of a 9 × 13-inch pan. Place roast in center of foil.

In a bowl, combine soup, soup mix, Worcestershire sauce, and garlic. Spread soup mixture over roast. Fold foil over roast and seal all edges. Bake 3–3½ hours, or until done in center. To make sure center is not pink, cut roast open. MAKES 6–8 SERVINGS.

Creamy Tender Cube Steaks

    4 **cube steaks**

    ½ **teaspoon pepper**

    1 **can (12 ounces) lemon-lime soda**

    ¼ **cup chopped onion**

    2 **cans (10.5 ounces each) cream of mushroom soup, condensed**

Preheat oven to 325 degrees.

Place steaks on bottom of a greased 9 × 13-inch pan. Sprinkle pepper over steaks. Pour soda over top and then sprinkle steaks with onion. Spread soup over the top. Bake 1 hour, or until done. MAKES 4 SERVINGS.

Main Dish Bread Pudding

16   ounces mild Italian sausage

 1   bunch green onions, sliced (about 1 cup)

 2   cloves fresh garlic, minced

 8   cups day-old white bread cubes

 1   cup grated provolone or Monterey Jack cheese

 6   large eggs

 3   cups milk

 1   can (10.75 ounces) cream of mushroom soup, condensed

Preheat oven to 350 degrees.

Remove casings from sausages and crumble into a large frying pan. Cook about 3 minutes. Remove sausage and drain pan, leaving about 2 tablespoons of oil. Add onions and garlic to the pan and cook another 2 minutes. Spray a 3½- to 4-quart casserole dish with nonstick cooking spray. Spread half the bread cubes in the bottom. Sprinkle meat mixture and cheese evenly over top. Spread remaining bread cubes over meat.

In a bowl, mix together eggs, milk, and soup. Pour over top, making sure each bread cube is saturated. Bake 40–50 minutes, or until set in the middle and bubbling on edges. Let stand 10 minutes before serving. MAKES 6–8 SERVINGS.

SOUTHWEST BREAD PUDDING VARIATION: *Replace sausage with 2 boneless, skinless chicken breasts, diced. Replace garlic with 3 tablespoons minced jalapeños or green chiles. Replace soup with southwest pepper jack soup.*

GARDEN VEGETABLE VARIATION: *Replace sausage with 2 cups diced fresh vegetables. Replace soup with cream of asparagus soup.*

Saucy Pork Chops

4 sirloin pork chops

1 tablespoon olive oil

½ bag (16 ounces) medium egg noodles

1 can (10.5 ounces) cream of celery soup, condensed

½ cup apple juice

2 tablespoons spicy mustard

1 tablespoon honey

½ teaspoon pepper

In a frying pan, brown pork chops in oil. Cook noodles according to package directions. While noodles cook, combine soup, juice, mustard, honey, and pepper. Pour mixture over pork chops and bring to a boil. Cover and simmer over medium heat for 5 minutes. Serve pork chops over hot cooked noodles. MAKES 4 SERVINGS.

Pork Chops and Potatoes

2 cans (10.5 ounces each) cream of mushroom soup, condensed*

1 cup milk

4 potatoes, peeled and thinly sliced

½ medium onion, chopped

salt and pepper, to taste

1½ teaspoons Italian seasoning

6 to 7 boneless thin-cut pork chops

Preheat oven to 400 degrees.

In a bowl, combine soup and milk. Place potatoes evenly on bottom of a greased 9 × 13-inch pan. Sprinkle onion evenly over potatoes. Season with salt and pepper. Sprinkle Italian seasoning over vegetables. Lay pork chops over vegetables. Pour soup mixture over top. Bake, covered, 50 minutes. Uncover and bake 10 minutes more, or until potatoes are tender. MAKES 6–7 SERVINGS.

*Condensed cream of celery soup can be substituted.

Shredded Barbecue Pork Sandwiches

3½- to 4-pound boneless pork roast

1 can (10.5 ounces) French onion soup, condensed

1 cup ketchup

¼ cup cider vinegar

¼ cup brown sugar

14 to 16 hamburger buns

Place roast in a greased 3- to 4½-quart slow cooker.

In a bowl, combine soup, ketchup, vinegar, and sugar. Pour mixture over roast. Cover and cook on high heat 4–5 hours or on low heat 8–10 hours. With two forks, shred pork. Stir pork to coat with sauce. Cook for an additional 30 minutes with the lid off. Serve on hamburger buns. MAKES 14–16 SANDWICHES.

Slow-Cooked Potatoes and Sausage

8 cups cubed potatoes

1 package (16 ounces) smoked sausage, sliced

1 can (10.5 ounces) cream of mushroom soup, condensed

1 can (10.5 ounces) vegetable beef soup, condensed

1 teaspoon crushed rosemary

Combine potatoes, sausage, soups, and rosemary in a greased 5- to 6-quart slow cooker. Cover and cook on low heat for 6–8 hours. MAKES 6–8 SERVINGS.

Beef and Bean Burritos

2 pounds ground beef

1 can (10.75 ounces) tomato soup, condensed

1 can (16 ounces) refried beans

2 envelopes taco seasoning

¼ cup water

12 large flour tortillas

2½ cups grated cheddar cheese

In a large frying pan, brown and crumble beef until no longer pink; drain if necessary. Stir in soup, beans, seasoning, and water. Simmer over low heat 5–10 minutes. Spread filling over center of warm tortillas. Sprinkle cheese over filling and roll up burritos. Garnish with salsa, guacamole, and sour cream if desired. MAKES 12 SERVINGS.

VARIATION: *Replace soup with creamy ranchero tomato soup.*

NACHO VARIATION: *Hot filling can also be served over tortilla chips. Garnish with cheese, salsa, guacamole, and sour cream.*

Polynesian Pork and Rice

3 pounds boneless pork loin or chops

2 tablespoons canola oil

1 can (10.75 ounces) golden mushroom soup, condensed

1 tablespoon minced garlic

¼ cup soy sauce

2 tablespoons brown sugar

1 can (20 ounces) pineapple chunks, with juice

1 red bell pepper

1 green bell pepper

1 large yellow onion

8 cups hot cooked rice

Preheat oven to 350 degrees.

Cut pork into 2-inch cubes, removing visible fat. Heat oil in a large frying pan and sauté pork cubes over medium-high heat, stirring often, until well browned on all sides.

In a bowl, stir together soup, garlic, soy sauce, sugar, and pineapple juice (drained from the can of pineapple). Stir pork and sauce together and pour into a 9 × 13-inch pan. Bake 1 hour. Cut bell peppers and onion into 1-inch chunks. Remove pork from oven and stir in vegetables. Bake another 30 minutes. Remove from oven and stir in pineapple chunks. Let stand 5 minutes before serving. Serve over hot cooked rice. MAKES 6–8 SERVINGS.

Family Favorites

Specialty Sauces

For easy weeknight family meals, use one of these quick and delicious sauces to top broiled or grilled meats, or your family's favorite pasta!

Tangy Tomato Mustard Sauce

- ¼ cup butter
- ½ cup sugar
- 1 tablespoon mustard
- ¼ cup vinegar
- 1 can (10.75 ounces) tomato soup, condensed
- 3 egg yolks

In a small saucepan over medium-high heat, melt butter and then stir in sugar until dissolved. Stir in mustard, vinegar, and soup. Heat until sauce begins to simmer. Stir in egg yolks and whisk until sauce is thickened, 3–5 minutes; serve warm. Excellent as a sauce for roasted meats or baked ham slices. MAKES 2 CUPS.

Three Cheese Sauce

- 1 can (10.75 ounces) cheddar cheese soup, condensed
- ⅔ cup milk
- ¼ cup grated Parmesan cheese
- ½ cup grated mozzarella or provolone cheese
- ½ teaspoon garlic powder

Combine all ingredients in a small saucepan over medium heat and whisk until cheeses are melted and sauce is smooth. A perfect topping for steamed vegetables or pasta.

Mushroom Roasted Garlic Sauce

1 can (10.75 ounces) mushroom and roasted garlic soup, condensed

1 cup cream

5 or 6 large button mushrooms, finely minced

Combine soup and cream in a small saucepan over medium heat. Whisk until it begins to simmer. Stir mushrooms into saucepan and simmer a few minutes more, stirring occasionally. Great for pastas and broiled meats.

Creamy Pesto Sauce

1 can (10.75 ounces) cream of potato soup, condensed

1 cup cream

1 jar (6 ounces) pesto

1 teaspoon garlic powder

Process soup and cream in a food processor or blender until creamy. Pour into a small saucepan and bring to a simmer over medium heat. Stir in pesto and garlic powder and simmer a few minutes more. Use for pasta or broiled fish or chicken.

Seafood Newburg Sauce

1 can (15 ounces) New England clam chowder, condensed

1 cup cream

1 package (3.5 ounces) crabmeat

1 package (3.4 ounces) shrimp, with liquid

2 tablespoons grated Parmesan cheese

Process soup and cream in a food processor or blender until creamy. Pour into a small saucepan and bring to a simmer over medium heat. Add crabmeat and shrimp. Stir in cheese. Simmer for a few minutes until well heated. Serve over broiled fish or pasta.

Winter Chili

2 pounds ground beef

1 medium onion, chopped

1 envelope chili seasoning mix

½ cup water

1 can (6 ounces) tomato paste

1 can (15.5 ounces) chili beans, with sauce

1 can (16 ounces) baked beans

1 can (10.75 ounces) tomato soup, condensed

1 can (10 ounces) diced tomatoes with green chiles, with liquid

In a frying pan, brown ground beef and onion together until done. Stir in chili seasoning and water. Place beef mixture in a greased 3½- to 5-quart slow cooker. Stir in remaining ingredients. Cover and cook on high heat 1½–2 hours or on low heat 3–4 hours. MAKES 8–10 SERVINGS.

Upside-Down Pizza Casserole

2 cans (19 ounces each) ready-to-serve minestrone soup

2 cans (6 ounces each) tomato paste

1 teaspoon garlic powder

2 teaspoons dry Italian seasoning

2 cups diced pepperoni or cooked Italian sausage

2 cups grated mozzarella cheese

1½ cups grated Parmesan cheese, divided

1 tube (13 ounces) refrigerated pizza dough

Preheat oven to 350 degrees.

Drain and discard ½ cup liquid from each of the cans of soup, and then pour remainder in a 9 × 13-inch pan. Stir in tomato paste, garlic powder, seasoning, and meat, spreading mixture evenly in pan. Sprinkle mozzarella and 1 cup Parmesan on top. Unroll pizza dough and lay on top of cheese; cut to fit. Make a few slits in dough to allow steam to escape while baking. Bake 40–50 minutes, or until crust is browned. Remove from oven and let sit 5 minutes. Cut in squares and turn upside down on each plate as you serve. Garnish with remaining cheese. MAKES 8–10 SERVINGS.

Classic Tuna Noodle Casserole

    1 cup diced fresh mushrooms

    ½ cup thinly sliced green onions

    1 tablespoon butter

    1 can (10.75 ounces) cream of mushroom soup, condensed

    ½ cup sour cream

    1 cup frozen peas

    2 cans (6 ounces each) water-packed solid chunk tuna, drained

    1 bag (16 ounces) egg noodles, cooked until just tender and drained

    1 cup crushed potato chips

Preheat oven to 375 degrees.

Sauté mushrooms and onions in butter 2–3 minutes over medium-high heat, or until onions are limp.

In a large mixing bowl, combine soup, sour cream, peas, and tuna. Stir in mushrooms and onions. Stir in cooked noodles. Spread in a 3-quart casserole dish and sprinkle potato chips on top. Bake uncovered 25–30 minutes, or until bubbly on sides and cooked through. MAKES 6–8 SERVINGS.

SOUTHWEST-STYLE VARIATION: *Replace soup with southwest pepper jack soup. Replace mushrooms and peas with 1 can (4 ounces) diced green chiles. Add 1 cup grated pepper jack cheese. Replace potato chips with crushed tortilla chips.*

CHEESY-STYLE VARIATION: *Replace soup with cream of onion soup. Add 1 cup grated sharp cheddar cheese. Replace potato chips with crushed cheese puffs.*

Do-It-Yourself Quesadillas

    3 cups cooked ground turkey or beef

    3 cups minced onion and/or peppers

 1½ cups diced fresh tomatoes

    1 can (10.75 ounces) nacho cheese soup, condensed

  12 (8-inch) flour tortillas

    2 cups grated Mexican-style cheese blend

Place meat, onion, peppers, and tomatoes in separate bowls. Allow each person to choose the amounts and types of fillings, as suggested below. Heat a 10-inch frying pan to medium heat. Spread 1 tablespoon soup on a tortilla and place it dry side down in pan. Sprinkle ½ cup ground meat, ½ cup peppers and/or onions, ¼ cup tomatoes, and ⅓ cup cheese on top. Spread another tortilla with 1 tablespoon soup. Place soup side down on top. Press with a spatula to remove any air bubbles. Cook uncovered for about 2 minutes and then turn over and cook another 2–3 minutes. Tortillas should be golden brown and crisp on the outside. Cut into wedges with a pizza cutter. Garnish with guacamole, sour cream, and/or salsa, if desired. MAKES 6 QUESADILLAS.

VARIATION: *Replace soup with chicken chile verde or Southwest pepper jack soup.*

Sloppy Joes

3 pounds ground beef

1 can (10.75 ounces) tomato soup, condensed

1 can (10.5 ounces) French onion soup, condensed

½ cup ketchup

1 tablespoon mustard

¼ cup packed brown sugar

10 to 14 hamburger buns

In a large frying pan, brown ground beef until crumbled and no longer pink; drain if necessary. Stir in soups, ketchup, mustard, and brown sugar. Simmer over medium heat 20–30 minutes. Spoon meat mixture onto buns. MAKES 10–14 SANDWICHES.

Debbie's Mushroom Burgers

1 pound ground beef

1 can (10.5 ounces) cream of mushroom soup, condensed

1 can (4 ounces) sliced mushrooms, drained

   salt and pepper, to taste

8 hamburger buns

In a frying pan, brown ground beef until no longer pink; drain if necessary. Stir in soup and mushrooms. Season with salt and pepper. Serve hot on buns. MAKES 6–8 SERVINGS.

Yummy Meatballs

1 green bell pepper, seeded and chopped

½ medium onion, chopped

1 tablespoon butter

1 can (10.75 ounces) tomato soup, condensed

1 can (10.5 ounces) chicken and rice soup, condensed

½ cup water

25 frozen fully cooked meatballs, thawed

In a large frying pan, sauté bell pepper and onion in butter until tender. Stir in soups and water. Bring to a boil. Add meatballs and return sauce to a boil. Reduce heat and simmer 15 minutes, or until meatballs are thoroughly heated. MAKES 5–6 SERVINGS.

Easy Chicken Potpie

2 boneless, skinless chicken breasts, cooked and cubed

2 cans (10.75 ounces each) cream of chicken soup with herbs, condensed

1 bag (16 ounces) frozen mixed vegetables, thawed

1 package (2 count) 9-inch refrigerated piecrust dough

Preheat oven to 375 degrees.

Combine chicken, soup, and vegetables. Place one pie shell into pie pan. Spread chicken mixture into pie. Cover with the second crust. Seal edges and make slits in top of crust. Bake 40 minutes, or until crust is golden brown. MAKES 4–6 SERVINGS.

Hamburger Vegetable Pie

1   pound ground beef

1   medium onion, chopped

1   can (10.5 ounces) condensed vegetable beef soup

1   can (10.5 ounces) cream of mushroom soup, condensed

1   tablespoon Worcestershire sauce

3   medium potatoes, peeled and cut into small cubes

4   carrots, peeled and thinly sliced

½   teaspoon pepper

1   package (2 count) 9-inch refrigerated piecrust dough

Preheat oven to 350 degrees.

In a large frying pan, brown ground beef and onion together until meat is done; drain if necessary. Stir in soups, Worcestershire sauce, potatoes, carrots, and pepper. Divide filling between two 9-inch pie pans. Cover each pie with a crust and tuck crust inside pan's edge. Make slits in top of crusts. Bake 45–50 minutes, or until golden brown. Cool 10 minutes before serving.

MAKES 8–12 SERVINGS.

Chile Relleno Casserole

6 large Anaheim green chiles, cleaned and diced

1 large yellow onion, diced

3 tablespoons butter

6 corn tortillas, cut into 1-inch squares

½ teaspoon salt

16 ounces Monterey Jack cheese, grated

4 large eggs, at room temperature and separated

1 teaspoon cream of tartar

1 can (10.75 ounces) southwest pepper jack soup, condensed

Preheat oven to 350 degrees.

In a large frying pan over medium-high heat, sauté chiles and onion in butter until onion is translucent, about 3 minutes. Add tortilla pieces and sauté another 2 minutes. Spread this mixture in a greased 3- to 4-quart baking pan. Sprinkle salt on top. Spread cheese evenly on top. Whip egg whites and cream of tartar until stiff.

In a small saucepan, cook soup and egg yolks over medium heat, stirring constantly until thickened, about 3 minutes. Remove from heat and fold in egg whites. Spread soup mixture on top. Bake 30–40 minutes, or until solid in the center and golden brown on top. MAKES 8–10 SERVINGS.

Harvest Veggie
Stuffing Casserole

- 1 box (12 ounces) seasoned stuffing
- 2 cups water, divided
- 2 cups grated zucchini
- 1 cup diced onion
- 1 cup grated carrot
- 3 tablespoons butter
- 1 can (10.75 ounces) cream of mushroom and roasted garlic soup, condensed
- 1 cup sour cream

Preheat oven to 350 degrees.

Spray a 9 × 13-inch pan with nonstick cooking spray. Spread stuffing in pan; sprinkle 1 cup water evenly over stuffing. Spread zucchini over top.

In a small frying pan over medium-high heat, sauté onion and carrot in butter for about 3 minutes, or until onion is limp. Spread onion and carrot mixture on top of zucchini.

In a small mixing bowl, mix together soup, sour cream, and 1 cup water. Pour on top of casserole and spread with a spoon to make sure edges are sealed. Bake 40–45 minutes, or until bubbly on edges and cooked through in center.

MAKES 6–8 SERVINGS.

Potluck Potatoes

1 bag (20 ounces) frozen seasoned hash brown potatoes

1 can (10.5 ounces) cream of chicken soup, condensed

⅔ cup sour cream

1 cup grated cheddar cheese

¾ medium onion, chopped

Preheat oven to 375 degrees.

In a bowl, combine all ingredients. Transfer to a greased 9 × 13-inch pan. Bake about 1 hour, or until bubbly and golden on top. MAKES 8 SERVINGS.

Never-Fail Veggie Soufflé

1 cup steamed and mashed vegetables*

2 green onions, chopped

8 ounces Swiss or Havarti cheese, finely grated

1 can (10.75 ounces) cream of celery soup, condensed

6 eggs, at room temperature and separated

½ teaspoon nutmeg

1 teaspoon cream of tartar

Preheat oven to 350 degrees.

Whirl vegetables, onions, and cheese in food processor until mixture is coarsely crumbled.

In a medium saucepan, cook soup until simmering. Stir in egg yolks and nutmeg and whisk until thickened, about 2 minutes. Remove from heat and stir in vegetable mixture. Whip egg whites and cream of tartar until stiff. Gently fold egg whites into mixture in saucepan. Pour into a 2-quart soufflé pan or baking pan that has been oiled on the bottom only. Pour water about 2 inches deep in a large baking pan. Place soufflé pan into water in large baking pan. Bake 50–55 minutes. Check to make sure middle is set. When done, turn off oven and let sit about 10 minutes. MAKES 4–6 SERVINGS.

*Try using steamed spinach, zucchini, butternut squash, broccoli, or cauliflower.

Creamy Pasta Primavera

2 tablespoons peanut oil

2 cups fresh asparagus pieces (2-inch)

2 cups green onion pieces (2-inch)

1 red bell pepper, julienned

2 cans (10.75 ounces each) cream of asparagus soup, condensed

2 tablespoons lemon juice

2 cups sour cream

½ cup grated Parmesan cheese

24 ounces penne pasta, cooked until just tender and drained

2 cups fresh spinach, cut in thin strips

½ cup pine nuts or sliced almonds

In a large frying pan or wok, heat peanut oil and stir-fry asparagus, onions, and bell pepper for 2–3 minutes, or until just done. Stir together soup, lemon juice, sour cream, and cheese. Stir soup mixture into vegetables; bring to a simmer. Stir in pasta and spinach and remove from heat. Garnish with nuts and serve warm. MAKES 6–8 SERVINGS.

Florentine Lasagna Rolls

- 1 box (16 ounces) lasagna noodles
- 1 box (10 ounces) frozen chopped spinach, thawed and drained
- 2 large eggs, lightly beaten
- 1 cup ricotta cheese
- ½ cup grated Parmesan cheese
- 1 can (10.75 ounces) cream of onion soup, condensed
- 2 teaspoons garlic powder
- 1 jar (26 ounces) spaghetti sauce, divided

Preheat oven to 350 degrees.

Boil lasagna noodles until just tender. Remove from heat and cool.

In a small bowl, mix together remaining ingredients except spaghetti sauce. Pour 1 cup spaghetti sauce in the bottom of a 9 × 13-inch pan. Place a lasagna noodle on a flat surface and spread ⅓ cup spinach mixture on top. Roll up noodle, being careful not to let spinach mixture leak out, making bundles about 4 inches in diameter, with ruffle edges facing out. Place in pan seam side down. Repeat with remaining noodles. Pour remaining spaghetti sauce over top of rolls. Bake 30–40 minutes, or until cooked through and bubbly.

MAKES 6–8 SERVINGS.

Cheesy Stuffed Mushrooms

4 large portobello mushrooms*

4 tablespoons canola oil, divided

1 cup thinly sliced green onions

1 medium tomato, diced

1 box (10 ounces) frozen chopped spinach, thawed and drained

1 can (10.75 ounces) cream of celery soup, condensed

½ cup grated mozzarella cheese

¼ cup grated Parmesan cheese

½ cup seasoned dry breadcrumbs

Preheat oven to 425 degrees.

Remove stems from mushrooms and clean. Brush mushrooms on all sides with 2 tablespoons oil and then place in a 9 × 13-inch pan.

In a medium frying pan, heat remaining oil and sauté onions, tomato, and spinach until liquid has mostly evaporated. Remove from heat and stir in soup and mozzarella cheese. Spoon spinach mixture into caps of mushrooms, mounding and using all the mixture. Bake 15 minutes. Remove from oven. Stir together Parmesan cheese and breadcrumbs. Sprinkle this mixture over the tops of the stuffed mushrooms. Return to oven and broil about 4 inches from broiler for 4–6 minutes, or until topping is golden brown. MAKES 4 SERVINGS.

*If portobello mushrooms are not available, use about 12 large brown or white button mushrooms.

Family Favorite Meat Loaf

1½ pounds ground beef

1 egg, beaten

1 cup sour cream

2 tablespoons Worcestershire sauce

1 envelope dry onion soup mix

½ cup grated Parmesan cheese

1½ cups seasoned breadcrumbs

1 can (10.75 ounces) tomato soup, condensed

Preheat oven to 375 degrees.

In a large bowl, combine all ingredients except tomato soup. Press meat mixture into a greased 9 × 5-inch bread pan to form a loaf. Spread condensed soup over meat loaf. Bake 55–60 minutes, or until internal temperature reaches 165 degrees. MAKES 8 SERVINGS.

Breakfast or Brunch

Canadian Bacon and Egg English Muffins

1 can (10.5 ounces) cream of chicken soup, condensed

1 cup milk

8 round slices Canadian bacon

8 eggs

salt and pepper, to taste

4 English muffins, split and toasted

In a saucepan, combine soup and milk over low heat. Heat bacon in a large frying pan until lightly browned on both sides. Remove bacon and cover with foil to keep warm.

In same pan, cook eggs according to personal preference. Season with salt and pepper. Place toasted muffin halves on a serving platter. Layer Canadian bacon and cooked eggs evenly over muffin halves. Spoon hot soup over individual servings. MAKES 4–6 SERVINGS.

Spinach and Sausage Breakfast Casserole

- 1 pound spicy ground pork sausage
- 1 bag (6 ounces) seasoned small croutons
- 4 eggs
- 2¼ cups milk
- 1 can (10.5 ounces) cream of mushroom soup, condensed
- 1 package (10 ounces) frozen chopped spinach, thawed
- 1 can (4.5 ounces) sliced mushrooms, drained
- 1 bag (8 ounces) grated colby cheese, divided
- ½ teaspoon dry mustard

Brown, crumble, and drain sausage. Spread croutons over bottom of a greased 9 × 13-inch pan. Spoon cooked sausage over the croutons.

In a bowl, blend eggs and milk. Stir in soup, spinach, mushrooms, 1 cup cheese, and dry mustard. Pour egg mixture over sausage layer. Sprinkle remaining cheese over top. Refrigerate for 3 hours or overnight.

Preheat oven to 350 degrees. Remove casserole from refrigerator 20 minutes before baking. Bake 50–60 minutes, or until set and browned on top.
MAKES 8–10 SERVINGS.

VEGETARIAN VARIATION: *Add a red and a green bell pepper in place of sausage.*

Breakfast Pizzas

1   pound ground sausage

12 eggs

½   cup milk

    salt and pepper, to taste

1   can (10.5 ounces) cream of celery soup, condensed

2   (12-inch) prebaked ready pizza crusts

½   cup real bacon bits

1   small onion, finely chopped

1   green bell pepper, seeded and chopped

4   cups grated cheddar cheese

Preheat oven to 400 degrees. Brown, crumble, and drain sausage; set aside.

In a large frying pan, combine eggs, milk, salt, and pepper. Scramble eggs over medium-low heat until firm. Spread ½ can soup over each crust. Spoon half the scrambled eggs over each crust. Sprinkle cooked sausage over one and bacon bits over the other. Sprinkle half the onion and bell pepper over each pizza. Top each with 2 cups cheese. Bake 25 minutes, or until golden brown. MAKES 12–16 SERVINGS.

Baked Hash Brown and Ham Casserole

6 eggs, beaten

1 teaspoon pepper

1 can (10.5 ounces) cream of mushroom soup, condensed

1 cup sour cream

1 package (30 ounces) frozen country-style hash brown potatoes, thawed

1 medium onion, chopped

1 package (16 ounces) cooked ham, cubed

1¾ cups grated cheddar cheese

Preheat oven to 350 degrees.

In a large bowl, combine all ingredients. Pour mixture into a greased 9 × 13-inch pan. Bake, uncovered, for 1 hour, or until set in the center. MAKES 6–8 SERVINGS.

Cheesy Egg and Sausage Casserole

  1 tube (16 ounces) spicy sausage

 12 eggs

  1 can (10.5 ounces) cream of mushroom soup, condensed

1¼ cups milk

  1 teaspoon dry mustard

  ½ medium onion, chopped

  1 green bell pepper, seeded and chopped

  1 package (30 ounces) frozen potato rounds, partially thawed

  1 cup grated cheddar cheese

Preheat oven to 350 degrees. Brown, crumble, and drain sausage.

In a large bowl, scramble eggs, soup, milk, and dry mustard. Stir onion, bell pepper, and sausage into egg mixture. Fold in potato rounds. Spread mixture into a greased 9 × 13-inch pan and bake 55 minutes. Sprinkle top with cheese and then bake 10 minutes more, or until cheese is melted and casserole is set. MAKES 8–10 SERVINGS.

VARIATION: *1 can (4 ounces) drained sliced mushrooms can be added.*

Mix 'n' Match Quiche

2 deep-dish frozen piecrusts, thawed

1 cup diced vegetables*

½ cup cooked diced meat*

2 cups grated cheese*

½ teaspoon spice*

6 large eggs

1 can (12 ounces) evaporated milk

1 can (10.5–10.75 ounces) condensed cream soup*

Preheat oven to 350 degrees. Layer in the thawed piecrusts in the following order: vegetables, meat, cheese, and spice.

In a medium bowl, mix together eggs, milk, and soup. Pour into piecrusts, stirring slightly to make sure egg mixture is evenly distributed and there are no air pockets. Bake 45–50 minutes, or until middle of each quiche is firm. Turn off oven and wait another 5 minutes. Serve warm. MAKES 2 QUICHES, 8–10 SERVINGS.

*Choose any combination of the following ingredients that blend well together, according to your tastes:

Vegetables: broccoli, cauliflower, green onion, bell pepper, asparagus, spinach.

Meats: chicken, crab, smoked salmon, ham, sausage, bacon.

Cheeses: Swiss, Havarti, provolone, Monterey Jack, Parmesan.

Spices: nutmeg, chili powder, basil, garlic powder.

Soups: cream of mushroom, celery, asparagus, onion, southwest pepper jack, shrimp, cheddar.

Baked Brunch Enchiladas

  2 **tablespoons butter**

  ½ **cup milk**

12 **large eggs**

  2 **cups diced ham**

  ½ **cup thinly sliced green onions**

  1 **can (10.75 ounces) nacho cheese soup, condensed**

  1 **can (14 ounces) red or green enchilada sauce**

  2 **cups grated cheddar cheese, divided**

10 **medium-sized flour tortillas**

Preheat oven to 350 degrees.

Heat butter in a large frying pan. Mix milk and eggs with a fork and pour into pan. Scramble eggs until done. Stir in ham and onions. Mix together soup and enchilada sauce and then pour 1 cup into a 9 × 13-inch baking pan. Roll a little of the eggs and a little of the cheese in a tortilla, being careful to make sure the same amount is used in all 10 tortillas. Place seam side down in pan. Pour remaining sauce over top. Bake covered 20 minutes. Uncover and bake another 10–15 minutes, or until cooked through and bubbly. Garnish with a little extra cheese. Let stand 5 minutes before serving. MAKES 8–10 SERVINGS.

Ham and Asparagus Rolls

  2   cans (10.75 ounces each) cheddar cheese soup, condensed

1⅓   cups milk

  ½   cup grated Parmesan cheese

  1   cup grated Swiss cheese

  1   teaspoon garlic powder

  2   cups cooked rice

  8   slices cooked ham, ⅛ inch thick

 24   fresh asparagus spears, lightly steamed

Preheat oven to 350 degrees.

Combine first five ingredients in a small saucepan and whisk until cheeses are melted and sauce is smooth. Remove from heat. Spread ½ cup of the sauce in the bottom of a 9 × 13-inch pan. Mix ½ cup sauce into the cooked rice. Lay a slice of ham on cutting board, with longest edge to the front. Spread ¼ cup of rice mixture on ham slice, leaving ½-inch edge all the way around. Place 3 asparagus spears on top of rice. Roll ham slice up like a jellyroll. Place seam side down in pan. Repeat for all ham slices. Pour remaining sauce on top of rolls. Bake 20–30 minutes, or until heated through and sauce is bubbly. Garnish with additional cheese(s) sprinkled on top, if desired. MAKES 8 SERVINGS.

Baked Goods

Tomato Soup Cake

1 box (18 ounces) spice cake mix

1 teaspoon baking soda

1 can (10.75 ounces) tomato soup, condensed

½ cup water

¼ cup canola oil

2 large eggs

1 container (16 ounces) cream cheese frosting

Combine all ingredients except frosting and beat for 2–3 minutes, or until batter becomes lighter. Bake as directed on back of cake mix box. Cool and frost. MAKES 10–12 SERVINGS.

VARIATION: *Add up to ½ cup chopped walnuts, chopped dates, or raisins to batter before baking.*

Cheesy Mexicali Cornbread

1 can (10.75 ounces) southwest pepper jack soup, condensed

2 large eggs, beaten lightly with a fork

1 cup milk

1 can (4 ounces) mild diced green chiles

2 cups frozen corn, thawed

2 cups grated cheddar cheese

1½ cups cornmeal

1½ cups flour

1 teaspoon salt

1 tablespoon baking powder

Preheat oven to 400 degrees. Spray a 9 × 13-inch baking pan with nonstick cooking spray.

In a large mixing bowl, mix soup, eggs, and milk. Stir in chiles, corn, and cheese.

In a separate bowl, mix dry ingredients together and then add to soup mixture. Pour into pan and spread evenly. Bake 20–25 minutes, or until middle is set and top is lightly browned. Serve warm with butter. MAKES 9–12 PIECES.

Savory Mushroom Muffins

1 can (10.75 ounces) cream of mushroom soup, condensed

⅓ cup milk

1 large egg

¼ cup melted butter

4 white or brown button mushrooms, cleaned

2 cups cake flour

1 tablespoon baking powder

1 teaspoon garlic salt

2 tablespoons dried parsley flakes

Preheat oven to 425 degrees.

Place soup, milk, egg, and butter in a food processor or blender. Chop mushrooms in fourths and add to mixture in food processor. Process until smooth and mushrooms are cut into tiny pieces. Pour into a medium-sized mixing bowl. Add dry ingredients and stir until just mixed and no dry streaks remain. Do not overstir. Batter will be slightly lumpy. Spoon batter into greased muffin tins. Bake 20–25 minutes, or until set and lightly browned on top. MAKES 12 MUFFINS.

Baked Potato Biscuits

2½ cups cake flour

1 tablespoon baking powder

1 can (10.75 ounces) cream of potato soup, condensed

4 tablespoons sour cream

2 tablespoons water

¼ cup minced chives or green onion tops

½ cup grated sharp cheddar cheese

3 tablespoons cooked crumbled bacon

Preheat oven to 375 degrees.

In a large mixing bowl, stir together flour, baking powder, soup, sour cream, and water until dough begins to form a ball. Add chives, cheese, and bacon. Turn onto a floured surface and roll out to 1-inch thickness. Cut into 2- to 3-inch circles and place in a pie pan or small baking pan that has been sprayed with nonstick cooking spray. Bake 16–18 minutes, or until lightly browned. MAKES ABOUT 12 BISCUITS.

No-Knead French Onion Bread

1½ cups flour

2 tablespoons sugar

2 tablespoons fast-rising yeast

¼ cup butter

1 can (10.75 ounces) French onion soup, condensed

1 large egg

1 cup grated cheddar cheese

1½ cups whole wheat flour

In a large mixing bowl, combine regular flour, sugar, and yeast.

In a small saucepan, bring butter and soup to a simmer. Remove from heat and pour into flour mixture. Beat with mixer at medium speed 1 minute. Add egg, cheese, and wheat flour and beat 2 minutes more, or longer, until smooth. Spray a large metal bowl with nonstick cooking spray and pour batter into metal bowl. Cover and let rise in a warm place 1½ hours or more, until doubled in size. Grease a loaf pan. Remove from mixing bowl and place in loaf pan. Let rise again until doubled, about 1 hour. Preheat oven to 350 degrees. Bake 50–60 minutes, or until done in center and browned on top. MAKES 10 SERVINGS.

Sweet Potato Pies

1 can (29 ounces) sweet potatoes or yams

¼ cup milk

1 can (10.75 ounces) tomato soup, condensed

1 cup light brown sugar

3 large eggs

1 teaspoon vanilla

½ teaspoon cinnamon

¼ teaspoon nutmeg

2 (9-inch) frozen piecrusts, thawed

Preheat oven to 350 degrees.

Drain sweet potatoes well and then blend with milk in a food processor or blender until smooth. Pour into a mixing bowl and mix with remaining ingredients except crusts. Pour half the mixture into each crust and bake 60 minutes. Turn off oven and let sit until cooled. Serve at room temperature. MAKES 12 SERVINGS.

Chocolate Zucchini Cake

1⅓ cups brown sugar

¼ cup butter, softened

2 large eggs

1 can (10.75 ounces) tomato soup, condensed

2 cups pureed zucchini

2½ cups flour

1 tablespoon baking powder

2 teaspoons baking soda

1 teaspoon cinnamon

½ cup cocoa powder

½ cup diced walnuts

Preheat oven to 350 degrees.

Cream sugar and butter together. Stir in eggs, soup, and zucchini. Add remaining ingredients, mixing until smooth. Spray a 9 × 13-inch pan with nonstick cooking spray. Pour in batter and bake 30–40 minutes, or until done in center. Cool and frost or sprinkle with confectioners' sugar, if desired.

MAKES 12 LARGE PIECES.

CHAPTER 2

101 Ways with
Mac 'n' Cheese

Soups

Easy Italian Vegetable Soup 87 • Tomato Soup 87 • Bean Soup 88 • Miracle Soup 89 • Oaxaca Soup 90 • Tavern Soup 91 • Garlicky Soup 92 • Lazarus Soup 92 • Hungarian Bean Soup 93 • Chicken Soup 93 • Onion Soup 94 • Vegetable Picante Soup 94 • Quick Minestrone 95 • Pomodoro e Zucchina Minestra 95

Salads

Macaroni Salad with Peas and Ham 96 • Mexican Salad 97 • Simple Ranch Salad 97 • Egg Pasta Salad 98 • Spinach and Tomato Salad 98 • Confetti Salad 99 • Chicken Curry Party Salad 99 • Classic Macaroni Salad 100 • Cheddar Mac Salad 100 • Fruit Salad 101 • Tomato Basil Cannellini Salad 102 • Herbed Macaroni and Cucumber 103 • Macaroni, Tomato, Corn, and Basil Salad 104 • Seafood Pasta with Lemon Herb Dressing 105 • Quick Mac Salad 106 • Shrimp and Macaroni Salad 106 • Catalina Salad 107 • Macaroni Chef Salad 108 • Chicken Macaroni Salad 109 • Michelle's Special Salad 110 • Cucumber Dill Pasta Salad 111

Casseroles

Baked Macaroni and Cheese 112 • Four Cheese Casserole 113 • Mark's Mega Macaroni 114 • Macaroni Pie 115 • Crispy Macaroni and Cheese 115 • Chicken Potpie 116 • Dr. Pepper Bake 117 • Fajita Macaroni and Cheese 118 • Baked Tomato Macaroni 118 • Mom's Mac and Cheese 119 • Chicken Casserole 119 • Mac and Cheese Custard 120 • Curried Macaroni 121 • Potato Macaroni Gratin 122 • Macaroni and Cheese with Mushrooms and Bacon 123 • Corned Beef and Kraut 124 • Cavatini 125 • Creamy Mushroom Casserole 126 • Dried Beef Casserole 126 • Mac and Cheese with Mustard and Worcestershire 127

Skillet Dishes

Hot Dog Casserole 128 • Italian-Style Macaroni and Beef 128 • Chili Mac 129 • Savory Bacon Mac 129 • Cheeseburger Pasta 130 • Goulash 130 • Greek Chicken Pasta 131 • Cheesy Pea Pasta 132 • Tex-Mex Macaroni and Cheese 133 • Spicy Hamburger Mac 133 • Chop Suey 134 • Chicken Stuff 134 • Spicy Mac and Cheese 135 • Beefy Macaroni and Cheese 135 • Wisconsin Mac 136 • Mexican Mac and Cheese 137

Saucepan Dishes

Salsa Macaroni and Cheese 138 • Stadium Mac and Cheese 138 • Balsamic Chicken 139 • Salsa Verde 139 • Bacon and Macaroni 140 • Rachel's Macaroni 140 • Broccoli and Turkey Macaroni 141 • Spiced-Up Macaroni 141 • Mac and Green Chiles 142 • Bacon and Tomato Mac 142 • Fiesta Mac 143 • Creamy Sage Macaroni 143 • Frito Pie 144 • Italian Chicken 144 • Creamy Pesto 145 • Paladin Blue Macaroni 145 • Creamy Basil and Almonds 145

Family Favorites

Fried Macaroni and Cheese 146 • Chicken Parmesan 147 • Pizza Mac 147 • Mock Mashed Potatoes 148 • Macaroni Cake 148 • Christmas Stew 149 • Cheesy Triangles 149 • Denver Omelet 150 • Chili Dogs 150 • Meat Loaf 151 • Taco Salad 151 • Salsa Balls 152 • Pan-Fried Mac and Cheese 152

Soups

Easy Italian Vegetable Soup

1 can (14.5 ounces) Italian-style stewed tomatoes
1 can (15.25 ounces) whole kernel sweet corn
1 can (15.25 ounces) cut green beans
2 cans (14.5 ounces each) vegetable broth
1 box macaroni and cheese
1 teaspoon sweet basil

Combine all canned vegetables and their liquids and the broth with the cheese packet and basil in a large pot; bring to a boil. Reduce heat to medium-low, cover, and simmer for 15 minutes. Add macaroni and simmer 5 minutes more. Remove from heat and serve. MAKES 2–3 SERVINGS.

Tomato Soup

3 cans (14.5 ounces each) vegetable broth
½ cup chopped fresh parsley
4 large cloves garlic, minced
1 teaspoon thyme
1 teaspoon sage
2 cups spicy tomato juice
1 box macaroni and cheese

Combine vegetable broth, parsley, garlic, thyme, and sage in a large pot. Bring to a boil and then reduce heat to medium-low; simmer for 15 minutes. Add tomato juice and cheese packet. Bring to a boil again, then add macaroni and let simmer 5 minutes more; serve immediately. MAKES 4 SERVINGS.

Bean Soup

4 cups canned kidney beans

1 teaspoon salt

1 clove garlic, pressed

¼ cup chopped parsley

1 zucchini, sliced

2 stalks celery, chopped

3 tablespoons butter

2 bay leaves

¼ teaspoon pepper

1 tablespoon oil

1 carrot, diced

5 leaves spinach or chard, chopped

1 can (8 ounces) tomato sauce or stewed tomatoes

1 box macaroni and cheese

1 teaspoon basil

Mash 3 cups beans and leave the remaining beans whole. Combine all remaining ingredients, including cheese packet, except macaroni and basil; bring to a boil. Turn down heat and simmer for 45 minutes. Add basil and macaroni and cook 5 minutes more. MAKES 4–6 SERVINGS.

COOKING TIP

Boxed macaroni is made to be prepared
faster than regular pasta, so be sure not
to overcook it.

Miracle Soup

2 large onions

1 green bell pepper

1 can (14.5 ounces) diced tomatoes

⅓ head cabbage

2 stalks celery

2 cans (14 ounces each) vegetable broth

1 envelope dry onion soup mix

1 box macaroni and cheese

Cut vegetables into medium-size pieces and add with vegetable broth to a large pot. Add water until vegetables are covered. Boil over medium heat for 10 minutes. Turn heat to low and simmer until vegetables are soft. Add dry soup mix, cheese packet, and macaroni. Simmer 5 minutes, or until macaroni is tender; serve immediately. MAKES 4–6 SERVINGS.

FOOD FACT

First made in the 19th century, macaroni and cheese originally consisted of boiled noodles that were layered in a buttered baking dish and topped with grated American, Cheddar, or Swiss cheese. The dish was then baked until the cheese melted. Today, most macaroni and cheese recipes call for the cheese sauce to be made separately.

Oaxaca Soup

     1   can (4 ounces) whole green chiles
     ½   large onion, chopped
     2   cloves garlic, minced
     2   cans (14.5 ounces) stewed tomatoes
     1   tablespoon vegetable oil
     4   to 6 cups water
         salt
     3   tablespoons granulated chicken bouillon
     1   teaspoon chopped parsley
     1   box macaroni and cheese
     ½   teaspoon baking soda
    2½   cups milk
     4   cups diced Oaxaca or mozzarella cheese

Slit chiles and remove seeds. Rinse chiles in water and then cut in long strips. In a 6- to 8-quart pan, fry the onion, garlic, tomatoes, and chile strips in oil until the onion is soft. Measure 1½ cups of the vegetable mixture and then puree in a blender. Pour pureed vegetables back in pan and add 4 cups water, salt, bouillon granules, parsley, cheese packet, and baking soda.

In a separate pan, bring the milk to a boil; remove any "skin" from the top and then add milk to the other mixture. Add the diced cheese and stir until melted. Once mixture comes to a boil, add macaroni and simmer 5 minutes. Add remaining 2 cups water if too thick. Serve immediately. MAKES 4 SERVINGS.

COOKING TIP

Once water is boiling, it generally takes 4½ minutes at sea level or 5 minutes if you are in the high country to make al dente (tender) macaroni.

Tavern Soup

¼ cup chopped celery

¼ cup chopped carrots

¼ cup chopped green bell pepper

¼ cup chopped onion

4 cans (14 ounces each) chicken broth

2 tablespoons butter or margarine

1 box macaroni and cheese

1 teaspoon salt

¼ teaspoon pepper

⅓ cup flour

3 cups grated sharp cheddar cheese

1 can (12 ounces) beer, at room temperature

Combine celery, carrots, bell pepper, and onion in a pot. Add broth, butter, cheese packet, salt, and pepper. Boil over medium heat for 10 minutes. Reduce heat and simmer until vegetables are soft; puree mixture. Return to pot and cook over high heat. Dissolve flour in ¼ cup water and add to broth. Add cheese ½ cup at a time, stirring until blended; pour in pasta and beer and cover. Cook over high heat for 15–20 minutes. MAKES 4–6 SERVINGS.

COOKING TIP

When making soups, add the macaroni just prior to serving. If you are making the soup ahead of time, reheat the broth a few minutes before serving and then add the pasta.

Garlicky Soup

1 tablespoon butter or margarine

8 teaspoons minced garlic

3 cans (14 ounces each) chicken broth

1 can (14 ounces) vegetable broth

1 can (14 ounces) Italian diced tomatoes, with liquid

1 box macaroni and cheese

5 ounces spinach, stems removed

8 to 10 fresh basil leaves, coarsely chopped

   grated Parmesan cheese

Melt butter in a large saucepan over medium-high heat. Add garlic and sauté about 2 minutes. Add broth, tomatoes, and cheese packet. Bring to a boil and then reduce heat to a simmer. Stir in macaroni, spinach, and basil; cook until pasta is done, about 5 minutes. Sprinkle each bowl with Parmesan cheese just before serving. MAKES 4 SERVINGS.

Lazarus Soup

6 cups turkey or chicken broth

2 heads garlic, cloves separated, peeled, and minced

4 jalapeños, seeded and coarsely chopped (or fewer if desired)

1 box macaroni and cheese

1 teaspoon dried oregano

1 teaspoon dried thyme

Combine broth, garlic, jalapeños, cheese packet, oregano, and thyme in a saucepan and bring to a boil. Reduce heat and simmer until the garlic is very soft, about 30 minutes. Transfer to a blender and puree until smooth. Return to pan and bring to a boil. Add macaroni and simmer 5 minutes more. MAKES 4–6 SERVINGS.

Hungarian Bean Soup

1 pound Polish sausage, cut into bite-size pieces

½ large onion, chopped

1 clove garlic, crushed

salt and pepper

½ pound carrots, thinly sliced

1 can (14 ounces) tomato juice

1 can (14 ounces) red kidney beans

¼ cup flour

¼ cup water

1 box macaroni and cheese

½ pint sour cream

Place sausage, onion, garlic, salt, and pepper in a large pot. Fill with water until ingredients are completely covered and then boil about 30 minutes. Add carrots, tomato juice, and beans and more water if necessary to cover ingredients completely. Continue boiling until carrots are tender. Mix together flour, water, cheese packet, and sour cream to make a thin paste. Slowly add to boiling soup. Add macaroni and boil 5 minutes more; serve hot. MAKES 4–6 SERVINGS.

Chicken Soup

2 stalks celery, sliced

3 cubes chicken bouillon

2 carrots, sliced

2 chicken breasts, cooked and diced

1 teaspoon salt

¼ teaspoon pepper

1 box macaroni and cheese

Bring 3 cups water to a boil. Add celery, bouillon, and carrots. Cook until carrots are tender. Add chicken, salt, pepper, and cheese packet. Bring to a boil. Add macaroni and continue to boil 5 minutes more; serve immediately. MAKES 2–3 SERVINGS.

Onion Soup

1 cup diced white onions

2 cloves garlic, crushed

4 tablespoons butter or margarine

2 cans (10.75 ounces each) beef broth

1 box macaroni and cheese

Sauté onion and garlic in butter for about 5 minutes, or until golden. Do not let the onions or garlic get too brown. Add broth and cheese packet. Heat through, for about 20 minutes, or up to 30 minutes if covered. Add macaroni and simmer 5 minutes more. MAKES 2–3 SERVINGS.

VARIATION: *Top with a ½-inch slice of Italian or French bread and some grated mozzarella cheese. Place under the broiler for about 2–3 minutes.*

Vegetable Picante Soup

½ large onion, coarsely chopped

2 teaspoons minced garlic

½ tablespoon olive oil

2 cans (14.5 ounces each) beef broth

½ can (14.5 ounces) Italian-style stewed tomatoes with liquid

¼ cup picante sauce or salsa

1 box macaroni and cheese

½ teaspoon dried basil, crushed

½ green bell pepper, diced

¼ cup freshly grated Parmesan cheese

In a large saucepan or Dutch oven, cook onion and garlic in oil until tender, about 6 minutes. Add broth, tomatoes, picante sauce, cheese packet, and basil; bring to a boil. Stir in bell pepper and macaroni; simmer 5 minutes, or until macaroni is tender. Ladle into soup bowls and then sprinkle with Parmesan cheese. MAKES 2–3 SERVINGS.

Quick Minestrone

1 can (14.5 ounces) diced tomatoes

1 can (14.5 ounces) kidney beans

1 can (15.25 ounces) green beans

1 can (14.5 ounces) peas

2 cans (14 ounces each) vegetable broth

1 box macaroni and cheese

1 tablespoon basil

Combine all canned ingredients, including juices, in a pot with cheese packet and basil. Simmer for 15 minutes; add macaroni and continue to simmer 5 minutes more, or until macaroni is tender. MAKES 2–3 SERVINGS.

Pomodoro e Zucchina Minestra

1 can (14.5 ounces) Italian diced tomatoes

1 can (14.5 ounces) zucchini

1 can (14 ounces) chicken broth

2 cans (14 ounces each) vegetable broth

1 box macaroni and cheese

1 tablespoon oregano

1 tablespoon basil

Combine all canned ingredients in a pot with cheese packet, oregano, and basil. Simmer for 15 minutes and then add macaroni; simmer 5 minutes more, or until macaroni is tender. MAKES 2–4 SERVINGS.

Salads

Macaroni Salad with Peas and Ham

1 box macaroni and cheese

1¼ tablespoons white wine or white grape juice

¾ tablespoon lemon juice

¼ teaspoon garlic powder

3 tablespoons extra virgin olive oil

¾ cup diced ham

½ cup diced red bell pepper

½ cup frozen peas, thawed

¼ cup chopped celery

2 tablespoons diced shallots

2 tablespoons fresh parsley

Boil macaroni in 2 cups water until al dente; drain and rinse in cool water.

Whisk wine, lemon juice, garlic powder, oil, and cheese packet together; set aside.

In a large bowl, combine cooked macaroni, ham, vegetables, and parsley. Toss with the dressing and chill for 2–6 hours. MAKES 4–6 SERVINGS.

COOKING TIP

Always rinse the macaroni if the recipe calls for it; don't if it doesn't.

Mexican Salad

1 box macaroni and cheese

¾ cup chunky salsa

½ cup mayonnaise

½ teaspoon garlic powder

½ teaspoon salt

   pepper

¼ cup chopped green bell pepper

1 can (3 ounces) sliced black olives

Boil macaroni in 2 cups water until al dente; drain and rinse in cool water.

Mix salsa, mayonnaise, garlic powder, salt, pepper, and cheese packet together; set aside.

In a large bowl, combine cooked macaroni, bell pepper, and olives. Toss with dressing and chill for at least 1 hour. MAKES 4–6 SERVINGS.

Simple Ranch Salad

1 box macaroni and cheese

¼ cup sour cream

¼ cup mayonnaise

1 envelope ranch dressing mix

2 tablespoons milk

1 stalk celery, chopped

1 can (10 ounces) chicken chunks, drained

1 can (2.25 ounces) chopped green olives

1 teaspoon paprika

Boil macaroni in 2 cups water until al dente; drain and rinse in cool water.

Mix sour cream, mayonnaise, dry ranch dressing mix, milk, and cheese packet; set aside.

In a large bowl, combine cooked macaroni, celery, chicken, and olives. Toss with dressing and sprinkle with paprika. Chill for at least 1 hour. MAKES 4–6 SERVINGS.

Egg Pasta Salad

1 box macaroni and cheese

½ cup mayonnaise

2 tablespoons mustard

½ cup sweet relish

4 hard-boiled eggs, sliced

Boil macaroni in 2 cups water until al dente; drain and rinse in cool water.

In a small bowl, mix together mayonnaise, mustard, and cheese packet. Stir in relish and then set aside.

In a large bowl, combine cooked macaroni and eggs; toss with dressing. Chill for at least 1 hour. MAKES 4–6 SERVINGS.

Spinach and Tomato Salad

1 box macaroni and cheese

½ cup Italian dressing

1 can (14.5 ounces) Italian diced tomatoes, drained

5 ounces fresh spinach

Boil macaroni in 2 cups water for 5 minutes; drain and rinse in cold water.

Mix Italian dressing with cheese packet and then toss dressing with cooked macaroni and remaining ingredients. Chill for at least 1 hour. MAKES 4–6 SERVINGS.

Confetti Salad

1 box macaroni and cheese

1 cup mayonnaise

2 tablespoons Mrs. Dash

1 teaspoon lemon juice

1 tomato, diced

1 green bell pepper, diced

1 red bell pepper, diced

1 yellow bell pepper, diced

Boil macaroni in 2 cups water for 5 minutes; drain and rinse in cold water.

Mix mayonnaise with the cheese packet, Mrs. Dash, and lemon juice. Toss dressing with cooked macaroni and remaining ingredients. Chill for at least 1 hour. MAKES 4–6 SERVINGS.

Chicken Curry Party Salad

1 box macaroni and cheese

½ cup mayonnaise

½ cup sour cream

1 clove garlic, chopped

1 teaspoon curry powder

   salt and pepper

1 can (4 ounces) sliced black olives, drained and chopped

1 apple, peeled, cored, and sliced

1 yellow bell pepper, thinly sliced

2 stalks celery, chopped

1 can (10 ounces) diced chicken, drained

Boil macaroni in 2 cups water for 5 minutes; drain and rinse in cold water.

Mix mayonnaise, sour cream, garlic, curry powder, salt, and pepper with the cheese packet. Toss dressing with cooked macaroni and remaining ingredients. Chill for at least 1 hour. MAKES 4–6 SERVINGS.

Classic Macaroni Salad

1 box macaroni and cheese

½ cup mayonnaise

3 tablespoons mustard

3 hard-boiled eggs

¼ cup sweet relish

½ onion, diced

Boil macaroni in 2 cups water for 5 minutes; drain and rinse.

Mix mayonnaise and mustard with the cheese packet. Toss dressing with cooked macaroni and remaining ingredients. Chill for at least 1 hour. MAKES 4–6 SERVINGS.

Cheddar Mac Salad

1 box macaroni and cheese

¼ cup mayonnaise

¼ cup sour cream

2 tablespoons milk

¼ cup cubed cheddar cheese

1 stalk celery

1 green bell pepper, chopped

½ cup frozen peas, thawed

⅓ cup chopped onion

2 tablespoons relish

Boil macaroni in 2 cups water for 5 minutes; drain and rinse in cold water.

Mix mayonnaise, sour cream, and milk with the cheese packet. Toss dressing with cooked macaroni and remaining ingredients. Chill for at least 1 hour. MAKES 4–6 SERVINGS.

Fruit Salad

- 1 box macaroni and cheese
- 1 can (8 ounces) mandarin oranges, with juice
- 1 can (11 ounces) pineapple chunks, with juice
- 1 egg, beaten
- ¼ teaspoon salt
- ¾ cup sugar
- 1 tablespoon flour
- ½ teaspoon lemon juice
- 1 cup frozen whipped topping, slightly thawed

Bring a large pot of lightly salted water to a boil. Add macaroni and cook for 4–5 minutes, or until al dente; drain.

In a medium saucepan over medium heat, combine reserved mandarin juice, reserved pineapple juice, egg, salt, sugar, flour, cheese packet, and lemon juice. Stir well and bring to a boil. Remove from heat and pour over cooked macaroni; chill overnight. Stir together macaroni mixture, oranges, pineapple chunks, and whipped topping; serve at once. MAKES 4–6 SERVINGS.

COOKING TIP

Low-fat ingredients, such as light soups, sour cream, and cream cheese, can be substituted.

Tomato Basil Cannellini Salad

1   box macaroni and cheese

1½ tablespoons extra virgin olive oil

3   tablespoons red wine vinegar

1   tablespoon basil

1   clove garlic, minced

    salt and pepper

1   pound plum tomatoes, halved lengthwise

1   can (15 ounces) cannellini beans, rinsed and drained

½   cup chopped red onion

¼   cup chopped pitted kalamata olives or other brine-cured olives

1   tablespoon chopped Italian parsley

Bring a large pot of lightly salted water to a boil. Add macaroni and cook for 4–5 minutes, or until al dente; drain. Transfer macaroni to large bowl and let cool.

In a small bowl, mix oil, vinegar, cheese packet, basil, and garlic. Season with salt and pepper. Add tomatoes, beans, onion, olives, and parsley to cooked macaroni and then toss with dressing. Chill at least 1 hour before serving.
MAKES 4–6 SERVINGS.

Herbed Macaroni and Cucumber

1 box macaroni and cheese

½ cup loosely packed fresh fine dill sprigs, rinsed and spun dry

½ cup loosely packed fresh parsley leaves, rinsed and spun dry

½ cup coarsely chopped green onions

½ cup mayonnaise

½ cup buttermilk

   salt

1 seedless cucumber, halved lengthwise and cut into ¼-inch-thick slices

In a blender or food processor, puree the cheese packet, dill, parsley, and green onions with the mayonnaise, buttermilk, and salt until the dressing is smooth.

In a pot of boiling salted water, cook the macaroni until tender; drain and rinse in cold water. Combine cucumber and cooked macaroni and then toss with dressing. Chill for at least 1 hour. MAKES 4–6 SERVINGS.

Macaroni, Tomato, Corn, and Basil Salad

1	box macaroni and cheese
1	cup packed fresh basil leaves
⅓	cup plain nonfat yogurt
3	tablespoons low-fat mayonnaise
1½	tablespoons fresh lime juice
2	cloves garlic, peeled
4	medium tomatoes, cut into thin wedges
½	cup thinly sliced green onions
1	cup thinly sliced and halved English hothouse cucumber
1	cup fresh (or frozen and thawed) corn

Boil macaroni in a medium saucepan in salted water until just tender; drain and rinse in cold water.

Blend basil, yogurt, mayonnaise, cheese packet, lime juice, and garlic in a food processor or blender until basil is evenly distributed. Combine cooked macaroni and vegetables in a large bowl and toss with dressing. Chill for at least 1 hour. MAKES 4–6 SERVINGS.

COOKING TIP

Fresh garlic adds great flavor to a dish, but when pushed for time, minced garlic from the jar works well. Use 1 teaspoon minced garlic for each clove of garlic.

Seafood Pasta with Lemon Herb Dressing

1 box macaroni and cheese

¼ cup mayonnaise

¼ cup sour cream

¼ cup thinly sliced green onions

1 tablespoon drained capers

1 tablespoon minced fresh tarragon

½ tablespoon minced fresh dill

½ teaspoon sugar

3½ tablespoons fresh lemon juice

3 tablespoons extra virgin olive oil

½ cup finely chopped celery

½ pound Dungeness crabmeat

½ pound cooked medium shrimp

Boil macaroni in a large pot of salted water until al dente, stirring occasionally.

In a medium bowl, combine mayonnaise, sour cream, green onions, capers, tarragon, dill, cheese packet, sugar, lemon juice, and oil; whisk to combine.

In a large bowl, combine cooked macaroni, celery, crabmeat, and shrimp; toss with dressing. Chill for at least 1 hour before serving. MAKES 4–6 SERVINGS.

Quick Mac Salad

1 box macaroni and cheese

1 tablespoon vinegar

½ cup mayonnaise

  salt and pepper

½ cup chopped celery

½ cup chopped green bell pepper

1 jar (4 ounces) pimientos, drained and diced

Boil macaroni in 2 cups water until tender; drain and rinse in cold water.

In a small bowl, combine vinegar, mayonnaise, cheese packet, salt, and pepper.

In a large bowl, combine remaining ingredients with cooked macaroni; toss with dressing. Chill at least 1 hour before serving. MAKES 4–6 SERVINGS.

Shrimp and Macaroni Salad

1 box macaroni and cheese

½ cup light mayonnaise

½ teaspoon seasoned salt

¼ teaspoon celery seed

½ teaspoon salt, or to taste

¼ teaspoon pepper

1 tablespoon brown spicy mustard

1 stalk celery, chopped

1½ large tomatoes, diced

½ bunch green onions, chopped

½ pound cooked shrimp

Boil macaroni in 2 cups water until tender; drain and rinse in cold water.

Combine mayonnaise, seasonings, cheese packet, and mustard in a large bowl; mix well. Add celery, tomatoes, and green onions; mix well. Add shrimp and cooked macaroni; mix well. Refrigerate about 2 hours before serving. MAKES 4–6 SERVINGS.

Catalina Salad

- 1 box macaroni and cheese
- 3 tablespoons mayonnaise
- 4 tablespoons Catalina salad dressing
- 1 pinch garlic salt
- ½ can (6 ounces) tuna
- ½ can (6 ounces) small shrimp, drained
- ¼ cup chopped onion
- ½ green bell pepper, chopped
- ¾ cup chopped celery
- 1½ tablespoons sweet pickle relish

Boil macaroni in 2 cups water until tender; drain and rinse in cold water.

Mix together mayonnaise, Catalina dressing, garlic salt, and cheese packet. Toss together cooked macaroni, tuna, shrimp, onion, bell pepper, celery, and relish with dressing. Add more mayonnaise to thin out, if desired. Chill 1 hour before serving. MAKES 4–6 SERVINGS.

COOKING TIP

Simple substitutions make meal preparation a breeze. Here are some common substitutions: ¼ cup fresh minced onion = 2 tablespoons dried minced onions; ¼ cup fresh herbs = 1 tablespoon dried herbs

Macaroni Chef Salad

1   box macaroni and cheese

½   tablespoon cider vinegar

½   cup mayonnaise

¼   cup chopped white onion

2   tablespoons sliced pimientos, drained

¼   cup chopped dill pickles

¼   cup chopped green bell pepper

3   slices processed American cheese, cut into ½-inch squares

½   can (6 ounces) whole black olives, pitted

2   hard-boiled eggs, chopped

½   cup diced ham

    salt and pepper

Boil macaroni in a large pot of water until tender; drain and rinse in cold water.

Blend the vinegar and mayonnaise thoroughly with cheese packet. Combine cooked macaroni, onion, pimientos, pickles, bell pepper, cheese, olives, eggs, and ham in a large bowl. Toss in the mayonnaise mixture. Season with salt and pepper to taste. Chill in the refrigerator until ready to serve. MAKES 4–6 SERVINGS.

Chicken Macaroni Salad

1   box macaroni and cheese

1½ cups mayonnaise

¼   tablespoon dried basil

     salt and pepper

1   pinch garlic powder

2   chicken breasts, cooked and diced

1   can (15 ounces) mixed vegetables, drained

2   cups shredded lettuce

Boil macaroni in a medium pot and cook until al dente; drain and rinse under cold water.

Mix mayonnaise with spices and cheese packet.

In a large bowl, mix together the cooked chicken, drained vegetables, lettuce, and mayonnaise; toss to coat. Chill 1 hour before serving. MAKES 4–6 SERVINGS.

Michelle's Special Salad

1 box macaroni and cheese

½ cup creamy Italian salad dressing

½ tablespoon cider vinegar

1 tablespoon milk

1 stalk celery, chopped

1 can (3 ounces) sliced black olives

¼ cup chopped Vidalia onion

¼ cup chopped green bell pepper

salt and pepper

Boil macaroni in a large pot of lightly salted water for 4–5 minutes, or until al dente; drain and rinse in cold water.

In a medium bowl, blend salad dressing, vinegar, and milk with cheese packet.

In a large bowl, mix the cooked macaroni, celery, olives, onion, and bell pepper. Toss with the dressing and then season with salt and pepper. Cover and chill at least 1 hour. MAKES 4–6 SERVINGS.

COOKING TIP

Steamed fresh or frozen vegetables can be substituted for canned vegetables in any of these recipes.

Cucumber Dill Pasta Salad

1 box macaroni and cheese

1 cup low-fat sour cream

½ cup skim milk

1 tablespoon chopped fresh dill weed

1 tablespoon distilled white vinegar

½ teaspoon salt

½ teaspoon coarse pepper

2 cups chopped cucumber

1 cup chopped tomatoes

Boil macaroni in salted water until al dente; drain and rinse in cold water. Transfer cooked macaroni to a large bowl.

In a separate bowl, mix together sour cream, cheese packet, milk, dill, vinegar, salt, and pepper; set aside. Mix cucumbers and tomatoes into the cooked macaroni. Pour in dressing and mix thoroughly. Cover, and refrigerate at least 1 hour and preferably overnight. Stir just before serving. MAKES 4–6 SERVINGS.

Casseroles

Baked Macaroni and Cheese

1 box macaroni and cheese

¼ cup milk

4 tablespoons butter, divided

½ cup diced onion

1 clove garlic, minced

5 slices bacon, cooked and crumbled

1 cup grated sharp cheddar cheese

Boil macaroni in water until al dente; drain. Add milk and 3 tablespoons butter. Sauté onion and garlic in remaining butter. Mix onion, garlic, and bacon into macaroni and spoon into an 8 × 8-inch casserole. Top with cheese and bake at 350 degrees for 15–20 minutes. MAKES 4–6 SERVINGS.

Four Cheese Casserole

1 box macaroni and cheese

¼ cup grated Muenster cheese

¼ cup grated cheddar cheese

¼ cup grated sharp cheddar cheese

¼ cup grated Monterey Jack cheese

1 egg, beaten

¾ cup half-and-half

¼ teaspoon salt

¼ teaspoon pepper

1 can (4 ounces) green chiles

Boil macaroni in 2 cups water for 5 minutes, or until al dente; drain. Combine all grated cheeses in a bowl; set aside.

In a small bowl, mix egg, half-and-half, salt, pepper, and cheese packet. Place cooked macaroni in an 8 × 8-inch casserole dish and cover with half the cheese mixture and all the green chiles. Pour egg mixture evenly over top and then sprinkle with remaining cheese. Bake at 350 degrees for 35 minutes, or until bubbling around the edges. MAKES 4–6 SERVINGS.

Mark's Mega Macaroni

1 box macaroni and cheese

4 tablespoons butter

¼ cup milk

   salt and pepper

¼ teaspoon cayenne pepper

¼ pound cubed ham

1¼ cups grated cheddar cheese

1¼ cups grated mozzarella cheese

1¼ cups grated Monterey Jack cheese

   paprika

Boil macaroni in 2 cups water for 5 minutes, or until al dente; drain and add butter while still warm. Stir until butter is melted. Mix together milk, salt, pepper, and cayenne. Add to macaroni with cheese packet. Stir in ham and cheeses. Pour into an 8 × 8-inch baking dish and top with some paprika. Bake at 350 degrees for 45–60 minutes, or until top is crispy; serve after cooling slightly. MAKES 4–6 SERVINGS.

Macaroni Pie

1 box macaroni and cheese

2¼ cups milk

4 eggs

½ cup dry pancake mix

½ teaspoon salt

1 teaspoon red pepper sauce, or to taste

¾ cup grated Colby Jack cheese, divided

Preheat oven to 400 degrees. Boil macaroni in 2 cups water until tender; drain. Put in a 9 × 9-inch greased baking dish. Beat milk, eggs, pancake mix, salt, red pepper sauce, ½ cup cheese, and the cheese packet until smooth, about 1 minute. Pour mixture over pasta. Bake for 40 minutes, or until knife comes out clean. Sprinkle with remaining cheese and bake 1–2 minutes more, or until cheese is melted. Let cool 10 minutes before serving. MAKES 4 SERVINGS.

Crispy Macaroni and Cheese

1 box macaroni and cheese

1 can (10.75 ounces) cream of mushroom soup, condensed

½ cup milk

½ teaspoon mustard

1 dash pepper

2 cups grated cheddar cheese, divided

1 can (2.8 ounces) french-fried onions

Boil macaroni in 2 cups water for 5 minutes; drain. Mix soup, milk, mustard, pepper, cheese packet, cooked macaroni, and 1½ cups cheese in a 1½-quart casserole. Bake at 400 degrees for 20 minutes, or until hot; stir. Sprinkle with onions and remaining cheese. Bake 1 minute more, or until onions are golden and cheese is melted. MAKES 4 SERVINGS.

Chicken Potpie

1 box macaroni and cheese

1 can (10.75 ounces) cream of broccoli soup, condensed

1 cup milk

¼ teaspoon garlic powder

⅛ teaspoon pepper

2 cups cubed cooked chicken or turkey

1 package (10 ounces) frozen peas and carrots, cooked and drained

½ cup herb-seasoned stuffing, crushed

2 tablespoons grated Parmesan cheese

2 tablespoons butter or margarine, melted

Preheat oven to 400 degrees. Boil macaroni for 5 minutes, or until al dente; drain. Mix soup, cheese packet, milk, garlic powder, and pepper in a 2-quart shallow baking dish. Stir in cooked macaroni, chicken, and vegetables. Bake 20 minutes; stir. Mix stuffing and Parmesan cheese with butter and then sprinkle over top. Bake 5 minutes more, or until hot. MAKES 4–6 SERVINGS.

Dr. Pepper Bake

1 box macaroni and cheese

1 pound lean ground beef

½ cup chopped onion

¼ teaspoon garlic powder

¼ teaspoon Italian seasoning

¼ teaspoon salt

¼ teaspoon pepper

¾ cup Dr. Pepper

1 can (8 ounces) tomato sauce

2 tablespoons Worcestershire sauce

1 cup grated mozzarella cheese, divided

Boil macaroni in water until tender; drain. Preheat oven to 350 degrees.

Brown beef in a large skillet; drain well. Add onion, cheese packet, and seasonings and cook about 5 minutes. Add Dr. Pepper, tomato sauce, and Worcestershire sauce; cook 5 minutes more. Stir in cooked macaroni. Stir in ¾ cup cheese. Pour mixture into a well-greased casserole dish. Sprinkle remaining cheese over top. Bake at 350 degrees for 20 minutes. MAKES 4–6 SERVINGS.

Fajita Macaroni and Cheese

1 box macaroni and cheese

1 pound ground beef

¼ cup sliced green onions

½ envelope fajita seasoning mix

1 jar (15.5 ounces) salsa con queso

3 taco shells, crushed

Boil macaroni in water until tender; drain. Brown ground beef in a large skillet, stirring until it crumbles; drain. Stir in cooked macaroni, green onions, fajita seasoning mix, cheese packet, and salsa con queso. Pour into a lightly greased 9 × 13-inch baking dish. Sprinkle with crushed taco shells. Bake at 350 degrees for 30 minutes, or until thoroughly heated. MAKES 4–6 SERVINGS.

Baked Tomato Macaroni

1 box macaroni and cheese

1 can (14.5 ounces) diced tomatoes

1 can (10.75 ounces) tomato soup, condensed

¾ cup milk

2 cups grated cheddar cheese

3 tablespoons butter

¼ cup dry breadcrumbs

Preheat oven to 350 degrees. Boil macaroni in lightly salted water for 5 minutes, or until al dente; drain.

In large bowl, combine cooked macaroni, tomatoes, soup, milk, cheese packet, cheese, and butter. Pour into 9 × 13-inch baking dish. Top with breadcrumbs. Bake for 45 minutes, or until golden brown and bubbly. MAKES 6 SERVINGS.

Mom's Mac and Cheese

1 box macaroni and cheese

1 can (14.5 ounces) stewed tomatoes, with juice

1 package (8 ounces) grated sharp cheddar cheese

Preheat oven to 350 degrees.

Boil macaroni in lightly salted water for 5 minutes; drain. Mix tomatoes with cheese packet and then add to cooked macaroni. Stir in the cheese. Pour into a 9 × 13-inch baking dish and bake for 30 minutes. MAKES 4–6 SERVINGS.

Chicken Casserole

1 box macaroni and cheese

2 cups diced cooked chicken

2 cups grated cheddar cheese

1 can (10.75 ounces) cream of chicken soup, condensed

1 cup milk

1 can (4.5 ounces) sliced mushrooms

Preheat oven to 350 degrees.

Boil macaroni in lightly salted water for 5 minutes, or until al dente; drain.

In a large bowl, combine cooked macaroni, cheese packet, chicken, cheese, soup, milk, and mushrooms. Place mixture in a 9 × 13-inch baking dish. Bake uncovered for 50–60 minutes; serve. MAKES 4–6 SERVINGS.

Mac and Cheese Custard

1 box macaroni and cheese

3 large eggs

1½ cups skim or low-fat milk

1 teaspoon salt

½ teaspoon paprika

2 cups grated cheddar cheese

¼ cup saltine cracker crumbs

Preheat oven to 325 degrees.

Grease a 10 × 7 × 2-inch casserole dish. Boil macaroni in large pot of water until tender; rinse in cold water and drain well.

In a mixing bowl, whisk together the eggs, milk, salt, cheese packet, and paprika. Stir in cheese and cooked macaroni. Pour into baking dish and then top with cracker crumbs. Bake for 30 minutes, or until a knife inserted in the center comes out clean. MAKES 4–6 SERVINGS.

Curried Macaroni

2½ cups cubed sourdough bread

1 box macaroni and cheese

1½ tablespoons cornstarch

1½ teaspoons dry mustard, divided

1½ teaspoons curry powder, divided

2¼ cups whole milk

6 tablespoons butter, divided

2¼ cups packed grated sharp cheddar cheese (about 10 ounces)

salt and pepper

Place bread on a cookie sheet. Bake at 225 degrees until bread has dried, about 15 minutes, and then crumble.

Boil macaroni in 2 cups water for 5 minutes, or until al dente; drain.

Preheat oven to 350 degrees. Butter an 8 × 8 × 2-inch glass baking dish. Combine cornstarch, cheese packet, 1 teaspoon dry mustard, and 1 teaspoon curry powder in a large heavy saucepan. Gradually whisk in milk and then add 2 tablespoons butter. Whisk over medium-high heat until sauce thickens and boils, about 1 minute; remove from heat. Add cheese and whisk until smooth; stir in cooked macaroni and then season with salt and pepper. Transfer to prepared baking dish. Melt remaining butter in a large heavy skillet over medium-high heat. Mix in remaining dry mustard and curry powder. Add breadcrumbs and stir until crumbs are crisp and golden, about 8 minutes. Sprinkle crumb mixture over macaroni and cheese. Bake until warmed through and bubbling at the edges, about 30 minutes; serve hot. MAKES 4–6 SERVINGS.

Potato Macaroni Gratin

1 (12-ounce) russet potato, peeled and cut into ½-inch pieces (about 2 cups)

1 box macaroni and cheese

2 tablespoons butter

1 pound onions (about 3 medium), sliced

¾ cup whipping cream

¾ cup milk (do not use low-fat or nonfat)

1½ cups grated Swiss cheese

salt and pepper

Preheat oven to 350 degrees. Butter an 8 × 8 × 2-inch baking dish.

Cook potato in large pot of boiling salted water until tender, about 10 minutes. Using slotted spoon, transfer potato to a large bowl. Add macaroni to same pot of boiling water and cook until tender; drain. Add cooked macaroni to potato. Meanwhile, melt the butter in a large heavy skillet over medium-high heat. Add onions and sauté until tender and brown, stirring often, about 15 minutes. Combine onions, cream, cheese packet, milk, and cheese with potato mixture and mix well. Season to taste with salt and pepper. Transfer to prepared dish. Bake until heated through and cheese melts, about 20 minutes. Let cool 5 minutes and then serve. MAKES 4–6 SERVINGS.

Macaroni and Cheese with Mushrooms and Bacon

1 box macaroni and cheese

1 cup chopped mushrooms

½ small onion, finely chopped

2 tablespoons butter, divided

½ tablespoon flour

¼ teaspoon dry mustard

¼ teaspoon salt

⅛ teaspoon pepper

¾ cup whole milk

1½ cups packed grated sharp cheddar cheese

1 tablespoon chopped fresh parsley

4 slices thick-cut bacon, chopped and cooked

½ cup fresh breadcrumbs

Preheat oven to 350 degrees. Butter a 9 × 13-inch glass baking dish.

Boil macaroni in large pot of water until tender, stirring occasionally; drain. Sauté mushrooms and onion in 1 tablespoon butter until tender, about 5 minutes. Stir in flour, cheese packet, dry mustard, salt, and pepper; cook 1 minute. Gradually whisk in milk. Cook until sauce is smooth and slightly thickened, whisking constantly, about 3 minutes; remove from heat. Add cheese and parsley; stir until cheese melts and then mix in cooked macaroni.

Mix half the bacon pieces into the macaroni mixture and transfer to prepared dish. Sprinkle with remaining bacon. Melt remaining butter in a small saucepan over medium heat; add breadcrumbs and sauté until beginning to brown, about 3 minutes. Sprinkle buttered breadcrumbs over macaroni and bake until heated through and golden brown, about 20 minutes. MAKES 4–6 SERVINGS.

Corned Beef and Kraut

1   box macaroni and cheese

1   can (10.75 ounces) cream of mushroom soup, condensed

1½ cups grated mozzarella cheese

1¾ cups sauerkraut

1   can (12 ounces) corned beef

Preheat oven to 325 degrees.

Boil macaroni in a large pot of lightly salted water for 5 minutes, or until al dente; drain off most of the water, but not all. Add the soup to the macaroni and mix well. Stir in cheese, cheese packet, sauerkraut, and corned beef. Pour mixture into a 9 × 13-inch baking dish and bake for 45–60 minutes.

MAKES 4–6 SERVINGS.

Cavatini

1 green bell pepper, chopped

1 yellow onion, chopped

1½ cups sliced and quartered pepperoni

12 ounces sliced fresh mushrooms

1 box macaroni and cheese

1 jar (20 ounces) spaghetti sauce

1 clove garlic, peeled and minced

1½ cups ricotta cheese

1½ cups grated mozzarella cheese, divided

¼ cup grated Parmesan cheese

In a large saucepan, combine bell pepper, onion, pepperoni, mushrooms, cheese packet, spaghetti sauce, and garlic. Cover and simmer for 15 minutes.

Boil macaroni in a large pot of lightly salted water for 5 minutes, or until al dente; drain. Preheat oven to 350 degrees. Mix together cooked macaroni with ricotta, 1 cup mozzarella, and Parmesan cheese. In a 9 × 13-inch baking dish, alternate macaroni and cheese mixture with sauce mixture, ending with sauce. Top with remaining mozzarella. Bake for 30 minutes and let stand for 5 to 10 minutes before serving. MAKES 4–6 SERVINGS.

Creamy Mushroom Casserole

 1 box macaroni and cheese

 ½ tablespoon butter

 ¼ cup milk

 1 can (10.75 ounces) cream of mushroom soup, condensed

 ½ pound Velveeta cheese, cubed

Boil macaroni in a large pot of lightly salted water for 5 minutes, or until al dente; drain.

Preheat oven to 350 degrees.

In a medium saucepan over medium heat, combine butter, milk, cheese packet, soup, and cheese. Stir until cheese is melted and mixture is smooth. Stir in cooked macaroni. Pour into a 2-quart baking dish and bake 20 minutes, or until top is golden. MAKES 4–6 SERVINGS.

Dried Beef Casserole

 1 box macaroni and cheese

 1 can (10.75 ounces) cream of mushroom soup, condensed

 1¼ cups milk

 ¼ cup sour cream

 1 jar (8 ounces) dried beef

 1 can (2 ounces) sliced black olives

 1 large onion, diced

 2 cups grated cheddar cheese

Boil macaroni in a large pot of lightly salted water for 5 minutes, or until al dente; drain. Preheat oven to 350 degrees.

Combine soup, milk, and sour cream with cheese packet in a large bowl. Cut beef into fourths. Combine beef, olives, and onion with soup mixture; stir in cooked macaroni. Pour into a 9 × 13-inch glass baking dish and top with cheese. Bake for 1 hour, or until cheese is golden brown. MAKES 4–6 SERVINGS.

Mac and Cheese with Mustard and Worcestershire

1 box macaroni and cheese

2 tablespoons butter

2½ cups grated extra-sharp cheddar cheese, divided

2 cans (5 ounces each) evaporated milk

3 large eggs

1 tablespoon mustard

1 teaspoon Worcestershire sauce

⅛ teaspoon cayenne pepper

Preheat oven to 350 degrees. Butter an 8 × 8 × 2-inch glass baking dish.

Boil macaroni in a pot of lightly salted water until al dente, stirring occasionally; drain and place in a large bowl. Add butter and toss until melted. Stir in 2 cups cheese. Beat milk, eggs, mustard, cheese packet, Worcestershire sauce, and cayenne pepper in a medium bowl to blend. Stir egg mixture into cooked macaroni. Transfer to prepared dish and then sprinkle remaining cheese over top. Bake until golden on top and set in center, about 1 hour.

MAKES 4 SERVINGS.

Skillet Dishes

Hot Dog Casserole

    1 **box macaroni and cheese**

    1 **tablespoon butter or margarine**

    8 **hot dogs, sliced**

   ½ **cup chopped onion**

    1 **can (12 ounces) Mexican-style corn, with liquid**

    1 **can (15 ounces) tomato sauce**

   ½ **teaspoon chili powder**

Boil macaroni in 2 cups water for 5 minutes; drain.

Melt butter in a pan. Add hot dog slices and onion. Cook until lightly browned. Stir in corn, tomato sauce, cheese packet, and chili powder; simmer 10 minutes. Add cooked macaroni, toss, and serve. MAKES 4–6 SERVINGS.

Italian-Style Macaroni and Beef

   ½ **onion, chopped**

   ½ **green bell pepper, chopped**

    1 **tablespoon olive oil**

   ½ **pound ground beef**

    1 **cup water**

    1 **cup marinara sauce**

    1 **box macaroni and cheese**

In a skillet, sauté onion and bell pepper in oil until onion is transparent; set aside. Brown ground beef in same skillet and drain. Add onion mixture, water, and marinara sauce; stir in cheese packet. Bring mixture to a simmer. Add macaroni and let simmer for 7 minutes, or until macaroni is tender. MAKES 4 SERVINGS.

Chili Mac

1 box macaroni and cheese

½ cup chopped green bell pepper

¼ cup chopped green onion

4 tablespoons butter

1 can (14 ounces) beanless chili

1 can (14.5 ounces) diced tomatoes with green chiles

¼ cup grated cheddar cheese

Boil macaroni in 2 cups water until al dente; drain. Sauté bell pepper and onion in butter. Stir in chili, tomatoes, and cheese packet. Simmer 10 minutes. Add cooked macaroni and serve topped with cheese. MAKES 4 SERVINGS.

Savory Bacon Mac

1 box macaroni and cheese

9 slices bacon

2 tablespoons butter

3 tablespoons flour

1 cup evaporated milk

1 tablespoon onion flakes

salt and pepper

1 teaspoon Worcestershire sauce

Boil macaroni in 2 cups water until tender; drain, reserving 1 cup water. Cook bacon and reserve 1 tablespoon bacon fat. Combine fat, butter, and flour. Slowly stir in reserved water, milk, and cheese packet. Add onion flakes, salt, pepper, and Worcestershire sauce. Simmer until sauce thickens, then toss with macaroni and bacon; serve immediately. MAKES 4–6 SERVINGS.

Cheeseburger Pasta

½ pound ground beef

1 box macaroni and cheese

1½ cups water

1 teaspoon mustard

½ cup ketchup

Cook ground beef in a skillet until browned; drain. Add remaining ingredients, including cheese packet, and heat to a boil. Cook over medium heat for 10 minutes, or until macaroni is done, stirring often. MAKES 4 SERVINGS.

Goulash

1 box macaroni and cheese

1 pound ground beef

1 medium onion, chopped (about ½ cup)

2 cups sliced celery

½ cup ketchup

1 jar (2.5 ounces) sliced mushrooms, with liquid

1 can (14.5 ounces) diced tomatoes, drained

2 teaspoons salt

¼ teaspoon pepper

Boil macaroni in a pot with lightly salted water until done; drain.

In the meantime, cook and stir beef and onion in a large skillet until meat is brown and onion is tender; drain off fat. Stir in cooked macaroni, celery, ketchup, mushrooms, tomatoes, cheese packet, salt, and pepper. Cover and simmer 30–45 minutes. MAKES 4 SERVINGS.

Greek Chicken Pasta

1 box macaroni and cheese

  olive oil

½ onion, diced

1 cup diced tomatoes (Roma work best)

2 chicken breasts, cooked and sliced

¼ cup balsamic vinegar

1 can (6 ounces) pitted whole black olives

½ cup crumbled feta cheese

Boil macaroni in a pot with lightly salted water until done; drain and rinse. Add the oil and onion to a large skillet. Cook over medium-high heat until the onion has wilted, then stir in the tomatoes. When the tomatoes begin to separate from their skins, add the chicken, cheese packet, and balsamic vinegar. Lower the heat and continue cooking for about 15–20 minutes, or until it becomes almost like a sauce. You may need to add more oil and/or balsamic vinegar to the mixture to keep it moist. When it reaches the desired consistency, combine with the cooked macaroni and black olives. Garnish with feta cheese and serve. MAKES 4 SERVINGS.

Cheesy Pea Pasta

1   onion, chopped

1   tablespoon olive oil

     salt and pepper

1   can (8 ounces) tomato sauce

1   cup water

1   can (8 ounces) peas, with liquid

1   box macaroni and cheese

Sauté onion in oil. Add salt, pepper, tomato sauce, and water; bring to a boil. Add peas and simmer 3 minutes.

Boil macaroni in 2 cups water until just tender; drain. Stir cooked macaroni and cheese packet into sauce mixture. Turn off heat and let stand 20 minutes. MAKES 4 SERVINGS.

Tex-Mex Macaroni and Cheese

1 box macaroni and cheese

¼ cup milk

4 tablespoons butter

1 pound ground beef

1 teaspoon salt

⅛ teaspoon pepper

1 medium onion, chopped

1 green bell pepper, chopped

1 can (12 ounces) whole kernel corn, drained

1 can (14.5–16 ounces) diced tomatoes, with liquid

1 can (6 ounces) tomato paste

Boil macaroni in a pot of lightly salted water until al dente; drain. Return to pot and stir in milk, butter, and cheese packet until cheese is dissolved.

Brown ground beef with salt and pepper in a large skillet. Add onion and bell pepper; continue cooking until onion is tender. Add corn, tomatoes, and tomato paste; heat through. Stir in prepared macaroni and cheese; simmer for 8 to 10 minutes. MAKES 4–6 SERVINGS.

Spicy Hamburger Mac

1 pound ground beef

1 can (10 ounces) tomatoes and green chiles with cilantro, with juices

1 can water

1 box macaroni and cheese

In a large nonstick skillet, brown beef and then drain. Add tomatoes, water, cheese packet, and macaroni. Mix together and bring to a boil. Cover and reduce heat to simmer for 7–8 minutes. MAKES 4 SERVINGS.

Chop Suey

- 1 box macaroni and cheese
- 1 pound ground Italian sausage
- 1 onion, diced
- 1 green bell pepper, diced
- 1 can (7 ounces) mushrooms, drained
- 1 can (14.5 ounces) stewed tomatoes

Boil macaroni in a large pot of lightly salted water for 5 minutes, or until al dente; drain. In the same pot, cook sausage over medium heat until brown; drain, leaving 2 tablespoons drippings. In the same pot, sauté onion and bell pepper over medium heat until softened. Add cheese packet, cooked macaroni, sausage, mushrooms, and tomatoes to pot and heat through, about 5 minutes; serve. MAKES 4 SERVINGS.

Chicken Stuff

- ½ cup butter or margarine
- 2 boneless, skinless chicken breasts, cut into 1-inch strips
  pinch garlic salt
- ⅛ teaspoon lemon pepper
- 1 box macaroni and cheese
- 1 can (10.75 ounces) cream of mushroom soup, condensed
- 1 can water
- ½ cup sliced fresh mushrooms (optional)

In a large skillet, melt butter over medium heat. Lay chicken strips in butter and then sprinkle with garlic salt and lemon pepper. Cook, turning frequently, until chicken is golden brown on all sides (the chicken should still be soft, not fried hard). When all the chicken is browned, add cheese packet, soup, water, and mushrooms to skillet; blend well with pan drippings and chicken strips. Add macaroni and just enough water to cover noodles; stir well. Lower heat and cover. Simmer until macaroni is done, stirring frequently. MAKES 4 SERVINGS.

Spicy Mac and Cheese

1 box macaroni and cheese

½ pound ground beef

¼ cup water

¼ cup ketchup

1 envelope chili seasoning mix

1 can (14.5 ounces) kidney beans, rinsed and drained

Boil macaroni in a pot with lightly salted water for 5 minutes, or until al dente; drain. Brown beef in a skillet; drain. Add water, ketchup, chili seasoning, cheese packet, and beans. Bring mixture to a simmer over medium-low heat. Add cooked macaroni and simmer for 5 minutes more. Add more water if necessary; serve. MAKES 3–4 SERVINGS.

Beefy Macaroni and Cheese

1 box macaroni and cheese

1 pound ground chuck

½ cup chopped onion

1¼ cups milk

¼ cup mayonnaise

1 can (4 ounces) chopped mild green chiles

Boil macaroni as directed on package; drain.

In a large skillet, brown beef with onion, stirring to break up; drain off excess fat. Stir in cheese packet, milk, and mayonnaise. Add chiles and cooked macaroni; bring to a boil, stirring occasionally. MAKES 4–6 SERVINGS.

Wisconsin Mac

1 box macaroni and cheese

1 slice whole wheat bread

2 tablespoons butter

2 tablespoons flour

¾ cup low-fat milk

¾ cup vegetable broth

2 green onions, thinly sliced

1½ cups packed grated sharp cheddar cheese

   salt and pepper

Boil macaroni in pot with lightly salted water until tender but still firm to bite; drain.

Meanwhile, grind bread in a food processor to fine crumbs; transfer to small bowl. Melt butter in a medium saucepan. Mix ½ tablespoon melted butter into crumbs. Add flour and cheese packet to remaining butter; whisk over medium heat 2 minutes. Gradually whisk in milk and broth. Preheat broiler. Mix cooked macaroni into sauce with onions and cheese. Season to taste with salt and pepper. Spoon into a 9-inch pie plate. Sprinkle crumbs over top and then broil until crumbs brown, about 2 minutes; serve. MAKES 2–3 SERVINGS.

Mexican Mac and Cheese

¾ pound lean ground beef

1 tablespoon dried onion flakes

1 box macaroni and cheese

1 scant cup nacho cheese dip

½ cup medium salsa

1 can (4 ounces) diced green chiles

In a medium skillet over medium-high heat, cook beef with onion flakes until beef is browned; drain.

In a large saucepan, cook the macaroni and cheese according to package directions. Stir in the meat mixture, nacho cheese dip, salsa, and green chiles. Reduce heat and simmer 15 minutes, or until heated through. MAKES 3–4 SERVINGS.

COOKING TIP

If you are making a dish to be reheated, undercook the pasta, as it will finish cooking upon reheating. When reheating, add a tablespoon of water to the dish.

Saucepan Dishes

Salsa Macaroni and Cheese

- 1 box macaroni and cheese
- ¼ cup sour cream
- 4 tablespoons butter
- 1 cup salsa
- ¼ cup grated cheddar cheese

Boil macaroni in a pot of lightly salted water for 5 minutes, or until pasta is al dente; drain. Return to pot and stir in sour cream, butter, and cheese packet until cheese is dissolved. Add salsa and cheese; mix well and serve. MAKES 4 SERVINGS.

Stadium Mac and Cheese

- 1 box macaroni and cheese
- ¼ cup milk
- 4 tablespoons butter
- ½ cup barbecue sauce
- 2 tablespoons applesauce
- 1 can (10 ounces) tomatoes
- 4 cooked hot dogs, sliced

Boil macaroni in a pot of lightly salted water for 5 minutes, or until pasta is al dente; drain. Return to pot and stir in milk, butter, and cheese packet until cheese is dissolved.

In a separate bowl, mix barbecue sauce and applesauce. Stir sauce into macaroni and toss with tomatoes and hot dogs and heat through. MAKES 4 SERVINGS.

Balsamic Chicken

1 box macaroni and cheese

¼ cup milk

4 tablespoons butter

2 chicken breasts, cooked and diced

1 cup diced green bell pepper

¼ cup balsamic vinaigrette dressing

Boil macaroni in a pot of lightly salted water for 5 minutes, or until pasta is al dente; drain. Return to pot and stir in milk, butter, and cheese packet until cheese is dissolved. Stir in chicken and bell pepper. Toss with balsamic vinaigrette and serve. MAKES 4 SERVINGS.

Salsa Verde

1 box macaroni and cheese

¼ cup milk

4 tablespoons butter

2 chicken breasts, cooked and diced

1 cup green chile sauce

Boil macaroni in a pot of lightly salted water for 5 minutes, or until pasta is al dente; drain. Return to pot and stir in milk, butter, and cheese packet until cheese is dissolved. Stir in chicken and green chile sauce; heat through and serve. MAKES 4 SERVINGS.

Bacon and Macaroni

1 box macaroni and cheese

¼ cup milk

1 cup grated Swiss cheese

4 tablespoons butter

9 slices bacon, cooked and crumbled

   dash Worcestershire sauce

Boil macaroni in a pot of lightly salted water for 5 minutes, or until pasta is al dente; drain. Return to pot and stir in milk, Swiss cheese, butter, and cheese packet until cheese is dissolved. Stir in bacon and Worcestershire sauce; serve. MAKES 4 SERVINGS.

Rachel's Macaroni

1 box macaroni and cheese

¼ cup milk

4 tablespoons butter

1 cup diced ham

1 cup frozen peas, thawed

Boil macaroni in a pot of lightly salted water for 5 minutes, or until pasta is al dente; drain. Return to pot and stir in milk, butter, and cheese packet until cheese is dissolved. Stir in ham and peas; heat through and serve. MAKES 4 SERVINGS.

Broccoli and Turkey Macaroni

1 box macaroni and cheese

¼ cup milk

4 tablespoons butter

1 cup steamed broccoli, well drained and chopped

1 cup diced turkey

Boil macaroni in a pot of lightly salted water for 5 minutes, or until pasta is al dente; drain. Return to pot and mix in milk, butter, and cheese packet until cheese is dissolved. Stir in broccoli and turkey; heat through and serve. MAKES 4 SERVINGS.

Spiced-Up Macaroni

1 box macaroni and cheese

¼ cup milk

4 tablespoons butter

1 teaspoon cayenne pepper

1 teaspoon garlic powder

Tabasco sauce, to taste

Boil macaroni in a pot of lightly salted water for 5 minutes, or until pasta is al dente; drain. Return to pot and stir in milk, butter, cayenne, garlic, and cheese packet until cheese is dissolved. Top with Tabasco sauce. MAKES 4 SERVINGS.

Mac and Green Chiles

1 box macaroni and cheese

1 cup diced green chiles

½ cup diced onion

½ cup diced green bell pepper

4 tablespoons butter, divided

¼ cup milk

Boil macaroni in a pot of lightly salted water for 5 minutes, or until pasta is al dente; drain. Sauté chiles, onion, and bell pepper in 2 tablespoons butter. Return macaroni to pot and stir in milk, remaining butter, vegetables, and cheese packet until cheese is dissolved. MAKES 4 SERVINGS.

Bacon and Tomato Mac

1 box macaroni and cheese

¼ cup milk

4 tablespoons butter

9 slices bacon, cooked and crumbled

1 cup diced tomatoes

Boil macaroni in a pot of lightly salted water for 5 minutes, or until pasta is al dente; drain. Return to pot and stir in milk, butter, and cheese packet until cheese is dissolved. Stir in bacon and tomatoes; heat through and serve. MAKES 4 SERVINGS.

Fiesta Mac

1 box macaroni and cheese

¼ cup milk

4 tablespoons butter

1 cup diced green bell pepper

1 cup black beans, rinsed and drained

1 cup corn

Boil macaroni in a pot of lightly salted water for 5 minutes, or until pasta is al dente; drain. Return to pot and stir in milk, butter, and cheese packet until cheese is dissolved. Stir in remaining ingredients and heat through. MAKES 4 SERVINGS.

Creamy Sage Macaroni

1 box macaroni and cheese

½ tablespoon butter

2 tablespoons breadcrumbs

1 teaspoon finely chopped sage

1 cup grated Parmesan cheese

Boil macaroni in a pot of lightly salted water for 5 minutes, or until pasta is al dente; drain. Melt butter in a skillet over low heat, add breadcrumbs, sage, and cheese packet. Return pasta to pot. Stir in breadcrumb mixture and Parmesan cheese. MAKES 4 SERVINGS.

Frito Pie

1 box macaroni and cheese

¼ cup milk

4 tablespoons butter

1 can (14 ounces) beanless chili

2 cups Fritos

Boil macaroni in a pot of lightly salted water for 5 minutes, or until pasta is al dente; drain. Return to pot and stir in milk, butter, and cheese packet until cheese is dissolved. Stir in chili and heat through. Crumble in Fritos and serve. MAKES 4 SERVINGS.

Italian Chicken

1 box macaroni and cheese

¼ cup milk

4 tablespoons butter

1 cup diced cooked chicken

1 can diced and seasoned tomatoes, with juice

⅓ cup diced green bell pepper

Boil macaroni in a pot of lightly salted water for 5 minutes, or until pasta is al dente; drain. Return to pot and stir in milk, butter, and cheese packet until cheese is dissolved. Stir in chicken and vegetables and heat thoroughly. MAKES 4 SERVINGS.

Creamy Pesto

1 box macaroni and cheese

½ cup whole cream

1 cup pesto

Boil macaroni in a pot with lightly salted water until tender; drain and rinse. Mix cheese packet into cream. Bring cream to a boil and then add pesto. Simmer 5 minutes and then add cooked macaroni. Toss and serve. MAKES 4 SERVINGS.

Paladin Blue Macaroni

1 box macaroni and cheese

¼ cup crumbled Paladin Blue Cheese

1 tablespoon butter

1 teaspoon chopped parsley

Boil macaroni in 2 cups water until tender; drain. Stir in blue cheese, cheese packet, and butter until cheese and butter are melted. Sprinkle with parsley and serve immediately. MAKES 4 SERVINGS.

Creamy Basil and Almonds

1 box macaroni and cheese

1 cup chopped fresh basil sprigs

4 tablespoons butter, chopped

2 tablespoons cream

⅓ cup toasted slivered almonds

Add macaroni to a large pot of boiling water. Boil, uncovered, for about 5 minutes, or until tender; drain. Return cooked macaroni to pot and gently stir in basil, butter, cream, cheese packet, and almonds. MAKES 4 SERVINGS.

Family Favorites

Fried Macaroni and Cheese

1 box macaroni and cheese

¼ cup milk

4 tablespoons butter

½ cup balsamic vinaigrette dressing

3 cups grated mozzarella cheese

4 cups cornflakes, crushed

4 cups vegetable oil

Boil macaroni in a pot of lightly salted water for 5 minutes, or until pasta is al dente; drain (do not rinse!). Return to pot and mix in milk, butter, and cheese packet until cheese is dissolved. Stir in the balsamic vinaigrette and cheese. Roll a spoonful of mixture into a ball; add some cornflakes if the mixture crumbles apart. Roll in crushed cornflakes until thoroughly coated.

In a skillet, heat oil over medium-low heat until hot. Add balls and fry until golden. (If balls do not hold their shape, add small amounts of flour to the macaroni and cheese until they become sticky.) You will need to turn the balls to reach all sides. MAKES ABOUT 35 BALLS.

VARIATIONS: *Try combining ranch dressing with cheddar, pepper jack, or mozzarella cheese; Thousand Island dressing with cheddar cheese; Italian dressing with cheddar or mozzarella; honey dijon dressing with cheddar or Monterey Jack cheese.*

Chicken Parmesan

1 tablespoon garlic powder

1 box macaroni and cheese

4 boneless, skinless chicken breasts

1 cup breadcrumbs

2 cups marinara sauce

4 thick slices fresh mozzarella

Preheat oven to 350 degrees.

In a small bowl, mix garlic powder and cheese packet. Rub chicken breasts with cheese mixture until thoroughly covered. Coat both sides of chicken with breadcrumbs and place in a greased glass casserole dish with enough room so the breasts are not touching. Bake for 35–40 minutes.

Heat marinara sauce according to directions. Boil macaroni in 2 cups water until al dente; drain and rinse in warm water. Before removing chicken from the oven, place a piece of mozzarella on each breast. Bake 5 minutes more. Serve macaroni topped with sauce and chicken. MAKES 4 SERVINGS.

Pizza Mac

1 box macaroni and cheese

¼ cup milk

4 tablespoons butter

1 cup diced pepperoni

1 can (7 ounces) mushrooms, drained

1 small onion, diced (about ½ cup)

1 can (14.5 ounces) sliced black olives, drained

Boil macaroni in a pot of lightly salted water for 5 minutes, or until pasta is al dente; drain. Return to pot and stir in milk, butter, and cheese packet until cheese is dissolved. Stir in remaining ingredients, heat through, and serve. MAKES 4 SERVINGS.

Mock Mashed Potatoes

1 head cauliflower, cut up

1 box macaroni and cheese

4 tablespoons butter

1 cup sour cream

Preheat oven to 350 degrees.

In a large saucepan, cook cauliflower until soft; drain. Boil macaroni in lightly salted water until done, about 5 minutes. Puree cauliflower, macaroni, butter, sour cream, and cheese packet in a food processor or blender until creamy. Pour into a 9 × 9-inch greased baking dish and bake for 30 minutes. MAKES 6–8 SERVINGS.

Macaroni Cake

1 box macaroni and cheese

1 cup sugar

1 teaspoon anise extract

6 eggs

½ pound ricotta cheese

Preheat oven to 350 degrees.

Boil macaroni in a pot of lightly salted water for 5 minutes, or until pasta is al dente; drain. Beat remaining ingredients, including cheese packet, in a bowl. Place pasta in a greased 8 × 8-inch pan. Pour mixture over pasta, making sure pasta is completely covered. Cover with foil and bake for 45 minutes. Remove foil and bake another 15 minutes. Allow cake to cool and then serve. MAKES 4–6 SERVINGS.

Christmas Stew

    2 carrots, sliced
    ½ cup green peas
    2 medium onions, chopped
    1 can (14.5 ounces) green beans, with juice
    3 cups water
    1 box macaroni and cheese
    2 teaspoons ground cinnamon
    1 teaspoon ground cloves
    1 tablespoon corn flour
    1 cup milk
    1 tablespoon sugar
    ½ teaspoon pepper
       salt

Boil carrots, peas, onions, and beans in the water until carrots are tender. Add cheese packet, cinnamon, and cloves. Mix corn flour with the milk and slowly add to the boiling mixture. Add sugar, pepper, and salt. Add macaroni and simmer 5 minutes more; serve immediately. MAKES 4–6 SERVINGS.

Cheesy Triangles

    1 box macaroni and cheese
    ¼ cup milk
    4 tablespoons butter
    1 cup grated cheddar cheese
    1 cup breadcrumbs

Preheat oven to 350 degrees.

Boil macaroni in a pot of lightly salted water until al dente; drain. Return to saucepan and stir in milk, butter, and cheese packet until cheese is dissolved.

On a baking sheet, thinly spread macaroni and top with cheese and bread-crumbs. Bake for 20 minutes. Cut into triangles. MAKES 6–8 SERVINGS.

Denver Omelet

- 1 box macaroni and cheese
- ¼ cup milk
- 4 tablespoons butter
- 12 eggs, beaten
- 1 teaspoon salt
- ⅛ teaspoon pepper
- 1 medium onion, chopped
- 1 cup sliced mushrooms
- 1 green bell pepper, chopped

Boil macaroni in a pot of lightly salted water until al dente; drain. Return to saucepan and stir in milk, butter, and cheese packet until cheese is dissolved.

In a bowl, beat eggs, salt, and pepper. Add onion, mushrooms, and bell pepper to eggs. Stir in macaroni and cheese and then pour into skillet; cook over medium heat until eggs are done. MAKES 6–8 SERVINGS.

Chili Dogs

- 1 box macaroni and cheese
- ¼ cup milk
- 4 tablespoons butter
- 4 hot dogs, cooked and sliced
- 1 cup beanless chili

Boil macaroni in a pot of lightly salted water for 5 minutes, or until pasta is al dente; drain. Return to pot and stir in milk, butter, and cheese packet until cheese is dissolved. Top with hot dogs and chili. MAKES 4 SERVINGS.

Meat Loaf

1 box macaroni and cheese

¼ cup ketchup

1 pound ground beef

Preheat oven to 350 degrees.

Boil macaroni in lightly salted water for 5 minutes; drain and rinse. Mix half of the cheese packet, ketchup, cooked macaroni, and beef until evenly dispersed. Place in a well-greased loaf pan. Cover with remaining cheese packet. Bake for 40 minutes. MAKES 4–6 SERVINGS.

Taco Salad

1 box macaroni and cheese

¼ cup milk

4 tablespoons butter

1 pound ground beef

1 envelope taco seasoning

1 head lettuce, chopped

1 tomato, diced

3 green onions, diced

4 tablespoons Thousand Island dressing

1½ cups tortilla chips, crushed

Boil macaroni in a pot of lightly salted water until al dente; drain. Return to pot and stir in milk, butter, and cheese packet until cheese is dissolved; chill for 1 hour. Brown beef with taco seasoning; drain and let cool for a few minutes.

In a large bowl, combine lettuce, tomato, onions, ground beef, and macaroni. Toss with dressing, sprinkle chips over top, and then serve. MAKES 4–6 SERVINGS.

Salsa Balls

1 box macaroni and cheese

¼ cup milk

4 tablespoons butter

1 cup salsa

3 cups grated Mexican-blend cheese

4 cups finely crushed corn chips

Preheat oven to 300 degrees.

Boil macaroni in a pot of lightly salted water until al dente; drain. Return to pot and stir in milk, butter, and cheese packet until cheese is dissolved. Add salsa and cheese. Roll into balls, adding more cheese if they fall apart. Roll in crushed corn chips and place on a baking sheet. Bake for 15 minutes. Let cool before serving. MAKES 35 BALLS.

Pan-Fried Mac and Cheese

1 box macaroni and cheese

½ teaspoon salt

¼ teaspoon pepper

⅛ teaspoon paprika (optional)

3 large eggs, beaten and at room temperature

1 tablespoon oil or bacon drippings

2 tablespoons butter, melted

8 ounces medium or sharp cheddar cheese, grated

Boil macaroni in lightly salted water until al dente; drain well and then place in a large bowl. Season with salt, pepper, and paprika, if using.

In a medium bowl, briskly beat eggs with cheese packet using a whisk, until light and fluffy and pale yellow.

In a large skillet over low heat, heat oil and butter together. Quickly mix together macaroni, grated cheese, and beaten eggs. Add mixture to skillet and then stir and fry until brown and crispy. Serve immediately. MAKES 4–6 SERVINGS.

Chicken and Broccoli Cups **33**

Meatballs with Apricot Hoisin Sauce 214

Ham and Egg Pizzas **262**

101 Ways with Meatballs

Appetizers & Sides

Mini Meatball Hamburgers 155 • Meatball Jalapeño Poppers 156 • Meatball Sliders 157 • Meatball Bruschetta 158 • Bacon-Wrapped Meatballs 158 • Thai Pizza 159 • Puff Pastry Meatball and Mushroom Pockets 160 • Malaysian Meatballs 161 • Crescent-Wrapped Meatballs 161 • Southwest Taco Salad 162 • Parmesan Meatball Biscuits 162 • Easy Meatball Nachos 163

Soups, Stews & Chilis

Meatball Minestrone 164 • Tortellini Meatball Stew 165 • Family Favorite Egg Noodle Soup 166 • Taco Soup 166 • Southwestern Cilantro Rice Soup 167 • Meatball Chowder 167 • Chinese Beef Noodle Soup 168 • Winter Stew 169 • Crowd-Pleasing Meatball Chili 169 • White Bean Salsa Chili 170 • Meatball Zucchini Orzo Soup 170 • Cheesy Rice and Hamburger Soup 171 • Garden Veggie Soup with Bow Tie Pasta 172

Sandwiches, Wraps & More

Philly Meatball Sub Sandwiches 173 • Saucy Meatball Grinders 174 • Coney Meatball Subs 175 • Pesto Meatball Baguette Sandwiches 176 • Piping Hot Buffalo Subs 177 • Roasted Pepper and Meatballs on Rye 177 • Mediterranean Meatball Sandwiches 178 • Italian Focaccia Meatball Sandwiches 179 • Swedish Meatball Hero 180 • Open-Faced Meatball Sub 180 • Fall Cranberry Wrap 181 • Yummy Stuffed Pitas 181 • Easy Sloppy Joes 182

Dressed-Up Meatballs

Crowd-Pleasing Meatballs 183 • Marinated Meatballs 184 • Sweet and Spicy Meatballs 184 • Cranberry Sauerkraut Meatballs 185 • Italian-Style Cocktail Meatballs 185 • Blue Cheese Buffalo Balls 186 • Sports Day Meatballs 186 • Magnificent Meatballs 187 • Saucy Meatballs 187 • Teriyaki Meatballs 188 • Maple Meatballs 188 • Feta Meatballs with Cucumber Yogurt Sauce 189 • Spicy Jamaican Jerk Meatballs 190 • Asian Meatball Appetizers 191 • Ginger Ale Meatballs 191 • Cheesy Meatballs 192 • Salsa Verde Meatballs 192 • Holiday Meatballs 193 • Sour Cream–Sauced Meatballs 193

Pasta Dinners

Meatball Fettuccine Alfredo 194 • Chipotle Meatball Pasta 195 • Florentine Meatballs and Noodles 196 • Meatballs in Blue Cheese Sauce 197 • Slow-Cooked Tomato Soup Meatballs 198 • Easy Meatball Lasagna 199 • Pesto Spaghetti and Meatballs 200 • Ricotta-Stuffed Shells and Meatballs 200 • Baked Ziti and Meatballs 201 • Eggplant Parmesan 202 • Italian-Tossed Tortellini 203 • Ravioli Meatball Stir-Fry 203 • Meatball Stroganoff 204 • Amazing Meatball Tortellini 205 • Cheesy Broccoli Meatballs 206

Dinners with Rice

Easy Rice and Meatballs 207 • Meatballs in Curry Sauce 208 • Sesame Stir-Fry 208 • Swiss Mushroom Meatball Casserole 209 • Creamy Meatball and Brown Rice Casserole 210 • Pineapple Meatballs and Rice 211 • Meatballs with Orange Peanut Sauce 211 • Cajun Shrimp and Meatball Goulash 212 • Creamy French Onion Meatballs 213 • Meatballs with Apricot Hoisin Sauce 214 • Enchilada Meatballs 215 • Creamy Rice and Meatballs 215 • Taste of the Islands Meatballs 216

Family Favorites

Meatballs in Tomato and Corn Sauce 217 • Sweet and Sour Meatball Kabobs 218 • Caesar Meatball Kabobs 219 • Breakfast Burritos 220 • Easy Meatball Pizza 220 • Southwest Crescent Pockets 221 • Meatball Pot Pie 222 • Instant Soft Taco 222 • Meatball Fajita Quesadillas 223 • Baked Beefy Mac and Cheese 224 • Stuffing-Covered Meatball Casserole 224 • Enchilada Casserole 225 • Spicy Meatball Burritos 226 • Tater Tot Kids' Casserole 226 • Hash Brown Meatball Casserole 227 • Kid-Friendly Taco Casserole 228

Appetizers & Sides

Mini Meatball Hamburgers

26 (1 pound) frozen, fully cooked meatballs

1 cup ketchup

3 tablespoons honey Dijon mustard

26 (2-inch) dinner rolls, sliced in half horizontally

1½ cups sweet pickle relish

Preheat oven to 400 degrees.

Place the meatballs in a 9 × 9-inch pan with ½ inch water. Bake for 30 minutes, or until thoroughly heated.

In a small bowl, combine ketchup and mustard. Place a heaping teaspoon of the mixture on the bottom of a roll and then top with a meatball. Add a teaspoon of pickle relish and cover with top half of roll. Repeat with remaining ingredients and serve immediately on a large platter. MAKES 26 APPETIZERS.

VARIATION: *Place a small slice of cheddar cheese over each meatball to make cheeseburgers.*

COOKING TIP

Choose the flavor you crave. The most common flavors of meatballs are original (also known as home style), Italian style, and Swedish.

Meatball Jalapeño Poppers

13 jalapeños, stemmed
 1 package (8 ounces) cream cheese, softened
13 frozen, fully cooked meatballs, thawed
13 slices (1 pound) bacon, cut in half

Preheat oven to 375 degrees.

Slice each pepper in half lengthwise, remove the seeds, and rinse out. Spread cream cheese in each jalapeño half. Cut the meatballs in half. Place each meatball half, cut side down, over cream cheese. Wrap a half slice of bacon around each stuffed jalapeño and secure with a toothpick. Place on a baking sheet and bake 25–30 minutes, or until bacon is browned. Serve immediately on a platter. MAKES 26 APPETIZERS.

COOKING TIP

Use plastic gloves when cutting and preparing jalapeño peppers to prevent skin irritation.

Meatball Sliders

½ medium onion, finely chopped

2 tablespoons olive oil

2 teaspoons minced garlic

1 can (28 ounces) crushed tomatoes

½ teaspoon sugar

2 teaspoons Italian seasoning

¾ teaspoon salt

20 frozen, fully cooked meatballs, thawed

20 (2-inch) soft buns or rolls, split

In a 4-quart pan, sauté onion in oil until tender. Add garlic and sauté 1 minute more. Stir in tomatoes, sugar, and seasonings. Simmer 10–15 minutes over medium heat, stirring occasionally. Add meatballs to the sauce. Cover pan and continue to cook over medium heat 10–15 minutes more, stirring occasionally, until meatballs are heated through. Place a meatball and 1 tablespoon sauce in the middle of each split roll. Secure each meatball to the bun with a toothpick. Serve immediately. MAKES 20 APPETIZERS.

NOTE: *Any leftover sauce can be used for dipping bread sticks or serving over hot cooked pasta later.*

Meatball Bruschetta

9 frozen, fully cooked meatballs, thawed

1 French baguette or loaf crusty Italian bread

2 tablespoons olive oil

1 jar (13.75 ounces) bruschetta topping

⅓ pound fresh full-fat mozzarella, thinly sliced

Cut meatballs in half and heat according to package directions. Cut bread into 18 slices. Lay slices evenly over a baking sheet and brush with oil. Broil 1–2 minutes, or until lightly toasted. Place a tablespoon of the bruschetta topping over each bread slice. Top with a meatball half, cut side down. Place cheese slices over the meatballs and broil 1–2 minutes, or until the cheese melts and lightly browns. MAKES 18 APPETIZERS.

VARIATION: *Use goat cheese instead of mozzarella.*

Bacon-Wrapped Meatballs

8 slices uncooked bacon, cut in half

16 frozen, fully cooked meatballs, thawed

honey mustard

barbecue sauce

ranch dressing

Preheat oven to 375 degrees.

Wrap a half slice bacon around each meatball and secure with a toothpick. Place on a baking sheet and bake 20–25 minutes, or until bacon is crisp. Serve with honey mustard, barbecue sauce, and ranch dressing for dipping. MAKES 16 APPETIZERS.

Thai Pizza

1 teaspoon dried ginger

2 tablespoons olive oil

1 tube (13.8 ounces) refrigerated pizza crust dough

3 tablespoons soy sauce

3 tablespoons peanut butter

juice from 1 lime

1 teaspoon Thai green curry paste

13 frozen, fully cooked meatballs, thawed and sliced into thirds

½ cup shredded carrots

1 can (8 ounces) pineapple tidbits, drained

1 tablespoon chopped fresh cilantro

1 tablespoon sliced green onion

Preheat oven to 425 degrees.

In a small bowl, combine ginger and oil; let sit 10 minutes. Spread dough on a baking sheet prepared with nonstick cooking spray. Brush olive oil mixture over dough and then bake for 5 minutes.

In a 2-quart bowl, whisk together the soy sauce, peanut butter, lime juice, and curry paste until fairly smooth. Spread mixture evenly over pizza crust. Top with remaining ingredients and bake 8–10 minutes more, or until crust is golden. Slice into six rows of four pieces. MAKES 24 APPETIZERS.

COOKING TIP

Thaw meatballs properly. Frozen meatballs should be thawed in the refrigerator, or they can be thawed using the defrost function on a microwave.

Puff Pastry Meatball and Mushroom Pockets

26 (1 pound) frozen, fully cooked meatballs, thawed

2 cups sliced mushrooms

½ cup chopped sweet onion

1 teaspoon minced garlic

1 tablespoon olive oil

   salt and pepper

1 box (17.3 ounces) frozen puff pastry dough, thawed

1 large egg, beaten

Preheat oven to 400 degrees.

Cut meatballs in half. In a frying pan, sauté meatball halves, mushrooms, onion, and garlic in oil for 10 minutes over medium heat; salt and pepper to taste. On a cutting board, cut each sheet of puff pastry into 9 (3-inch) squares. Place a heaping tablespoon of mushroom meatball filling in the center of each square. Pull corners up to the top center and overlap over the filling. With a pastry brush, brush the tops with the egg and press to seal the pockets. Place pockets on two baking sheets and bake 16–18 minutes, or until golden brown. MAKES 18 APPETIZERS.

Malaysian Meatballs

52 (2 pounds) frozen, fully cooked meatballs

¼ cup 100 percent natural peanut butter (no added sugar or oil)

½ cup warm water

½ cup hoisin sauce

2½ tablespoons sweet red chile sauce

Cook meatballs according to package directions. Meanwhile, stir peanut butter until smooth. In a bowl, combine peanut butter, water, and hoisin sauce until smooth. Stir in the chile sauce. Serve meatballs with toothpicks as an appetizer with the sauce on the side for dipping. MAKES 10–12 SERVINGS.

NOTE: *Hoisin sauce and sweet red chile sauce can be found in the Asian section of the grocery store.*

Crescent-Wrapped Meatballs

24 frozen, fully cooked meatballs, thawed

2 tubes (8 ounces each) refrigerated crescent roll dough

1¼ cups grated Italian-blend cheese or mozzarella and provolone

marinara sauce

Preheat oven to 400 degrees.

Cut meatballs in half. Unroll the crescent dough. Cut each crescent into 3 equal-size parts. Place a pinch of cheese over dough. Place meatball half over cheese. Wrap dough around the meatball, pinching and positioning to completely cover. Lay wrapped meatballs on a large baking sheet and bake 10–12 minutes, or until dough is golden brown. Serve with marinara sauce for dipping. MAKES 48 APPETIZERS.

Southwest Taco Salad

13 frozen, fully cooked meatballs, thawed

2 tablespoons taco seasoning

⅓ cup water

1 large head romaine lettuce, torn into bite-size pieces

1 cup cooked red kidney beans

1 cup grape tomatoes

1 cup grated sharp cheddar cheese

2 cups crushed Doritos, any flavor

1 bottle (16 ounces) Catalina dressing

Cut meatballs in half. In a frying pan, combine meatball halves, taco seasoning, and water. Simmer over medium heat for 8 minutes.

In a large bowl, layer lettuce, meatballs, beans, tomatoes, cheese, and chips. Serve with Catalina dressing on the side. MAKES 6–8 SERVINGS.

Parmesan Meatball Biscuits

1 tube (12 ounces) refrigerated biscuits

10 frozen, fully cooked meatballs, thawed

2 tablespoons grated Parmesan cheese

½ teaspoon dried Italian seasoning

¼ teaspoon garlic powder

marinara sauce

Preheat oven to 375 degrees.

Separate dough into 10 biscuits and flatten slightly. Place a meatball in the center of each biscuit and wrap dough completely around it, sealing the edges. Place the sealed side down in an 8-inch round pan. Evenly space the biscuits in the pan.

In a small bowl, combine the cheese, Italian seasoning, and garlic powder. Press a pinch of the cheese mixture into the top of each roll. Bake for 15–20 minutes, or until golden brown. Serve with warm marinara sauce for dipping. MAKES 10 SERVINGS.

Easy Meatball Nachos

16 frozen, fully cooked meatballs, thawed

1 medium onion, chopped

1 green bell pepper, seeded and chopped

1 tablespoon olive oil

1 envelope taco seasoning

1 can (14.5 ounces) sliced stewed tomatoes, with liquid

1 can (15 ounces) black beans, rinsed and drained

1 bag (10 ounces or larger) tortilla chips, any variety

   grated cheddar or Monterey Jack cheese

   sour cream (optional)

Cut meatballs into quarters. In a large frying pan, sauté the onion and bell pepper in oil over medium-high heat until tender. Stir in meatballs and cook for 3 minutes. Stir in taco seasoning, tomatoes, and beans. Reduce heat to medium and simmer 10 minutes, stirring occasionally and breaking apart tomato chunks. Spoon mixture over individual servings of tortilla chips. Sprinkle cheese over top and garnish with sour cream if desired. MAKES 8–10 SERVINGS.

VARIATION: *Filling can also be served burrito style in warm soft flour tortillas.*

Soups, Stews & Chilis

Meatball Minestrone

2 cans (15 ounces each) cannellini or great Northern beans, rinsed and drained, divided

1 box (32 ounces) chicken broth

2 cups water

1 tablespoon minced garlic

1 envelope dry vegetable soup or dip mix

26 (1 pound) frozen, fully cooked meatballs, thawed

1 can (14.5 ounces) diced tomatoes with basil, garlic, and oregano, with liquid

8 ounces uncooked rainbow rotini pasta

1 bag (9 ounces) fresh spinach, torn

grated Parmesan cheese, optional

In a 5- to 6-quart stockpot, combine 1 can beans, broth, water, and garlic over medium-high heat and bring to a boil. Add dry vegetable mix, stirring thoroughly. Stir in meatballs and tomatoes and return to a boil; stir in pasta. Cover and simmer over medium heat for 15 minutes, stirring occasionally. Add remaining can of beans and spinach; simmer 5 minutes more. Garnish with cheese if desired. MAKES 12–15 SERVINGS.

Tortellini Meatball Stew

1   container (32 ounces) beef broth

4   cups water

26 (1 pound) frozen, fully cooked meatballs

1   cup chunky salsa

1   teaspoon minced garlic

½   tablespoon Italian seasoning

1   bag (16 ounces) frozen Italian-style vegetable mix

1   bag (19 ounces) frozen cheese tortellini

    salt and pepper

In a 5- to 6-quart stockpot, combine broth, water, meatballs, salsa, garlic, and Italian seasoning; bring to a boil. Simmer over medium-high heat for 10 minutes. Add vegetables and return to a boil. Simmer over medium-high heat for 6 minutes. Stir in tortellini and bring to a boil. Boil for 5 minutes. Salt and pepper to taste. MAKES 8–10 SERVINGS.

Family Favorite Egg Noodle Soup

1 bag (16 ounces) frozen egg noodles

1 medium onion, diced

2 stalks celery, sliced into small pieces

2 tablespoons olive oil

26 (1 pound) frozen, fully cooked meatballs

1 box (32 ounces) beef broth

2 cups water

2 teaspoons dried parsley flakes (or 2 tablespoons fresh chopped parsley)

1 teaspoon salt

1 teaspoon pepper

Thaw noodles according to package directions. In a 4-quart soup pan, sauté the onion and celery in oil over high heat for 3 minutes, stirring occasionally. Add meatballs to the pan. Sauté for 3 minutes more, stirring occasionally. Mix in broth, water, parsley, salt, and pepper. Add the noodles and then bring to a boil over high heat. Reduce heat to medium-high and simmer 15 minutes, or until noodles are done. MAKES 5–6 SERVINGS.

Taco Soup

16 frozen, fully cooked meatballs, thawed

1 can (14.5 ounces) diced tomatoes with garlic and onion, with liquid

1 can (15.25 ounces) whole kernel corn, drained

1 can (15 ounces) black or kidney beans, rinsed and drained

1 can (8 ounces) tomato sauce

2 cups water

1 envelope taco seasoning

Cut meatballs in half and place in a 3- to 4-quart soup pan. Stir in the remaining ingredients and bring to a boil. Lower to medium heat and simmer for 20 minutes, stirring occasionally. MAKES 5–6 SERVINGS.

VARIATION: *This soup can be served over crushed tortilla chips, and garnished with cheese and a dollop of sour cream.*

Southwestern Cilantro Rice Soup

4 cans (14 ounces each) beef broth

2 cans (14.5 ounces each) diced tomatoes and green chiles, with liquid

26 (1 pound) frozen, fully cooked meatballs

1 cup chopped onion

½ cup chopped fresh cilantro

2 teaspoons Italian seasoning

½ cup uncooked long-grain rice

grated Mexican-blend cheese, optional

In a 5- to 7-quart slow cooker prepared with nonstick cooking spray, stir together broth, tomatoes, meatballs, onion, cilantro, and seasoning. Sprinkle rice evenly over the soup. Cover and cook over high heat for 3–4 hours or on low heat for 6–8 hours. Garnish with cheese, if desired. MAKES 10–12 SERVINGS.

NOTE: *Recipe can be halved and prepared in a 3- to 4-quart slow cooker.*

Meatball Chowder

13 frozen, fully cooked meatballs, thawed and sliced in half

2 cups frozen corn

2½ cups water

1 pound baking potatoes, peeled and cut into ½-inch pieces

½ tablespoon Old Bay seafood seasoning

1 cup half-and-half

½ cup grated sharp cheddar cheese

In a 4-quart soup pan, combine meatball halves, corn, water, potatoes, and seasoning over high heat and bring to a boil. Cover and reduce heat. Simmer for 10 minutes, or until potatoes are done. Turn off the heat and then stir half-and-half into the soup. Ladle into individual bowls, sprinkle cheese over top, and serve. MAKES 4–6 SERVINGS.

Chinese Beef Noodle Soup

1   medium white onion, thinly sliced

1   tablespoon olive oil

1   teaspoon minced garlic

1   tablespoon thinly sliced fresh ginger or 2 teaspoons dried ginger

4   cans (14 ounces each) vegetable broth

3½ cups water

3   tablespoons soy sauce

1   teaspoon Chinese five-spice powder

1   teaspoon paprika

26 (1 pound) frozen, fully cooked meatballs

1   package (6 ounces) uncooked chow mein stir-fry noodles

2   tablespoons chopped fresh cilantro (optional)

In a 5- to 7-quart stockpot, sauté onion in oil over high heat until translucent. Stir in garlic and ginger and cook for 1 minute. Pour in broth, water, and soy sauce. Stir in Chinese five-spice powder and paprika. Bring broth to a boil and then stir in meatballs and return to a boil. Lower heat to medium-high and simmer for 7–8 minutes. Stir in noodles and boil 6–10 minutes more. Garnish with cilantro, if desired. MAKES 7–9 SERVINGS.

Winter Stew

3 medium potatoes, peeled and cubed

1 bag (16 ounces) baby carrots, cut into thirds

2 to 3 stalks celery, sliced

½ medium onion, chopped

26 (1 pound) frozen, fully cooked meatballs

3 cups water

1 envelope beef stew seasoning mix

1 can (10.5 ounces) cream of mushroom soup, condensed

In a 5- to 7-quart slow cooker prepared with nonstick cooking spray, layer potatoes, carrots, celery, onion, and meatballs.

In a bowl, combine water, stew mix, and soup. Pour mixture over meatball layer. Cover and cook on high heat for 4–5 hours or on low heat for 8–10 hours. MAKES 8–10 SERVINGS.

Crowd-Pleasing Meatball Chili

1 medium onion, chopped

1 tablespoon olive oil

2 teaspoons minced garlic

1 can (28 ounces) diced tomatoes, with liquid

1 can (28 ounces) crushed tomatoes

4 cans (16 ounces each) chili beans in sauce, with liquid

1 can (4 ounces) diced green chiles

1 to 2 tablespoons chili powder

39 (1½ pounds) frozen, fully cooked meatballs, thawed

In a 6- to 8-quart stockpot, sauté onion in oil until translucent. Stir in remaining ingredients. Bring to a boil, stirring frequently. Simmer over medium-low heat for 20 minutes, stirring occasionally. MAKES 14–16 SERVINGS.

White Bean Salsa Chili

18 frozen, fully cooked meatballs

1 jar (16 ounces) chunky salsa

1 can (15.25 ounces) white kernel corn, with liquid

2 cans (15.5 ounces each) great Northern beans, drained and rinsed

1 can (14.5 ounces) diced tomatoes with green chiles, with liquid

Combine all ingredients in a 3- to 5-quart slow cooker prepared with non-stick cooking spray. Cover and cook on high heat for 3 hours or on low heat for 6–8 hours. MAKES 6 SERVINGS.

VARIATION: *Defrost meatballs. Combine all ingredients in a 3½- to 4-quart soup pan. Bring to a boil on the stovetop. Reduce heat and simmer for 15–20 minutes, stirring occasionally.*

VARIATION: *To add more heat to the chili, stir in 2 to 3 teaspoons chili powder.*

Meatball Zucchini Orzo Soup

26 (1 pound) frozen, fully cooked meatballs, thawed

1 small zucchini, shredded

4 cans (14.5 ounces each) chicken broth

1 cup uncooked orzo pasta

1 teaspoon pepper

1 teaspoon dried parsley flakes

¼ cup freshly squeezed lemon juice

2 eggs

In a 4-quart soup pan, combine meatballs and zucchini. Add the broth, orzo, pepper, and parsley and bring to a boil. Reduce heat to medium-low and simmer uncovered 25–30 minutes.

In a separate bowl, beat together lemon juice and eggs. Stir ¼ cup of the hot soup into the egg mixture. Pour egg mixture into the pot and simmer 2 minutes more. Serve immediately. MAKES 6–8 SERVINGS.

Cheesy Rice and Hamburger Soup

26 (1 pound) frozen, fully cooked meatballs, thawed

2 cans (10.5 ounces each) cheddar cheese soup, condensed

2 cans (10.5 ounces each) tomato soup, condensed

1 cup uncooked long-grain white rice

3½ cups water

½ envelope dry onion soup mix

Cut meatballs into quarters; set aside.

In a 4-quart soup pan, combine soups, rice, water, and dry soup mix over high heat. Stirring constantly, bring to a boil. Reduce to medium heat and then stir in meatballs. Cover and cook over medium heat for 30 minutes, stirring every 3–4 minutes to prevent rice from sticking to bottom of pan. Garnish with crushed saltine crackers and grated cheddar cheese if desired.

MAKES 6–8 SERVINGS.

Garden Veggie Soup with Bow Tie Pasta

26 (1 pound) frozen, fully cooked meatballs

1 can (14.5 ounces) diced tomatoes with garlic and onion, with liquid

½ tablespoon dried basil

1 box (32 ounces) beef or chicken broth

1 cup water

3 carrots, peeled and sliced

1 medium summer squash, cut in half lengthwise and sliced

1 medium zucchini, cut in half lengthwise and sliced

1 medium red or green bell pepper, seeded and chopped

1½ cups uncooked bow tie pasta

In a 5- to 7-quart slow cooker, combine all ingredients except pasta. Cover and cook on high heat for 3½–4 hours or on low heat for 7–9 hours. During the last half hour of cooking, cook bow tie pasta according to package directions; drain pasta and add to soup. Serve immediately. MAKES 8–10 SERVINGS.

Sandwiches, Wraps & More

Philly Meatball Sub Sandwiches

- 2 green or red bell peppers, sliced fajita style
- 1 medium yellow onion, sliced fajita style
- 1 tablespoon olive oil
- 16 frozen, fully cooked meatballs
- 2 tablespoons Worcestershire sauce
- ½ cup Heinz 57 sauce
- 4 hoagie rolls, split and lightly toasted
- 4 slices provolone cheese

In a frying pan, sauté bell peppers and onion in oil until tender and starting to brown. While vegetables are cooking, place meatballs in a microwave-safe bowl with 1–2 tablespoons water. Microwave on high for 4 minutes, stirring halfway through. Drain any excess liquid.

In a small bowl, combine the sauces. Stir mixture into the meatballs. Divide sautéed vegetables over rolls. Evenly divide hot meatballs and cheese over top. Serve immediately. MAKES 4 SERVINGS.

Saucy Meatball Grinders

  1 jar (14 ounces) pizza sauce

  4 tablespoons apple jelly

  ½ teaspoon Italian seasoning

  ½ teaspoon salt

  ½ teaspoon pepper

30 frozen, fully cooked meatballs

  6 hoagie rolls, split lengthwise

  1 cup grated mozzarella cheese

In a 2½- to 3-quart saucepan, combine pizza sauce, jelly, Italian seasoning, salt, and pepper. Bring to a slow boil over medium heat. Add meatballs to the sauce. Cover and simmer over medium heat for 18–20 minutes, stirring occasionally, until meatballs are heated through. Reduce heat if sauce is too bubbly. During the last 10 minutes of cooking, preheat oven to 375 degrees. Place split hoagie rolls open faced on a large baking sheet. Equally place meatballs on the bottom half of each roll. Drizzle desired amount of sauce over meatballs and sprinkle cheese over top. Bake uncovered for 2–3 minutes, or until cheese melts. MAKES 6 SERVINGS.

Coney Meatball Subs

40 frozen, fully cooked meatballs

1 medium onion, peeled and quartered

1 green bell pepper, seeded and quartered

1 can (15 ounces) pork and beans

1 can (10.75 ounces) tomato soup, condensed

1 envelope taco seasoning

1 tablespoon water

   lettuce, torn

8 slices cheddar or pepper jack cheese

8 hoagie buns

Place meatballs in a 3- to 4-quart slow cooker prepared with nonstick cooking spray.

In a blender or food processor, blend the onion and bell pepper. Add pork and beans, soup, seasoning, and water. Process until smooth and then pour mixture over meatballs. Cover and cook on low heat for 6–8 hours or on high heat for 3½–4 hours. Layer lettuce, 5 meatballs, and a cheese slice on individual hoagie buns. MAKES 8 SERVINGS.

VARIATION: *For a spicier sauce, add chopped hot peppers or hot sauce, to taste, before cooking.*

Pesto Meatball Baguette Sandwiches

¼	cup pesto
¾	cup mayonnaise
½	tablespoon olive oil
15	cherry tomatoes, sliced in half
25	frozen, fully cooked meatballs, thawed
5	(6-inch) baguettes, split
	lettuce, torn into large pieces

In a bowl, combine pesto and mayonnaise. Refrigerate until ready to use. In a frying pan, heat the oil. Sauté tomato halves in oil for 1–2 minutes. Add meatballs to pan and cook, stirring frequently, until meatballs are hot. Toast open-faced baguettes under broiler for 1–2 minutes or in a toaster oven. Spread mayonnaise mixture over both sides of baguettes. Spoon 5 meatballs evenly over each baguette. Add desired amount of lettuce and serve. MAKES 5 SANDWICHES.

VARIATION: *Hoagie buns can be used in place of baguettes.*

Piping Hot Buffalo Subs

25 frozen, fully cooked meatballs

 1 jar (12–16 ounces) buffalo wing sauce

 5 (6-inch) hoagie or sub rolls

    lettuce, torn into sandwich-size sections

10 thin slices tomato

 1 medium red onion, sliced

 5 tablespoons chunky blue cheese dressing, divided

Preheat oven to 400 degrees.

Place meatballs in an 8 × 8-inch pan. Pour buffalo wing sauce over meatballs and then cover with aluminum foil. Bake for 35 minutes, or until bubbly. Split rolls and broil open-faced on a baking sheet for 1–2 minutes, or until lightly toasted. Layer lettuce, 2 tomato slices, and red onion rings on rolls. Spoon 5 meatballs with desired amount of sauce on each sandwich. Spread 1 tablespoon dressing over top. Serve immediately. MAKES 5 SERVINGS.

Roasted Pepper and Meatballs on Rye

18 frozen, fully cooked meatballs

 1 container (8 ounces) chive-and-onion cream cheese

 6 slices rye bread

 6 tablespoons jarred sweet roasted red peppers

 3 romaine lettuce leaves, torn to fit sandwich

 6 deep-fried onion rings, plus more

Heat meatballs according to package directions. Spread desired amount of cream cheese over each slice of bread. Spoon 2 tablespoons roasted peppers over 3 slices of bread. Place 6 heated meatballs over pepper layer. Add a lettuce leaf, followed by 2 onion rings. Top with remaining bread slices, cream cheese side down. Serve immediately with additional onion rings. MAKES 3 SERVINGS.

Mediterranean Meatball Sandwiches

12 frozen, fully cooked meatballs

6 tablespoons sour cream

½ teaspoon minced garlic

6 slices multigrain or olive bread

½ bag (8 ounces) Mediterranean-blend salad

3 slices red onion

4½ tablespoons grated Parmesan cheese

Heat meatballs according to package directions and then cut each into 3 slices. Combine sour cream and garlic. Spread 1 tablespoon sour cream mixture over each slice of bread. Place a layer of salad over 3 pieces of bread. Layer the hot meatball slices, red onion, and Parmesan cheese over the top. Top with remaining bread, sour cream side down. Serve immediately with any remaining salad on the side. MAKES 3 SERVINGS.

Italian Focaccia Meatball Sandwiches

9 frozen, fully cooked meatballs

2 tablespoons water

1 rectangle (12 ounces) focaccia bread

3 tablespoons olive oil

6 tablespoons warm spaghetti sauce

3 tablespoons jarred sun-dried tomato pieces, drained and julienned

¾ cup grated mozzarella cheese

3 fresh basil leaves, chopped

In a microwave-safe bowl, microwave meatballs with the water on high for 3 minutes, or until hot. Cut meatballs in half; set aside.

Cut bread into 3 equal sections. Turn each piece on end and slice in half. Place the 6 slices cut side up on a baking sheet. Brush oil over top. Broil on high for 1–2 minutes, or until lightly toasted. Spoon 2 tablespoons spaghetti sauce over 3 bottoms. Sprinkle 1 tablespoon sun-dried tomatoes over sauce. Lay 6 meatball halves evenly over each bottom. Sprinkle ¼ cup cheese evenly over each meatball layer. Broil for 1–2 minutes more, or until cheese melts. Sprinkle one-third of the basil over top. Place remaining toasted halves over each sandwich. MAKES 3 SERVINGS.

Swedish Meatball Hero

30 frozen, fully cooked meatballs

2 jars (12 ounces each) brown beef gravy

6 (6-inch) hoagie or hero rolls, split

Preheat oven to 375 degrees.

Place frozen meatballs in an 8 × 8-inch pan. Pour gravy over the meatballs and cover the pan with aluminum foil. Bake 45–55 minutes, or until bubbly. Spoon 5 meatballs and desired amount of sauce inside each roll. MAKES 6 SANDWICHES.

VARIATION: *Bake meatballs and gravy following the instructions above. Serve over hot cooked noodles or mashed potatoes.*

Open-Faced Meatball Sub

30 frozen, fully cooked meatballs

1 jar (26 ounces) spaghetti or marinara sauce

6 hoagie or sub rolls, split

1 cup grated mozzarella cheese

In a 2½- to 3-quart saucepan, combine meatballs and sauce. Bring to a boil, stirring occasionally; reduce heat. Cover and simmer for 10 minutes, or until meatballs are thoroughly heated. Spoon 5 meatballs and some sauce over each roll. Sprinkle cheese evenly over meatballs and serve immediately. MAKES 6 SERVINGS.

VARIATION: *Sub rolls can be toasted in a toaster oven or broiled in a regular oven for 2 minutes before topping with meatballs and cheese.*

Fall Cranberry Wrap

10 frozen, fully cooked meatballs

2 (10-inch) flour tortillas

4 tablespoons whole cranberry sauce

4 tablespoons grated sharp cheddar cheese

6 thin apple slices

sprouts, optional

In a microwave oven, heat meatballs in a microwave-safe bowl in 1 table-spoon water on high for 1½–2 minutes, or until meatballs are hot. Place 5 meatballs down the center of each tortilla. Spread 2 tablespoons cranberry sauce alongside the meatballs. Sprinkle cheese evenly over top. Place 3 apple slices down the center of each tortilla, as well as the sprouts. Roll or wrap burrito style and then serve immediately. MAKES 2 SERVINGS.

Yummy Stuffed Pitas

9 frozen, fully cooked meatballs

½ teaspoon minced garlic

½ container (8 ounces) plain yogurt

3 pita bread pockets, warmed

1 Roma tomato, diced

½ cup shredded lettuce

3 tablespoons crumbled feta cheese, any variety

3 tablespoons sliced black olives

3 tablespoons chopped red onion

Heat meatballs according to package directions. Stir garlic into yogurt. Place 3 heated meatballs in each pita pocket. Fill pitas with tomato, lettuce, cheese, olives, and onion. Spoon desired amount of garlic yogurt sauce over top. MAKES 3 PITAS.

Easy Sloppy Joes

39 (1½ pounds) frozen, fully cooked meatballs, thawed

1¼ cups ketchup

1 tablespoon dried minced onion

1 tablespoon sugar

2 tablespoons yellow mustard

1 tablespoon apple cider vinegar

8 large hamburger buns

Crumble meatballs using a food processor or by hand. In a frying pan, sauté crumbled meatballs for 5–8 minutes over medium-high heat, stirring frequently. Stir in ketchup, dried onion, sugar, mustard, and vinegar. Reduce heat to medium-low. Cover and simmer for 25 minutes, stirring occasionally. Serve on warmed buns. MAKES 8 SERVINGS.

COOKING TIP

Be sure to cook the meatballs properly. While frozen meatballs are already fully cooked, they should be reheated to at least 160 degrees to ensure they are safe for eating. Heating meatballs can be done by baking, microwaving, heating in a sauce, or even grilling.

Dressed-Up Meatballs

Crowd-Pleasing Meatballs

1	cup grape juice
1	cup apple jelly
1	cup ketchup
1	cup spicy barbecue sauce
1	can (8 ounces) tomato sauce
2	teaspoons crushed red chili pepper flakes
104	(4 pounds) frozen, fully cooked meatballs

In a 2-quart saucepan, combine juice, jelly, ketchup, barbecue sauce, tomato sauce, and crushed pepper flakes. Heat over medium heat until jelly is melted into the sauce. Place meatballs in a 5-quart slow cooker prepared with non-stick cooking spray. Pour sauce evenly over meatballs. Cover and cook on low heat for 4–6 hours. Serve as an appetizer with toothpicks. MAKES 25–30 SERVINGS.

VARIATION: *This recipe can also be turned into a main dish by serving over a bed of rice with grated Swiss cheese sprinkled over top.*

NOTE: *This recipe can be halved and cooked on low heat for 4–6 hours in a 3-quart slow cooker.*

Marinated Meatballs

39 (1½ pounds) frozen, fully cooked meatballs

3 cups beef or vegetable broth

½ teaspoon lemon zest

1 teaspoon lemon juice

1 tablespoon dried parsley

½ teaspoon paprika

½ teaspoon fresh grated nutmeg

¼ teaspoon ground allspice

Place the meatballs in an 8-cup-capacity plastic bowl that has a tight lid. In a saucepan, combine the remaining ingredients. Bring the broth mixture to a boil. Lower temperature to medium and simmer for 15 minutes. Pour mixture over meatballs. Cover and refrigerate for 24 hours or more. Place the meatballs and marinade in a large frying pan and bring to a boil; boil 10 minutes and then remove meatballs to a serving dish. Boil sauce 5 minutes more, or until thickened. Pour sauce over meatballs. Serve as an appetizer with toothpicks or over buttered egg noodles. MAKES 6–8 SERVINGS.

Sweet and Spicy Meatballs

1 can (16 ounces) jellied cranberry sauce

1 jar (10 ounces) chili sauce

1 tablespoon brown sugar

1 tablespoon lemon juice

52 (2 pounds) frozen, fully cooked meatballs, thawed

In a 4-quart saucepan, combine cranberry sauce, chili sauce, brown sugar, and lemon juice. Cook over medium-high heat, stirring frequently until cranberry sauce melts and sauce is mostly smooth. Stir in meatballs. Simmer over medium heat for 10–15 minutes, or until meatballs are hot. Serve as an appetizer with toothpicks or over hot cooked rice as a main dish. MAKES 10 SERVINGS.

Cranberry Sauerkraut Meatballs

1 can (14.5 ounces) sauerkraut, with liquid

1 can (16 ounces) jellied cranberry sauce

½ cup packed brown sugar

½ jar (26 ounces) spaghetti sauce with onion and garlic

78 (3 pounds) frozen, fully cooked meatballs

In a bowl, combine sauerkraut, cranberry sauce, brown sugar, and spaghetti sauce. Place the meatballs in a 4- to 6-quart slow cooker prepared with non-stick cooking spray. Spoon sauerkraut mixture evenly over meatballs. Cover and cook on low heat for 4–6 hours, or until fully heated. Serve with toothpicks as an appetizer or over hot cooked pasta as a main dish. MAKES 12–16 SERVINGS.

Italian-Style Cocktail Meatballs

2 cans (8 ounces each) tomato sauce

⅓ cup packed brown sugar

½ cup red wine or apple cider vinegar

39 (1½ pounds) frozen, fully cooked meatballs

In a 2- to 3-quart pan, combine tomato sauce, brown sugar, and vinegar. Fold in meatballs. Cover and bring to a low boil. Reduce heat to medium and simmer for 15–20 minutes, stirring occasionally. Serve as an appetizer with toothpicks or over hot cooked angel hair pasta. MAKES 7–9 SERVINGS.

Blue Cheese Buffalo Balls

30 frozen, fully cooked meatballs

1 jar (12–16 ounces) buffalo wing sauce

1 bottle (12 ounces) chunky blue cheese dressing

Preheat oven to 375 degrees.

Place meatballs in an 8 × 8-inch pan and pour buffalo wing sauce over top. Cover pan with aluminum foil. Bake for 45–50 minutes, or until bubbly. Serve with toothpicks and blue cheese dressing on the side for dipping. MAKES 6–7 SERVINGS.

Sports Day Meatballs

2 jars (12 ounces each) chili sauce

2 tablespoons water, divided

1½ cups grape jelly

60 (2¼ pounds) frozen, fully cooked meatballs

Pour chili sauce into a 3- to 5-quart slow cooker that has been prepared with nonstick cooking spray. Add 1 tablespoon water to each jar, then replace the lid and shake the jar to release the chili sauce from sides of jar; pour remaining sauce into slow cooker. Stir grape jelly into chili sauce mixture. Add meatballs to slow cooker and stir to coat. Cover and cook on low heat for 4–6 hours, or until meatballs are heated through. Serve as an appetizer with toothpicks. MAKES 12–15 SERVINGS.

VARIATION: *Combine all ingredients in a 3- to 5-quart saucepan. Cover and simmer over medium-low heat on the stove for 50–55 minutes, stirring occasionally until meatballs are heated through. Serve in a chafing dish to keep warm during a party.*

Magnificent Meatballs

52 (2 pounds) frozen, fully cooked meatballs

1 jar (18 ounces) apricot preserves

1 jar (16 ounces) medium salsa

1 tablespoon cinnamon

Place meatballs in a 3- to 4½-quart slow cooker that has been prepared with nonstick cooking spray. In a bowl, combine the remaining ingredients. Pour sauce over meatballs. Cover and cook on low heat for 4–6 hours, or until meatballs are heated through. Serve as an appetizer with toothpicks or over rice as a main dish. MAKES 10–12 SERVINGS.

VARIATION: *Combine all ingredients in a 3- to 4-quart saucepan. Cover and simmer over medium-low heat on the stove for 55–60 minutes, stirring occasionally until meatballs are heated through.*

Saucy Meatballs

1 cup ketchup

2 tablespoons apple cider vinegar

2 tablespoons Worcestershire sauce

1 tablespoon sugar

½ teaspoon onion powder

½ teaspoon minced garlic

26 (1 pound) frozen, fully cooked meatballs, thawed

In a saucepan, combine ketchup, vinegar, Worcestershire sauce, sugar, onion powder, and garlic. Simmer over medium heat until bubbly. Stir meatballs into the sauce. Cover and cook over medium-low heat 15–20 minutes, stirring occasionally until meatballs are heated through. Serve as an appetizer with toothpicks or on hoagie buns with Monterey Jack cheese. MAKES 5–6 SERVINGS.

Teriyaki Meatballs

39 (1½ pounds) frozen, fully cooked meatballs

1 can (8 ounces) crushed pineapple, with liquid

1 jar (20 ounces) teriyaki sauce

Place frozen meatballs in a 2½- to 3½-quart slow cooker prepared with non-stick cooking spray. Spoon pineapple evenly over meatballs and pour teriyaki sauce over top. Cover and cook on low heat for 6–8 hours or on high heat for 3 hours. Serve as an appetizer with toothpicks or over hot cooked rice. MAKES 7–9 SERVINGS.

VARIATION: *Defrost meatballs. In a 3- to 4-quart saucepan, combine crushed pineapple and teriyaki sauce. Bring to a low boil, stirring constantly. Stir in thawed meatballs. Simmer over medium heat for 10–15 minutes, stirring frequently until meatballs are heated.*

Maple Meatballs

½ cup real maple syrup

½ cup chili sauce

2 teaspoons dried chives (or 2 tablespoons fresh chives)

1 tablespoon soy sauce

½ teaspoon ground mustard

26 (1 pound) frozen, fully cooked meatballs, thawed

In a saucepan, combine syrup, chili sauce, chives, soy sauce, and ground mustard. Bring to a low boil. Add meatballs and then return to a boil. Simmer over medium heat for 8–10 minutes, stirring occasionally until meatballs are thoroughly heated. Serve as an appetizer with toothpicks or over hot cooked rice. MAKES 5–6 SERVINGS.

Feta Meatballs with Cucumber Yogurt Sauce

26 (1 pound) frozen, fully cooked meatballs

1 container (4 ounces) crumbled tomato basil feta cheese

CUCUMBER YOGURT SAUCE:

1½ cups nonfat plain yogurt

4 ounces low-fat cream cheese

½ cup diced seedless cucumber

1 teaspoon minced garlic

1½ teaspoons dried dill seasoning

1 teaspoon fresh lemon juice

1 teaspoon lemon zest

Preheat oven to 375 degrees. Place meatballs in the bottom of an 8 × 8-inch pan with ½ inch of water and bake 40 minutes. While meatballs cook, place all yogurt sauce ingredients in a blender or food processor and blend until smooth. Pour the sauce in a bowl for dipping and refrigerate until ready to serve. Place baked meatballs on a serving platter and sprinkle with the cheese. Serve immediately with toothpicks and the yogurt sauce on the side.

MAKES 4–6 SERVINGS.

Spicy Jamaican Jerk Meatballs

39 (1½ pounds) frozen, fully cooked meatballs, thawed

JERK SEASONING:

1 tablespoon brown sugar

1 teaspoon ground allspice

1 teaspoon ground cinnamon

½ teaspoon ground ginger

½ teaspoon onion powder

½ teaspoon garlic powder

½ teaspoon pepper

¼ teaspoon cayenne pepper

¼ teaspoon ground cloves

JERK SAUCE:

½ cup ketchup

⅔ cup honey

1 tablespoon Jamaican jerk seasoning

1 cup white vinegar

Preheat oven to 375 degrees.

Place meatballs in a gallon-size ziplock bag. In a bowl, combine all jerk seasoning ingredients. Pour seasoning over meatballs. Seal bag and shake well to cover.

In a saucepan, combine jerk sauce ingredients and bring to a boil. Place meatballs in a 7 × 11-inch pan prepared with nonstick cooking spray. Pour sauce over the top and then cover pan with aluminum foil. Bake for 35–40 minutes. Serve as an appetizer with toothpicks or over hot cooked rice. MAKES 8–10 SERVINGS.

Asian Meatball Appetizers

1 bottle (18 ounces) honey barbecue sauce

1 can (8 ounces) crushed pineapple, with liquid

1½ teaspoons sugar

26 (1 pound) frozen, fully cooked meatballs, thawed

Preheat oven to 350 degrees.

In a bowl, combine barbecue sauce, pineapple, and sugar. Place meatballs in a deep 8 × 8-inch baking dish and pour sauce over top. Bake uncovered for 35–40 minutes, or until bubbly. Serve as an appetizer with toothpicks or over hot cooked rice garnished with crunchy chow mein noodles. MAKES 6–8 SERVINGS.

Ginger Ale Meatballs

39 (1½ pounds) frozen, fully cooked meatballs

2 cups ginger ale

2 cups ketchup

1 teaspoon minced garlic

Place frozen meatballs in a 3- to 4-quart slow cooker prepared with nonstick cooking spray.

In a bowl, combine ginger ale, ketchup, and garlic. Pour mixture over meatballs. Cover and cook on low heat for 6–8 hours or on high heat for 3 hours. Serve with toothpicks as an appetizer, on hoagie buns, or over hot cooked noodles. MAKES 8–10 SERVINGS.

Cheesy Meatballs

26 (1 pound) frozen, fully cooked meatballs

½ cup water

1 jar (15 ounces) Cheez Whiz

sliced green onions (optional)

Place frozen meatballs in a 2-quart pan and drizzle the water over top. Bring to a boil. Cover and simmer for 8–10 minutes over medium-high heat, stirring occasionally. Pour Cheez Whiz into a microwave-safe bowl and microwave on high heat for 2–3 minutes, stirring occasionally until cheese is melted. Fold melted cheese dip into meatballs. Serve with toothpicks or individually over snack crackers. Garnish with green onions, if desired. MAKES 26 APPETIZERS.

NOTE: *1 jar (16 ounces) Ragu cheese sauce can be used in place of Cheez Whiz.*

Salsa Verde Meatballs

39 (1½ pounds) frozen, fully cooked meatballs

1 jar (16 ounces) salsa verde

1 medium onion, chopped

2 teaspoons minced garlic

½ cup chicken or beef broth

½ teaspoon ground cumin

Place frozen meatballs in a 3- to 4-quart slow cooker prepared with nonstick cooking spray.

In a bowl, combine the remaining ingredients. Pour mixture over meatballs. Cover and cook on high heat for 3 hours or on low heat for 6–8 hours. Serve as an appetizer with tortilla chips or toothpicks or in a tortilla with beans and rice. MAKES 6–8 SERVINGS.

VARIATION: *Defrost meatballs. In a 3½- to 4-quart pan, combine the remaining ingredients and bring to a low boil. Stir in meatballs. Return to a low boil. Simmer over medium heat for 15 minutes.*

Holiday Meatballs

52 **(2 pounds) frozen, fully cooked meatballs**

1 **can (16 ounces) whole berry cranberry sauce**

1 **cup barbecue sauce**

Place frozen meatballs in a 3½- to 5-quart slow cooker prepared with nonstick cooking spray.

In a bowl, stir together cranberry sauce and barbecue sauce. Pour mixture over meatballs. Cover and cook on low heat for 5–6 hours or on high heat for 2½–3 hours. During a party, meatballs can be left in the slow cooker on the warm or low setting. Serve as appetizers with toothpicks.

VARIATION: *Combine all ingredients in a 3- to 4-quart saucepan. Cover and simmer over medium-low heat on the stove for 55–60 minutes, stirring occasionally until meatballs are heated through.*

Sour Cream–Sauced Meatballs

1 **container (16 ounces) sour cream**

1 **envelope dry onion soup mix**

26 **(1 pound) frozen, fully cooked meatballs, thawed**

In a 2- to 3-quart pan, combine sour cream and dry soup mix. Stir in meatballs. Bring to a low boil. Reduce heat to medium and simmer for 10 minutes, stirring occasionally until meatballs are heated through. Serve as an appetizer with toothpicks, over hot cooked pasta, or over mashed potatoes. MAKES 5–6 SERVINGS.

Pasta Dinners

Meatball Fettuccine Alfredo

  ½ **tablespoon olive oil**

  ½ **teaspoon salt**

  1 **box (12 ounces) fettuccine pasta**

  1 **jar (16 ounces) Alfredo sauce**

 20 **frozen, fully cooked meatballs, thawed**

  2 **tablespoons chopped fresh parsley**

In a 4- to 6-quart stockpot, bring 4 quarts water, oil, and salt to a boil. Add pasta and cook according to directions.

In a separate saucepan, combine Alfredo sauce and meatballs and bring to a boil. Lower heat and cover. Simmer for 10 minutes, stirring occasionally. Drain pasta and then place noodles on a large serving platter. Spoon meatballs and sauce evenly over top. Garnish with the parsley and serve. MAKES 6 SERVINGS.

Chipotle Meatball Pasta

    1   can (29 ounces) tomato sauce
    1   can (28 ounces) crushed tomatoes
    1   tablespoon onion powder
    1   teaspoon minced garlic
    ½   teaspoon cinnamon
    ½   teaspoon oregano
    ¼   cup chopped chipotle honey-roasted green chiles
   26   (1 pound) frozen, fully cooked meatballs
    9   cups hot cooked pasta
        grated Parmesan or Monterey Jack cheese

In a 4-quart saucepan, combine tomato sauce, tomatoes, onion powder, garlic, cinnamon, oregano, and chiles over medium-high heat. Once bubbly, add the meatballs. Bring mixture to a low boil. Cover and reduce to medium heat. Simmer for 20–25 minutes, stirring occasionally. Serve over pasta and garnish with cheese. MAKES 6 SERVINGS.

VARIATION: *If you cannot find jarred chopped chipotle chiles, you can use a can of chipotle peppers in adobo sauce, found in the Hispanic food section of your grocery store. Chop 4 peppers and toss them into the sauce.*

COOKING TIP

If you've run out of chili powder, here's a quick mix to get you by: 1 tablespoon ground cumin; 1 teaspoon *each* dried oregano, garlic powder, and onion powder; ½ teaspoon *each* ground red pepper and paprika; and ¼ teaspoon ground allspice. Makes about 2½ tablespoons.

Florentine Meatballs and Noodles

½   package (10 ounces) frozen chopped spinach, partially thawed

1   can (10.5 ounces) cream of mushroom soup, condensed

½   cup butter or margarine

1   cup heavy whipping cream

1   can (4 ounces) sliced mushrooms, drained

26   (1 pound) frozen, fully cooked meatballs, thawed

⅓   cup grated Parmesan cheese

8   cups hot cooked egg noodles

In a 3- to 4-quart saucepan, cook spinach and soup over medium heat until spinach is heated. Stir in butter, cream, and mushrooms until butter is completely melted. Add meatballs to the sauce. Simmer over medium heat for 6–8 minutes, stirring every 2–3 minutes to ensure the sauce doesn't burn. Stir in the cheese until it melts and then pour the sauce over the noodles. Serve immediately. MAKES 6–8 SERVINGS.

Meatballs in Blue Cheese Sauce

¼ cup butter or margarine

1 teaspoon minced garlic

4 tablespoons flour

1 can (14.5 ounces) chicken broth

1 cup half-and-half

1 container (5 ounces) crumbled blue cheese

39 (1½ pounds) frozen, fully cooked meatballs, thawed

¼ cup chopped fresh parsley

8 to 10 cups hot cooked pasta

In a 3-quart saucepan, melt butter over medium-high heat. Sauté garlic in butter for 1 minute. Stir in flour until completely blended. Gradually mix broth into flour mixture until completely dissolved. Stir in half-and-half and heat until sauce begins to bubble. Stir in blue cheese until melted. Add meatballs and then reduce heat to medium. Cover and simmer for 15 minutes, stirring occasionally, until meatballs are heated through. Sprinkle parsley over the sauce and serve over pasta or mashed potatoes. MAKES 8–10 SERVINGS.

VARIATION: *Use 52 (2 pounds) meatballs with the sauce. Serve with toothpicks as an appetizer in a chafing dish with cooked, crumbled bacon sprinkled over the top.*

Slow-Cooked
Tomato Soup Meatballs

26 (1 pound) frozen, fully cooked meatballs

½ cup chopped white onion

⅛ cup chopped green bell pepper

1 can (10.5 ounces) tomato soup, condensed

2 tablespoons brown sugar

1 tablespoon apple cider vinegar

1 tablespoon Worcestershire sauce

1 teaspoon mustard

6 to 8 cups hot cooked linguine or rotini pasta

Place meatballs in a 3- to 4-quart slow cooker prepared with nonstick cooking spray. Sprinkle onion and bell pepper over meatballs.

In a bowl, combine soup, brown sugar, vinegar, Worcestershire sauce, and mustard. Pour sauce over meatballs and vegetables. Cover and cook on low heat for 6–8 hours or on high heat for 3 hours. Serve over the pasta. MAKES 5–6 SERVINGS.

Easy Meatball Lasagna

26 (1 pound) frozen, fully cooked meatballs, thawed and halved or quartered

2 jars (26 ounces each) spaghetti sauce, divided

¾ cup water, divided

1 egg, beaten

1 container (15 ounces) ricotta cheese

2 cups grated mozzarella cheese, divided

1 box (12 ounces) oven-ready lasagna noodles, uncooked

½ cup grated Parmesan cheese

Preheat oven to 400 degrees.

Place meatballs in a large bowl. Reserve 2½ cups spaghetti sauce, and then pour the remaining over meatballs and stir in ½ cup water.

In a separate bowl, combine the egg, ricotta cheese, and 1 cup mozzarella cheese. Spread 1 cup of the reserved sauce in a 9 × 13-inch pan prepared with nonstick cooking spray. Lay 5 to 6 noodles over sauce and spread half the cheese mixture over the noodles. Spoon half the meatball mixture over the cheese. Repeat layers once. Add a final layer of noodles and spoon remaining sauce over top. Drizzle remaining water over top. Cover with heavy-duty aluminum foil. Bake for 55–60 minutes. Sprinkle remaining mozzarella and the Parmesan cheese over top and bake, uncovered, 5 minutes more. Let stand 5 minutes before serving. MAKES 8 SERVINGS.

Pesto Spaghetti and Meatballs

1 package (16 ounces) spaghetti

20 frozen, fully cooked meatballs

1 jar (26 ounces) spaghetti sauce

1 jar (6–7 ounces) pesto

1 cup grated mozzarella cheese

Cook spaghetti according to package directions. While water for spaghetti heats to a boil, combine meatballs and spaghetti sauce in a 2- to 3-quart saucepan and bring to a boil, stirring occasionally; reduce heat. Cover and simmer for 8–10 minutes. Drain spaghetti. Stir pesto into cooked spaghetti. Spoon sauce and hot meatballs over the pesto noodles and sprinkle cheese over top. MAKES 5 SERVINGS.

Ricotta-Stuffed Shells and Meatballs

8 frozen ricotta cheese–stuffed pasta shells

26 (1 pound) frozen, fully cooked meatballs, thawed

1 jar (26 ounces) spaghetti sauce

1¼ cups grated Italian-blend cheese

Preheat oven to 400 degrees.

Arrange pasta and meatballs in a 9 × 13-inch pan prepared with nonstick cooking spray. Pour spaghetti sauce evenly over top. Sprinkle cheese over sauce. Cover with aluminum foil and bake for 35–40 minutes. Uncover and bake 5 minutes more, or until cheese is melted. MAKES 6–8 SERVINGS.

Baked Ziti and Meatballs

20 frozen, fully cooked meatballs

 1 package (16 ounces) ziti or other pasta

 1 jar (26 ounces) spaghetti sauce

 2 cups grated mozzarella cheese, divided

    chopped fresh basil or parsley (optional)

Preheat oven to 350 degrees.

Heat meatballs according to package directions. Cook pasta according to package directions and drain. Stir in the spaghetti sauce, meatballs, and half the cheese. Place pasta mixture in a 9 × 13-inch pan prepared with nonstick cooking spray. Bake for 20 minutes. Sprinkle remaining cheese over top and bake 5 minutes more. Garnish with the basil or parsley if desired. MAKES 8 SERVINGS.

Eggplant Parmesan

- 1 large eggplant, peeled and diced
- 2 teaspoons minced garlic
- 1 teaspoon Italian seasoning
- 1 jar (26 ounces) spaghetti sauce
- 30 frozen, fully cooked meatballs, thawed
- 1 cup seasoned breadcrumbs
- ½ cup grated Parmesan cheese
- 8 to 10 cups hot cooked pasta

Place eggplant in a 4- to 5-quart stockpot. Cover with water and bring to a boil, stirring occasionally. Reduce heat to cook at a low boil for 8 minutes, stirring frequently; drain.

Preheat oven to 350 degrees.

In a bowl, stir together the eggplant, garlic, Italian seasoning, spaghetti sauce, and meatballs. Pour into a 9 × 13-inch pan prepared with nonstick cooking spray.

In a separate bowl, combine the breadcrumbs and cheese. Sprinkle mixture evenly over the eggplant mixture. Bake for 30–35 minutes, or until bubbly and golden. Serve over the pasta. MAKES 6–8 SERVINGS.

Italian-Tossed Tortellini

- ½ cup chopped red onion
- ½ cup chopped red bell pepper
- ½ cup chopped green bell pepper
- 1 tablespoon olive oil
- 20 frozen, fully cooked meatballs, thawed
- 2 bags (13 ounces each) frozen cheese tortellini
- 1 bottle (16 ounces) Italian dressing

In a large frying pan, sauté the onion and bell peppers in hot oil for 3 minutes. Quarter meatballs and then add to the vegetables and cook 4 minutes more. Cook tortellini according to package directions. Drain tortellini and stir Italian dressing into pasta while still hot. Gently toss vegetable and meat mixture with the warm tortellini. Serve hot or cold. MAKES 8 SERVINGS.

Ravioli Meatball Stir-Fry

- 2 tablespoons peanut or olive oil
- 1 bag (16 ounces) frozen stir-fry vegetables
- 13 frozen, fully cooked meatballs, thawed
- 1 bottle (12 ounces) stir-fry sauce
- 1 bag (25 ounces) frozen cheese ravioli, thawed

In a wok or stir-fry pan, heat oil until hot. Add frozen vegetables and stir-fry over high heat for 3 minutes. Stir in meatballs and cook 4 minutes more. Add the stir-fry sauce and toss in the ravioli. Stir-fry for 3–4 minutes, or until ravioli are heated through. Serve immediately. MAKES 6 SERVINGS.

Meatball Stroganoff

39 (1½ pounds) frozen, fully cooked meatballs

 2 cans (10.5 ounces each) cream of mushroom soup, condensed

 1 teaspoon Worcestershire sauce

 ¼ cup water

 1 dash Tabasco sauce

 1 cup sour cream

 1 can (7 ounces) mushroom stems and pieces, drained

 8 to 10 cups hot cooked egg noodles

Place meatballs in a 3- to 4½-quart slow cooker prepared with nonstick cooking spray.

In a medium bowl, combine the soup, Worcestershire sauce, water, and Tabasco sauce. Spoon mixture over the meatballs. Cover and cook on low heat for 4–4½ hours. Stir in sour cream and mushrooms. Cover and cook 30 minutes more. Serve over the egg noodles. MAKES 8 SERVINGS.

VARIATION: *Heat meatballs according to package directions for stovetop in a 4-quart saucepan. Drain any excess liquid. In a medium bowl, combine all remaining ingredients. Add soup mixture to meatballs. Simmer over medium heat for 20 minutes, stirring occasionally. Serve over egg noodles.*

Amazing Meatball Tortellini

- ¼ cup raisins
- 2 tablespoons olive oil
- ½ cup chopped onion
- 1 cup jarred julienned sun-dried tomatoes, drained
- 1 teaspoon crushed red pepper
- ½ tablespoon minced garlic
- 26 (1 pound) frozen, fully cooked meatballs, thawed
- 2 cans (14.5 ounces each) diced tomatoes, with liquid
- 1 bunch curly endive, leaves only
- 2 bags (13 ounces each) frozen cheese tortellini, thawed
- ⅓ cup pine nuts

In a small bowl, soak raisins in some water for 25 minutes; set aside.

In a 5- to 6-quart soup pan, heat the oil. Sauté the onion, sun-dried tomatoes, crushed red pepper, and garlic in the oil until onions are tender. Stir in meatballs and tomatoes. Simmer over medium-high heat for 5 minutes. Stir in the endive leaves and simmer 5 minutes more. Stir in drained raisins, tortellini, and pine nuts. Simmer over medium heat for 5–10 minutes, stirring occasionally, until tortellini are heated. MAKES 8–10 SERVINGS.

VARIATION: *Use 1 bag (9 ounces) spinach leaves in place of curly endive.*

Cheesy Broccoli Meatballs

  1 **box (16 ounces) bow tie pasta**

26 **(1 pound) frozen, fully cooked meatballs**

  2 **tablespoons water**

⅔ **cup half-and-half**

  2 **boxes (10 ounces each) frozen broccoli with cheese sauce**

Cook pasta according to package directions; drain.

In a large frying pan, sauté meatballs in the water over medium-high heat for 5–6 minutes. Stir in half-and-half. Place blocks of frozen broccoli and sauce in the frying pan, vegetable side down. Cover and cook 10–12 minutes, stirring occasionally, until vegetables are thoroughly heated. Serve over the pasta. MAKES 6 SERVINGS.

VARIATION: *This recipe can also be served over hot cooked rice.*

FOOD FACT

The British learned to make ketchup condiments from the Chinese (who called it *ke-tsiap*), but it was Mr. Heinz who borrowed the idea from Great Britain, adding tomato to please American tastebuds. Before that, ketchup was a runnier concoction, often made from mushrooms or walnuts.

Dinners with Rice

Easy Rice and Meatballs

26 (1 pound) frozen, fully cooked meatballs

3 cups water

1 envelope dry onion soup mix

½ cup chopped white onion

½ cup chopped green bell pepper

1 can (4 ounces) mushroom pieces, drained

1 can (14.5 ounces) petite-cut diced tomatoes, with liquid

2 cups uncooked white long-grain rice

In a 4-quart saucepan, combine meatballs, water, and dry soup mix, and bring to a boil. Simmer over medium-high heat for 8–10 minutes. Add the remaining ingredients and return to a boil. Reduce heat to medium-low. Stir and then cover and simmer for 25 minutes. Let cool for 5 minutes and then stir again right before serving. MAKES 6 SERVINGS.

Meatballs in Curry Sauce

 2 tablespoons butter or margarine

 ½ cup chopped red onion

 1 teaspoon curry powder

 1 can (10.5 ounces) cream of celery soup, condensed

 ½ cup sour cream

 26 (1 pound) frozen, fully cooked meatballs, thawed

 6 cups hot cooked rice

In a 2½- to 3-quart saucepan, melt the butter. Stir in onion and sauté until tender. Stir in curry powder and cook for 1½–2 minutes. Stir in soup and sour cream. Return to a low simmer. Once bubbly, stir in meatballs. Cook over medium heat for 8–10 minutes, stirring often. Serve over rice. If desired, garnish with shredded coconut and chopped peanuts. MAKES 4–6 SERVINGS.

Sesame Stir-Fry

 2 tablespoons olive or sesame oil

 1 bag (16 ounces) frozen vegetable stir-fry mix

 13 frozen, fully cooked meatballs, thawed

 ½ cup beef broth

 2 tablespoons soy sauce

 2 teaspoons seasoned rice vinegar

 ⅓ cup drained canned pineapple chunks

 2 tablespoons sesame seeds

 6 cups cooked long-grain rice

In a stir-fry pan or wok, heat oil over medium-high. Toss in vegetables and fry for 5 minutes, stirring frequently. Add meatballs, broth, soy sauce, and vinegar. Stir-fry for 6–7 minutes, or until vegetables are tender. Add the pineapple and stir-fry 3–4 minutes more. Sprinkle sesame seeds over top and serve immediately over hot cooked rice. MAKES 4 SERVINGS.

Swiss Mushroom Meatball Casserole

26 (1 pound) frozen, fully cooked meatballs, thawed

1 can (10.5 ounces) cream of mushroom soup, condensed

¾ cup milk

1 can (4 ounces) sliced mushrooms, drained

2 teaspoons minced garlic

1½ cups grated Swiss cheese

3 cups cooked long-grain white rice

¼ cup grated Parmesan cheese

Preheat oven to 350 degrees.

In a 9 × 13-inch pan prepared with nonstick cooking spray, combine meatballs, soup, milk, mushrooms, garlic, Swiss cheese, and rice. Sprinkle Parmesan evenly over top and bake 25–30 minutes until bubbly. MAKES 6–8 SERVINGS.

NOTE: *One and one-half cups water plus ¾ cup rice yields 3 cups hot cooked rice.*

Creamy Meatball and Brown Rice Casserole

1   cup uncooked brown rice

13 frozen, fully cooked meatballs, thawed

1   cup sliced mushrooms

1   can (10.5 ounces) cream of mushroom soup, condensed

1   cup sour cream

½   teaspoon pepper

⅓   cup grated Parmesan cheese

1½ cups crushed Ritz crackers

Cook brown rice according to package directions. Preheat oven to 350 degrees.

In a large bowl, combine the cooked rice, meatballs, mushrooms, soup, sour cream, and pepper. Spoon mixture into a 9 × 9-inch or 2-quart dish prepared with nonstick cooking spray. Sprinkle Parmesan over top and then cover with crushed crackers. Bake 35–40 minutes, or until bubbly. MAKES 5–6 SERVINGS.

Pineapple Meatballs and Rice

½ cup brown sugar

1½ tablespoons cornstarch

1 can (20 ounces) pineapple chunks, with juice drained and reserved

⅓ cup rice vinegar

1 tablespoon soy sauce

1 green bell pepper, seeded and chopped

13 frozen, fully cooked meatballs, thawed

4 cups hot cooked rice

In a 2-quart saucepan, combine the brown sugar and cornstarch. Stir in reserved pineapple juice, vinegar, and soy sauce and bring to a boil, stirring every 2 minutes. Add bell pepper and meatballs to the sauce and return to a boil. Reduce heat to medium-high and then cover and simmer 5 minutes. Stir and reduce heat to medium. Stir in pineapple chunks. Simmer 5 minutes more and then serve over the rice. MAKES 2–3 SERVINGS.

Meatballs with Orange Peanut Sauce

¾ cup orange marmalade

¼ cup peanut butter

3 tablespoons soy sauce

3 tablespoons water

2 tablespoons lemon juice

1 teaspoon minced garlic

26 (1 pound) frozen, fully cooked meatballs, thawed

6 to 8 cups hot cooked rice

Combine all ingredients except meatballs and rice in a 2- to 3-quart saucepan and bring to a boil, stirring frequently. Fold in the meatballs and return to a boil. Reduce heat to medium and simmer for 8 minutes, or until meatballs are heated through. Serve over the rice. MAKES 5–6 SERVINGS.

Cajun Shrimp and Meatball Goulash

2 cans (14.5 ounces each) diced tomatoes with herb seasoning, with liquid

⅓ cup chopped onion

1 teaspoon Cajun seasoning*

26 (1 pound) frozen, fully cooked meatballs

1 can (14 ounces) chicken broth

1 teaspoon minced garlic

1¼ cups uncooked long-grain white rice

½ pound frozen, fully cooked, peeled, and deveined medium shrimp, thawed

In a 4-quart stockpot, combine the tomatoes, onion, seasoning, meatballs, broth, and garlic and bring to a boil. Stir in the rice and return to a boil. Reduce heat to medium-low and cover. Simmer for 25 minutes, or until rice is tender. Remove tails from shrimp. Stir in shrimp and cook 3–4 minutes. Serve immediately. MAKES 8 SERVINGS.

*To make Cajun seasoning, combine ½ teaspoon chili powder and ½ teaspoon paprika.

Creamy French Onion Meatballs

78 (3 pounds) frozen, fully cooked meatballs

1 can (10.5 ounces) French onion soup, condensed

1 can (10.5 ounces) cream of celery soup, condensed

½ teaspoon pepper

1 cup sour cream

16 cups hot cooked rice

Place the meatballs in a 4- to 6-quart slow cooker prepared with nonstick cooking spray.

In a bowl, stir together the soups and pepper. Spoon mixture evenly over meatballs. Cover and cook on low heat for 4–5 hours. Stir in sour cream. Cover and cook 20–30 minutes more. Serve over the rice. MAKES 12–16 SERVINGS.

VARIATION: *Thaw meatballs. In a 4- to 6-quart stockpot, combine soups and pepper over medium-high heat on the stovetop, stirring occasionally until bubbly. Stir in meatballs. Cover and cook over medium heat for 15 minutes, until meatballs are heated through. Stir in sour cream. Continue to cook 5 minutes more. Serve over the rice.*

Meatballs with Apricot Hoisin Sauce

    1 jar (18 ounces) apricot preserves
    1 package (6 ounces) dried apricots, diced
    ½ cup hoisin sauce
    ½ cup rice vinegar
    ⅛ teaspoon crushed red pepper
    1 red bell pepper, diced
    1 green bell pepper, diced
   52 (2 pounds) frozen, fully cooked meatballs, thawed
   10 cups hot cooked rice

In a 4-quart saucepan, combine the preserves, apricots, hoisin sauce, vine-gar, crushed red pepper, and bell peppers. Bring to a boil, stirring occasion-ally. Stir in meatballs and return to a boil. Reduce heat to medium. Cover and cook for 15 minutes, stirring occasionally. Serve over hot cooked rice. MAKES 8–10 SERVINGS.

Enchilada Meatballs

52 (2 pounds) frozen, fully cooked meatballs, thawed

1 jar (16 ounces) chunky salsa

1 can (16 ounces) red enchilada sauce

10 cups hot cooked rice

grated Monterey Jack cheese

Place meatballs in a 3- to 4½-quart slow cooker prepared with nonstick cooking spray. Pour salsa and enchilada sauce over meatballs. Cover and cook on high heat for 2–3 hours or on low heat for 4–6 hours. Serve over the rice with cheese sprinkled over top. MAKES 8–10 SERVINGS.

VARIATION: *Thaw meatballs. In a 3- to 5-quart pot, combine meatballs, salsa, and enchilada sauce. Bring to a boil on the stovetop. Cover and cook over medium heat for 15–20 minutes, stirring occasionally, until meatballs are heated through. Serve over the rice and sprinkle with cheese.*

Creamy Rice and Meatballs

30 frozen, fully cooked meatballs, thawed

1 can (10.5 ounces) cream of mushroom soup, condensed

½ cup grape jelly

6 to 8 cups hot cooked rice

Preheat oven to 350 degrees. Place meatballs in an 8 × 8-inch pan.

In a bowl, combine soup and jelly. Pour mixture evenly over meatballs. Bake, uncovered, for 35 minutes, or until meatballs are heated through. Serve over the rice. MAKES 6 SERVINGS.

VARIATION: *This recipe can also be served as an appetizer with toothpicks, minus the rice.*

Taste of the Islands Meatballs

26 (1 pound) frozen, fully cooked meatballs

1 cup chopped onion

2 green or red bell peppers, sliced

1 cup beef broth

1 can (20 ounces) pineapple chunks, with liquid

1 tablespoon lemon juice

1 tablespoon soy sauce

1 tablespoon water

2 tablespoons cornstarch

1 can (11 ounces) mandarin oranges, drained

6 to 8 cups hot cooked rice

Place meatballs in a 3½- to 4-quart slow cooker prepared with nonstick cooking spray. Sprinkle onion and bell peppers over top. Pour broth and pineapple chunks with liquid over vegetable layer. Do not stir. Cover and cook on low heat for 6–7 hours or on high heat for 3 hours.

In a bowl, thoroughly mix the lemon juice, soy sauce, water, and cornstarch until smooth. Stir lemon juice mixture and mandarin oranges into cooked meatballs. Cover and cook on high heat for 20 minutes, or until sauce thickens. Serve over the rice. MAKES 6–8 SERVINGS.

Family Favorites

Meatballs in Tomato and Corn Sauce

  1 can (15.25 ounces) whole kernel corn, with liquid

  1 can (14.75 ounces) cream-style corn

  3 tomatoes, seeded and diced

 ½ teaspoon crushed red pepper

  1 tablespoon chopped dried cilantro

 ¼ cup crumbled cooked bacon

30 frozen, fully cooked meatballs, thawed

Add all ingredients except meatballs in the order listed above to a 4-quart saucepan. Bring mixture to a boil and then stir in meatballs. Simmer over medium heat for 10 minutes, or until meatballs are heated through. MAKES 6–8 SERVINGS.

Sweet and Sour Meatball Kabobs

1 can (8 ounces) pineapple chunks, with juice

1 tablespoon cornstarch

½ cup maple syrup

¼ cup vinegar

2 tablespoons soy sauce

2 tablespoons ketchup

½ teaspoon minced garlic

1 medium red or green bell pepper

1 red onion, peeled

18 frozen, fully cooked meatballs, thawed

12 medium whole mushrooms, with stems

Preheat oven to 350 degrees.

Drain pineapple juice into a saucepan; whisk in cornstarch until smooth. Stir in syrup, vinegar, soy sauce, ketchup, and garlic and bring to a boil. Reduce heat and allow to softly boil for 2 minutes; remove from heat. Cut bell pepper in half and clean out. Cut each half into 6 equal pieces. Cut onion into 12 equal pieces. On 6 metal skewers, place a meatball, a mushroom, then an onion, bell pepper, and pineapple chunk. Repeat one more time, ending with the meatball. Place skewers on a large baking sheet and brush with half of the prepared sauce. Bake for 10 minutes; turn and brush with remaining sauce. Bake 10–15 minutes more, or until done. Serve immediately. MAKES 6 SERVINGS.

VARIATION: *Place kabobs on a hot grill. Baste with sauce. Every 2–3 minutes give kabobs a quarter turn, basting with more sauce. Grill until done.*

NOTE: *If using bamboo skewers, soak in water for 30 minutes prior to assembling kabobs.*

Caesar Meatball Kabobs

18 frozen, fully cooked meatballs, thawed

 1 medium yellow or green bell pepper, seeded and cut into 12 equal pieces

 1 large or 2 small yellow summer squash, cut into 12 (1½- to 2-inch) slices

12 whole mushrooms

12 cherry tomatoes

½ cup Caesar dressing

¼ teaspoon pepper

On a long metal skewer, thread a meatball, bell pepper slice, yellow squash slice, mushroom, and tomato. Repeat pattern, ending with a meatball. Repeat for 5 more skewers. Combine Caesar dressing and black pepper. Place meatball skewers directly on a hot grill. Baste the kabobs with the dressing. Grill for 6–8 minutes, turning and basting every 2–3 minutes until done.
MAKES 6 KABOBS.

NOTE: *If using bamboo skewers, soak in water for 30 minutes prior to assembling kabobs.*

Breakfast Burritos

½ cup chopped onion

½ cup chopped green or red bell pepper

1 teaspoon olive oil

7 frozen, fully cooked meatballs, thawed and finely chopped

4 eggs

¼ teaspoon pepper

4 (6-inch) flour tortillas

4 tablespoons grated cheddar cheese

4 tablespoons fresh salsa, divided

In a frying pan over medium-high heat, sauté the onion and bell pepper in oil until tender. Add meatball pieces to vegetables and sauté 2 minutes. Scramble eggs and black pepper into vegetable and meat mixture. Continue to stir until egg mixture is completely cooked. Divide egg mixture over individual warm tortillas. Sprinkle 1 tablespoon each of cheese and salsa over mixture. Fold to form a burrito. MAKES 4 SERVINGS.

Easy Meatball Pizza

1 (12-inch) premade pizza crust

1 jar (14 ounces) pizza sauce, divided

1½ cups grated mozzarella or cheddar cheese, divided

13 frozen, fully cooked meatballs

¼ teaspoon Italian seasoning

Preheat oven to 400 degrees.

Place pizza crust on a pizza pan. Spread 1 cup pizza sauce over crust. Sprinkle half the cheese over sauce. Place meatballs and 2 teaspoons water in a microwave-safe bowl and microwave on high for 3 minutes; drain any excess liquid. Cut each meatball in half and then toss with the remaining sauce. Spoon meatballs over cheese layer, ensuring the cut side is down. Layer remaining cheese over meatballs. Sprinkle Italian seasoning evenly over pizza. Bake for 12–15 minutes, or until cheese is melted and sauce is bubbly. Cut pizza into 8 slices. MAKES 4–6 SERVINGS.

Southwest Crescent Pockets

18 frozen, fully cooked meatballs, thawed

2 tubes (8 ounces each) refrigerated crescent rolls

1 can (4 ounces) diced green chiles, drained

8 tablespoons grated cheddar or Mexican-blend cheese, divided

4 tablespoons finely chopped onion, divided

salsa and sour cream (optional)

Preheat oven to 375 degrees.

Crumble meatballs into a large frying pan and sauté 6–8 minutes until browned. Roll crescent dough from 1 tube onto a baking sheet. Separate dough into 4 rectangles, pressing the triangle edges together to form rectangles. Spoon chiles evenly over each rectangle, leaving ½ inch around the edge. Divide crumbled cooked meatballs evenly over chiles. Sprinkle 1 tablespoon cheese and 1 tablespoon onion over meat. Unroll remaining crescent roll dough and separate dough into 4 rectangles. Place rectangles over the top of each filled rectangle. Press dough around the edges to seal. Sprinkle 1 tablespoon cheese over each crescent pocket. Bake 13 minutes, or until golden brown. Garnish with salsa and sour cream if desired. MAKES 4 SERVINGS.

Meatball Pot Pie

2 cups frozen mixed vegetables, thawed and drained

13 frozen, fully cooked meatballs, thawed

2 cans (10.5 ounces each) cream of mushroom soup, condensed

1 can (15 ounces) diced potatoes, drained

1 teaspoon chopped dried rosemary

⅓ cup milk

2 frozen or refrigerated piecrusts, at room temperature

Preheat oven to 400 degrees.

In a 2-quart bowl, combine all the ingredients except the crusts. Place one piecrust evenly over the bottom and sides of a deep-dish pie pan, pressing it up the sides. Fill the piecrust with the meatball mixture. Cover with the second crust, sealing the edges and cutting slits in the top to vent steam. Bake 45 minutes, or until golden brown. Allow to cool 5 minutes before serving. MAKES 6 SERVINGS.

Instant Soft Taco

5 frozen, fully cooked meatballs

1 flour tortilla

1 tablespoon grated Monterey Jack cheese

2 tablespoons salsa

1 tablespoon guacamole

½ tablespoon sour cream

chopped fresh cilantro (optional)

Cook meatballs in the microwave according to package directions. Serve hot meatballs in a warm flour tortilla with cheese, salsa, guacamole, and sour cream. Garnish with cilantro if desired. MAKES 1 SERVING.

NOTE: *This recipe can be doubled, tripled, or quadrupled depending on the number of tacos needed.*

Meatball Fajita Quesadillas

       1 small onion, sliced
       1 red bell pepper, sliced
       1 tablespoon olive oil
       ½ teaspoon garlic salt
      20 frozen, fully cooked meatballs
       4 (10-inch) burrito-size flour tortillas
       1 cup grated Colby Jack cheese
          salsa and guacamole (optional)

In a frying pan, sauté the onion and bell pepper in oil until tender. Sprinkle garlic salt over top. While vegetables are sautéing, place meatballs in a microwave-safe dish. Drizzle 1 tablespoon water over top and microwave on high for 3 minutes, stirring once in the middle of cooking time. Cut each heated meatball into three slices.

Prepare a large frying pan with nonstick cooking spray. On half of each tortilla, layer 2 tablespoons cheese, 15 meatball slices, and one-fourth of the sautéed vegetable mixture. Fold the empty half of the tortilla over the layered half. Place the quesadilla in the heated pan and cook 2–3 minutes on each side, or until golden-crisp. Repeat for the remaining quesadillas. Cooked quesadillas can be placed in a pan and put in a preheated 180-degree oven to keep warm until ready to be served. Cut each quesadilla in half and serve with salsa and guacamole if desired. MAKES 4 SERVINGS.

Baked Beefy Mac and Cheese

26 (1 pound) frozen, fully cooked meatballs

2 boxes (7.25 ounces each) macaroni and cheese dinner

2 cans (10.5 ounces each) cream of mushroom soup, condensed

1½ cups milk

2 medium tomatoes, thinly sliced

3 tablespoons grated Parmesan cheese

Preheat oven to 350 degrees.

Cook frozen meatballs on a baking sheet for 20 minutes. While meatballs bake, cook macaroni according to package directions. Drain the water from the pan. Stir soup, milk, and cheese packets into the cooked macaroni. Place meatballs in a 9 × 13-inch pan prepared with nonstick cooking spray. Spoon mixture evenly over the meatball layer. Lay tomato slices over top and then sprinkle the Parmesan cheese over top. Bake, uncovered, for 25–30 minutes. MAKES 6–8 SERVINGS.

Stuffing-Covered Meatball Casserole

1 box (6 ounces) stuffing mix, any variety

1 can (10.5 ounces) cream of mushroom soup, condensed

¼ cup milk

2 cups frozen mixed vegetables

26 (1 pound) frozen, fully cooked meatballs, thawed

1 cup grated Colby Jack cheese

Preheat oven to 400 degrees.

Prepare stuffing according to package directions. In a 9 × 13-inch pan prepared with nonstick cooking spray, combine the soup and milk. Stir in the vegetables. Evenly place meatballs over the vegetable mixture. Sprinkle cheese over top. Spoon prepared stuffing evenly over casserole. Bake, uncovered, for 25–30 minutes. MAKES 6–8 SERVINGS.

Enchilada Casserole

39 (1½ pounds) frozen, fully cooked meatballs, thawed
1 medium red onion, finely chopped
1½ teaspoons ground cumin
1 can (28 ounces) enchilada sauce
18 corn tortillas
1 cup grated Colby Jack cheese

Preheat oven to 350 degrees.

Crumble meatballs into a large frying pan. Stir in onion and cumin. Sauté for 6–8 minutes, or until onion is tender. Place enchilada sauce in a round container deep enough to hold it, and wide enough to dip the tortillas. Dip both sides of each tortilla liberally in the enchilada sauce. Cover the bottom of a 9 × 13-inch pan prepared with nonstick cooking spray with 6 dipped tortillas. (Tortillas will overlap a little.) Sprinkle half the meatball mixture and one-third of the cheese over the tortillas. Cover with 6 more tortillas dipped in sauce. Sprinkle remaining meatball mixture and one-third of the cheese over tortilla layer. Cover with the remaining tortillas dipped in sauce. Pour remaining sauce evenly over tortillas and sprinkle remaining cheese on top. Bake for 25 minutes. MAKES 8–10 SERVINGS.

Spicy Meatball Burritos

  1 medium onion, chopped
  1 tablespoon olive oil
 13 frozen, fully cooked meatballs, thawed and halved
  1 can (7 ounces) diced green chiles
  1 envelope taco seasoning
  6 (8-inch) flour tortillas, warmed
  1 can (15 ounces) black beans, rinsed and drained
1½ cups grated Monterey Jack or Mexican-blend cheese
  6 tablespoons green enchilada sauce

In a large frying pan, sauté the onion in the oil over medium-high heat until tender. Stir meatball halves and chiles into the onion. Sprinkle taco seasoning evenly over top and stir. Cook for 5 minutes, or until mixture is hot. On individual tortillas, layer black beans, meatball mixture, cheese, and 1 tablespoon enchilada sauce. Fold ends over filling and wrap burrito style. Top with a dollop of sour cream and serve over a bed of shredded lettuce if desired.
MAKES 6 SERVINGS.

Tater Tot Kids' Casserole

 26 (1 pound) frozen, fully cooked meatballs, thawed and quartered
  1 can (14.5 ounces) cut green beans, drained
  1 can (10.5 ounces) cream of mushroom soup, condensed
  1 bag (27–32 ounces) frozen tater tots

Arrange meatball pieces in a 9 × 13-inch pan prepared with nonstick cooking spray. Evenly place green beans over meatball layer and then spread soup over top. Cover with tater tots, laying them on their sides. Bake 40–50 minutes. MAKES 6–8 SERVINGS.

VARIATION: *Sauté 1 chopped onion in 1 tablespoon olive oil. Layer over meatball layer and continue with the recipe as directed.*

Hash Brown Meatball Casserole

1   bag (28 ounces) frozen cubed hash brown potatoes with onions and peppers

1   cup sour cream

1   can (10.5 ounces) cream of mushroom soup, condensed

1½ cups grated Colby Jack or cheddar cheese

24 frozen, fully cooked meatballs

Preheat oven to 350 degrees.

In a large bowl, combine the hash browns, sour cream, soup, and cheese. Spread potato mixture in a 9 × 13-inch pan prepared with nonstick cooking spray. Evenly place meatballs over the top. Cover pan with aluminum foil and bake 45 minutes. Uncover and bake 20–25 minutes more, or until bubbly.

MAKES 6–8 SERVINGS.

Kid-Friendly Taco Casserole

26 (1 pound) frozen, fully cooked meatballs, thawed

 2 cans (8 ounces each) tomato sauce

 1 envelope taco seasoning mix

10 medium flour tortillas

 1 can (10.5 ounces) cream of chicken soup, condensed

¾ cup milk

1½ cups grated cheddar or Mexican-blend cheese

Preheat oven to 350 degrees.

Crumble the meatballs into a large frying pan and sauté over medium heat for 6 minutes, or until browned. Stir in tomato sauce and taco seasoning. Reduce heat to medium-low and simmer 5 minutes. Use 6 tortillas to cover bottom and sides of a 9 × 13-inch pan prepared with nonstick cooking spray. Spread meatball mixture over tortillas. Use remaining tortillas to cover, cutting to fit if necessary.

In a bowl, combine the soup and milk, and then pour over tortillas. Sprinkle cheese over top. Bake 20–25 minutes, or until edges turn golden brown. MAKES 6–8 SERVINGS.

VARIATION: *Sauté crumbled meatballs with 1 cup chopped onion until onion is tender. You can also add 1 can (4 ounces) diced green chiles for a spicier version.*

101 Ways with
Canned Biscuits

Appetizers

Turkey Empanadas 231 • Wrapped Smokies with Mustard Sauce 232 • Spinach Artichoke Dip in Bread Bowls 233 • Meatball Puffs 234 • Tasty Flowers 234 • Chicken and Dumplings 235 • Cheese Balls 235 • Shrimp and Pork Pot Stickers 236 • Cocktail Biscuits 237 • Zucchini and Cheese Roll-Ups 238 • Bruschetta 239 • Potato Turnovers 240 • Jalapeño Puffers 240 • Cheese Crescents 241 • Pepperoni Bites 241 • Feta Biscuits 242

Breads

Focaccia Bread 243 • Italian-Style Flatbread 243 • Cheesy Pull-Apart Bread 244 • Bubble Ring 244 • Cheese-Topped Biscuits 245 • Poppy-Onion Loaf 245 • Garlic Bread 246 • Herbed Biscuit Strips 246 • Cinnamon Nut Biscuits 247 • Cinnamon Biscuit Fans 248 • Caramel Apple Pull-Apart Biscuits 249 • Praline Meltaway Biscuits 249 • Lemon Pull-Apart Coffee Cake 250 • Maple Breakfast Rolls 251 • Pineapple Biscuits 251 • Cinnamon Pull-Apart Bread 252 • Monkey Bread 253

Breakfast

Breakfast Biscuit Sandwiches 254 • Cheddar Biscuit Quiche 255 • Sausage Quiche 255 • Herbed Biscuit Egg Bake 256 • Bacon Quiche Tarts 257 • Scrambled Eggs Alfredo Bake 258 • Roasted Vegetable Strata 259 • Breakfast Pockets 260 • Ham and Cheese Casserole 261 • Breakfast Sandwiches 261 • Ham and Egg Pizzas 262 • Sausage Biscuit Pinwheels 262 • Bear Claws 263 • Apple Coffee Cake 264 • Doughnuts 265 • Blueberry Monkey Bread 265

CHAPTER 4

Lunch

Beefy Pepper Biscuits 266 • Broccoli and Tuna on Biscuits 267 • Barbecue Pork Sandwiches 267 • Cheddar Biscuits with Ham Salad 268 • Buttermilk Biscuits with Tomato Gravy 269 • Tomato and Kielbasa Sandwiches 270 • Calzones 271 • Tex-Mex Sandwiches 272 • Meatball Biscuits 273 • Sammiches 273 • Mini Pizza Bites 274 • Hot Turkey Sandwiches 274 • Bacon Tomato Biscuit Melts 275 • Sesame Hot Dogs 275 • Ham Biscuiwiches 276 • Barbecups 276 • Krautburgers 277 • Crab Shortcakes 278 • Chicken Club Bake 279

Dinner

Italian Casserole 280 • Biscuits and Tuna 281 • Mexican Fiesta Bake 282 • Taco Casserole 283 • Southwestern Bean Bake 284 • Turkey Pot Pie 284 • Chicken and Biscuit Casserole 285 • Beef Pot Pie 285 • Turkey and Biscuits 286 • Pan Pizza 287 • Louisiana Shrimp Casserole 288 • Vegetable Casserole 289 • Turkey Salad with Biscuits 289 • Shrimp Newburg 290 • Beefy Cheese Bake 291 • Chicken with Biscuit Stuffing 292

Desserts

Mini Cherry Pies 293 • Fruity Biscuits 294 • Sweet and Tangy Apricot Biscuits 294 • Crunchy Peanut Ring 295 • Chocolate Oatmeal Bars 295 • Peach Pinwheels 296 • Chantilly Cream Strawberry Shortcake 297 • Apple Upside-Down Cake 297 • Orange Biscuits 298 • Marmalade Biscuits 298 • White Chocolate Berry Bread Pudding 299 • Caramel Biscuit Bites 300 • Sweet Potato Bread Pudding 301 • Biscuit Cookies 302 • Doughnut Parfait 302 • Apple Turnovers 303 • Fried Fruit Pies 303

Appetizers

Turkey Empanadas

1 pound ground turkey

1 large onion, diced

1 can (8 ounces) tomato sauce

4 teaspoons Cajun seasoning mix

   salt and pepper

½ cup grated Monterey Jack cheese

3 cans (7 ounces each) biscuits

1 egg, beaten

   oil, for deep frying

Sauté turkey in large frying pan over medium heat until brown, breaking up meat with fork, about 5 minutes. Using slotted spoon, transfer turkey to small bowl. Add onion to drippings in frying pan and sauté until light brown, about 7 minutes. Return turkey and any juices to frying pan. Add tomato sauce and Cajun seasoning; simmer until mixture is almost dry, stirring occasionally, about 8 minutes. Season with salt and pepper. Cool completely. Mix in cheese.

Flatten each biscuit into a 4-inch round. Place 1 tablespoon filling on round. Brush half of dough edge with egg. Fold dough over filling to create half circle and seal edges by pressing with tines of fork. Set empanada on baking sheet and cover with damp paper towel. Repeat with remaining biscuits and filling.

Pour oil to depth of ½ inch into heavy large frying pan. Heat oil over medium-high heat to 350 degrees. Fry empanadas in batches until golden brown, about 2 minutes per side. Transfer to a plate covered with paper towels. Serve warm or at room temperature. MAKES 30 EMPANADAS.

Wrapped Smokies
with Mustard Sauce

  1 can (12 ounces) biscuits

10 little smoked sausages

  2 tablespoons sugar

  1 tablespoon dry mustard

  2 tablespoons cornstarch

 ½ tablespoon garlic powder

 ½ tablespoon onion powder

  1 can beer

  1 tablespoon red wine vinegar

Preheat oven to 400 degrees.

Flatten each biscuit into a 6-inch round. Quarter biscuits and wrap around uncooked wieners. Roll and seal the edges, completely covering the wiener. Place on lightly greased baking sheet and bake for 10 minutes or until dough is golden brown.

In a medium saucepan, combine sugar, mustard, cornstarch, garlic powder, and onion powder. Cook on low heat until mixture combines, stirring constantly, about 1 minute. Add in beer and vinegar. Cook over medium heat, stirring constantly, until thickened. Serve as dipping sauce. MAKES 10 SERVINGS.

Spinach Artichoke Dip in Bread Bowls

1 package (8 ounces) cream cheese

½ cup mayonnaise

2 packages (9 ounces each) frozen creamed spinach, thawed

1 can (14 ounces) artichoke hearts, drained and chopped

½ cup grated Parmesan cheese

⅓ cup chopped onion

⅛ teaspoon cayenne pepper

2 cans (16.3 ounces each) biscuits

⅓ cup crushed herbed stuffing

½ cup chopped pecans

Preheat oven to 375 degrees. Grease 16 muffin cups.

Combine cream cheese and mayonnaise in a large bowl. Stir in creamed spinach, artichokes, Parmesan cheese, onion, and pepper.

Flatten each biscuit into a 6-inch round. Place in muffin cups, pressing firmly into the bottom and up the sides of cup. Spoon dip evenly into each cup. Combine stuffing and pecans; sprinkle on top. Bake for 17–20 minutes or until biscuits are golden brown. MAKES 16 SERVINGS.

COOKING TIP

As a quick reference to make it easier for you to choose the correct size of biscuits, the chart below lists the weight measurement with the biscuit count per can for the sizes used in the recipes in this cookbook. The ingredient lists only show the weight measurements.

16.3-ounce can = 8 jumbo-size biscuits

12-ounce can = 10 regular-size biscuits

10-ounce can = 5 jumbo-size biscuits

7-ounce can = 10 small-size biscuits

6-ounce can = 5 regular-size biscuits

Meatball Puffs

2 cans (16.3 ounces each) biscuits

⅔ cup grated mozzarella cheese

16 frozen Italian meatballs, thawed

1 cup marinara sauce

Preheat oven to 375 degrees.

Flatten each biscuit into a 5-inch round. Sprinkle with cheese and place a meatball in the center. Wrap dough around the meatball and pinch to seal. Place, pinched side down, on a slightly greased baking sheet. Bake for 17–20 minutes or until biscuits are golden brown. Serve warm with marinara sauce for dipping. MAKES 16 SERVINGS.

Tasty Flowers

¼ cup preserves, flavor of choice

¼ cup cream cheese

1 can (12 ounces) biscuits

Preheat oven according to package directions.

In a medium bowl blend preserves and cream cheese. Place biscuits on a lightly greased baking sheet. Make five slashes on each biscuit to form the petals. Make an indentation in the center of the biscuit and drop in a teaspoon of cream cheese mixture.

Bake according to package directions. MAKES 10 SERVINGS.

Chicken and Dumplings

3 cans (15 ounces each) chunky home-style chicken noodle soup

1 can (14 ounces) chicken or vegetable broth

1 can (12 ounces) biscuits

Combine soup and broth in large pot and bring to a boil.

Cut each biscuit into fourths. Drop biscuits into boiling soup and cook uncovered for 10 minutes at a medium boil. Cover and continue to cook for another 10 minutes until biscuits are fluffy. MAKES 8 SERVINGS.

Cheese Balls

1 can (12 ounces) biscuits

6 ounces cheddar cheese, cut into 40 cubes

¼ cup crushed cornflakes

¼ cup grated Parmesan cheese

¼ teaspoon garlic powder

⅓ cup butter, melted

Preheat oven to 400 degrees.

Cut each biscuit into fourths. Flatten each piece and place a cheese cube into center. Wrap dough around cheese and seal with a pinch. Shape into a ball.

Combine cornflakes, Parmesan cheese, and garlic powder. Roll each ball in butter, then in cornflake mixture. Place on a lightly greased baking sheet. Bake for 7–9 minutes or until golden brown. Serve hot. MAKES 40 BALLS.

Shrimp and Pork Pot Stickers

¼ pound ground pork

1 can water chestnuts, drained and diced

½ pound shrimp, peeled, deveined, and coarsely chopped

¾ cup chopped green onions

1½ tablespoons soy sauce

2 teaspoons minced fresh ginger

1 teaspoon Asian sesame oil

1 can (12 ounces) flaky biscuits

⅓ cup soy sauce

2 tablespoons Chinese vinegar

2 tablespoons water

1 teaspoon Asian chile oil

¼ cup peanut oil

In a medium frying pan, brown pork, stirring frequently to ensure pork is broken up into small pieces. Drain. In a large bowl, combine pork, chestnuts, shrimp, green onions, 1½ tablespoons soy sauce, ginger, and sesame oil. Mix well.

Split biscuits in half by pulling apart at center layers. On a floured surface and using a floured rolling pin, flatten biscuits into 4-inch rounds. Cut each biscuit in half. Place a tablespoon of pork mixture on each half. Moisten edges with water and fold dough over mixture. Seal edges firmly with a fork. In a medium bowl, combine ⅓ cup soy sauce, vinegar, water, and chile oil to make dipping sauce.

Place peanut oil in a medium frying pan. Over medium heat, fry biscuits until lightly brown. Serve pot stickers warm with soy dipping sauce. MAKES 40 POT STICKERS.

Cocktail Biscuits

    1 package (8 ounces) cream cheese

1½ tablespoons half-and-half

    1 teaspoon dill weed

    1 clove garlic, finely chopped

    ¾ teaspoon chives

    ⅛ teaspoon hot sauce

    ⅛ teaspoon pepper

    ¼ teaspoon salt

BISCUITS:

    2 teaspoons butter

    1 cup minced mushrooms

    2 shallots, minced

    ½ cup finely chopped ham

    2 green onions, finely chopped

       pepper, to taste

    1 can (12 ounces) biscuits

In a large bowl, combine cream cheese and half-and-half; mix well. Add rest of ingredients for cream cheese spread and mix well. Place in refrigerator and chill overnight.

Preheat oven to 400 degrees.

In medium frying pan, melt butter and then sauté mushrooms and shallots until tender. Add ham, onions, and pepper. Cook for 4 minutes. Remove from heat. Press each biscuit firmly into mushroom mixture, coating the entire top of biscuit. Place on a lightly greased baking sheet. Make an indentation in each biscuit by pressing a tablespoon firmly in the center. Bake for 12–15 minutes. Top with cream cheese mixture. MAKES 10 SERVINGS.

Zucchini and Cheese Roll-Ups

1 cup chopped zucchini

¼ cup chopped onions

1 tablespoon butter

½ teaspoon dried dill weed

½ teaspoon basil

1 can (12 ounces) flaky biscuits

1 cup grated sharp cheddar cheese

Preheat oven to 400 degrees.

In a large frying pan, sauté zucchini and onion in butter until tender. Remove from heat and stir in dill weed and basil.

Sprinkle flour on a large surface. Using a floured rolling pin, flatten biscuits into 5-inch rounds. Arrange biscuits so they are slightly overlapping, 2 across and 5 down. Flatten with the rolling pin to create a rectangle. Spread zucchini mixture evenly across biscuits and top with cheese.

Roll biscuits into a log beginning at the shortest edge and seal ends well. Cut into 10 pieces and place, cut side down, on a lightly greased baking sheet. Bake 15–20 minutes, until golden brown. Serve immediately. MAKES 10 SERVINGS.

Bruschetta

 1 cup olive oil

 ½ cup balsamic vinegar

 1 teaspoon basil

 1 teaspoon Dijon mustard

 1 clove garlic, minced

 6 large tomatoes, sliced

 1 can (12 ounces) flaky biscuits

12 ounces pesto

 6 ounces fresh mozzarella, sliced

Mix together oil, vinegar, basil, mustard, and garlic. Add tomatoes and place, covered, in refrigerator to marinate overnight.

Preheat oven to 400 degrees.

Cut biscuits in half horizontally. Flatten into 4-inch rounds and place on a greased baking sheet. Bake 10–15 minutes. Top each biscuit with pesto, tomato, and mozzarella. MAKES 20 SERVINGS.

Potato Turnovers

6 large potatoes, peeled and cut in large pieces

3 large onions, finely diced

3 tablespoons butter

2 cups grated cheddar cheese

1 can (12 ounces) flaky biscuits

In large pot, boil potatoes 20–25 minutes until soft. Drain.

Preheat oven to 400 degrees.

In a large frying pan, sauté onions in butter until clear. In a large bowl, combine potatoes, onions, and cheese. With a hand mixer, blend until creamy.

On a lightly floured surface, flatten biscuits into 7-inch rounds using a floured rolling pin. Place ½ cup potato mixture in the center of each biscuit. Moisten edges with water and fold into half circles. Use fork to seal edges. Bake for 15 minutes or until lightly golden. MAKES 10 SERVINGS.

Jalapeño Puffers

1 can (12 ounces) biscuits

10 slices jalapeño

½ cup grated cheddar cheese

Preheat oven to 375 degrees.

Flatten each biscuit into a 5-inch round. Place a slice of jalapeño and a large pinch of cheddar cheese in the center of each biscuit. Fold biscuit over and pinch to seal edges. Place seam side down on a lightly greased baking sheet. Bake until golden brown, about 15 minutes. MAKES 10 SERVINGS.

Cheese Crescents

    2 tablespoons butter
    2 teaspoons garlic powder
    ½ cup grated sharp cheddar cheese
    ½ cup grated mozzarella
    1 can (12 ounces) biscuits

Preheat oven to 375 degrees.

Melt butter and add garlic powder. In a separate bowl, mix cheeses.

Flatten each biscuit into a 6-inch round and cut in half. Brush top of biscuit with garlic butter. Top with cheese blend. Beginning at the narrowest point, roll biscuit into a crescent. Drizzle butter over top. Place on a lightly greased baking sheet and bake for 15 minutes. MAKES 20 CRESCENTS.

Pepperoni Bites

    1 cup grated mozzarella cheese
    ½ cup chopped pepperoni
    ½ cup pizza sauce
    2 cans (7 ounces each) biscuits
    1 tablespoon milk
    ¼ cup grated Parmesan cheese
    1 teaspoon oregano
    1 teaspoon basil

Preheat oven to 350 degrees.

In a bowl, combine mozzarella cheese, pepperoni, and sauce. Set aside.

Flatten each biscuit into a 3-inch round. Place about 1 rounded teaspoon of filling in the center of each circle. Bring edges of dough together. Pinch to seal. Place, seam side down, on greased baking sheets. Brush with milk. Sprinkle with Parmesan cheese, oregano, and basil. Bake for 12–15 minutes or until golden brown. MAKES 20 PIECES.

Feta Biscuits

¾ cup crumbled feta cheese

1 tablespoon lemon juice

1 tablespoon dill

1 green onion, finely chopped

1 can (7 ounces) biscuits

10 green olives with pimientos

Preheat oven to 400 degrees.

In a small serving bowl, combine cheese, lemon juice, dill, and onion.

Lightly grease 10 muffin cups. Cut each biscuit in half horizontally and arrange 1 layer in bottom of each muffin cup.

Place cheese mixture evenly among cups. Place one olive in the center of each. Top with remaining biscuit layer; press around edge of each biscuit to seal. Bake 8–10 minutes or until biscuits are golden brown. Let biscuits cool before serving. MAKES 10 SERVINGS.

Breads

Focaccia Bread

1 **can (16.3 ounces) buttermilk biscuits**
½ **cup pesto**
¼ **cup grated Parmesan cheese**
¼ **cup toasted pine nuts**

Preheat oven to 400 degrees.

Cut each biscuit in half horizontally. Flatten into 5-inch rounds. Place on lightly greased baking sheet. Top each with pesto, cheese, and pine nuts. Bake for 8–10 minutes or until edges are golden brown. MAKES 16 SERVINGS.

Italian-Style Flatbread

⅓ **cup mayonnaise**
⅓ **cup grated Parmesan cheese**
¼ **teaspoon basil**
¼ **teaspoon oregano**
3 **green onions, thinly sliced**
1 **teaspoon minced garlic**
1 **can (12 ounces) biscuits**
½ **cup grated mozzarella cheese**

Preheat oven to 400 degrees.

Combine mayonnaise, Parmesan cheese, basil, oregano, onions, and garlic.

Cut each biscuit in half horizontally. Flatten into 5-inch rounds. Place on a lightly greased baking sheet. Spread mixture over each biscuit. Top with mozzarella cheese. Bake 10–15 minutes or until biscuits are golden brown. MAKES 20 SERVINGS.

Cheesy Pull-Apart Bread

1   teaspoon garlic powder

¼   cup butter, melted

½   teaspoon dry mustard

1   can (16.3 ounces) biscuits

¼   cup grated Parmesan cheese

Preheat oven to 375 degrees.

Combine garlic powder, butter, and mustard in a bowl.

Cut each biscuit into fourths. Coat the bottom of a loaf pan with 2 table-spoons of the butter mixture. Dip each biscuit piece in butter mixture and place in bread pan. Drizzle remaining butter over top of biscuit pieces and top with cheese. Bake 30–40 minutes or until golden brown. MAKES 10 SERVINGS.

Bubble Ring

8   slices bacon, fried and crumbled

½   cup grated Parmesan cheese

¼   cup diced green bell pepper

¼   cup diced onion

1   can (16.3 ounces) flaky biscuits

¼   cup butter, melted

Preheat oven to 350 degrees.

Combine bacon, cheese, pepper, and onion in a large bowl. Cut each biscuit into fourths. Place pieces in the bowl and toss to mix. Distribute mixture evenly in a lightly greased Bundt pan. Bake for 20–30 minutes or until biscuits are golden brown. MAKES 10 SERVINGS.

Cheese-Topped Biscuits

2 cans (7 ounces each) biscuits
1 cup grated sharp cheddar cheese
2 tablespoons light cream
½ teaspoon poppy seeds
dash dry mustard

Preheat oven to 425 degrees.

Arrange 15 biscuits, overlapping, around outside of a 9-inch round cake pan. Arrange remaining biscuits to make inner circle. Combine cheese, cream, poppy seeds, and mustard. Crumble evenly over top of biscuits. Bake 12–17 minutes. Remove from pan immediately and serve hot. MAKES 8–10 SERVINGS.

Poppy-Onion Loaf

¼ cup butter, melted
2 tablespoons onion flakes
1 tablespoon poppy seeds
1 can (16 ounces) buttermilk biscuits

Preheat oven to 350 degrees.

Stir together butter, onion flakes, and poppy seeds.

Dip each biscuit into butter mixture, turning to coat. Arrange biscuits, standing on edge, in two rows in a 9 × 5-inch loaf pan. Brush with remaining butter mixture. Bake for 25–30 minutes or until golden brown. Let cool in pan for 10 minutes. MAKES 10 SERVINGS.

Garlic Bread

½ cup butter

¼ cup grated Parmesan cheese

½ teaspoon oregano

1 teaspoon garlic

3 cans (7 ounces each) biscuits

Preheat oven to 350 degrees.

Melt butter in Bundt pan. Sprinkle with cheese, oregano, and garlic.

Open cans of biscuits and place in Bundt pan, without separating biscuits. Bake 30–35 minutes. Invert onto a serving plate or wire rack. MAKES 10–15 SERVINGS.

Herbed Biscuit Strips

1 can (16.3 ounces) biscuits

¼ cup unsalted butter, melted

1½ teaspoons Italian seasoning

¼ teaspoon paprika

⅓ cup grated Parmesan cheese

Preheat oven to 400 degrees.

Cut each biscuit into 4 strips.

Pour melted butter in a 9 × 9-inch pan. Sprinkle in Italian seasoning, paprika, and cheese. Place biscuit strips evenly on top of butter. Bake 15–20 minutes or until golden brown. Recut strips and serve. MAKES 8–10 SERVINGS.

Cinnamon Nut Biscuits

1 can (16.3 ounces) flaky biscuits

3 tablespoons butter, melted

½ cup brown sugar

¾ teaspoon cinnamon

¼ cup chopped pecans

Preheat oven to 375 degrees.

Cut each biscuit in half horizontally. Mix butter, brown sugar, cinnamon, and pecans in a small bowl.

Place 4 biscuit halves along the bottom of a lightly greased loaf pan. Drizzle with one-third of the butter mixture. Repeat another two layers. Top with remaining 4 biscuits. Bake for 20–30 minutes or until golden brown. MAKES 8 SERVINGS.

Cinnamon Biscuit Fans

1 **can (16.3 ounces) flaky biscuits**

3 **tablespoons sugar**

1 **teaspoon cinnamon**

3 **tablespoons butter, melted**

ICING:

½ **cup confectioners' sugar**

¼ **tablespoon vanilla**

3 **teaspoons milk**

Preheat oven to 400 degrees.

Cut each biscuit in half horizontally. In a small bowl, mix sugar and cinnamon. Coat each biscuit half with butter and sprinkle with sugar mixture. Cut each half into 5 strips.

Lightly grease 8 muffin cups. Place 10 strips vertically in each cup so tips are sticking out. Bake 15–20 minutes or until golden brown. Remove from muffin cups.

In a medium bowl, combine confectioners' sugar, vanilla, and milk. Drizzle over warm biscuits. MAKES 8 SERVINGS.

Caramel Apple Pull-Apart Biscuits

2 cans (12 ounces each) biscuits

1 cup brown sugar

½ cup whipping cream

1 teaspoon cinnamon

1 medium apple, peeled and finely diced

Preheat oven to 350 degrees.

Cut each biscuit into fourths and arrange evenly in a lightly greased Bundt pan.

Combine brown sugar, cream, cinnamon, and apple. Pour over biscuits. Bake 30–35 minutes or until golden brown. Remove from oven and invert on serving plate. Leave pan over biscuits for at least 5 minutes. MAKES 10–12 SERVINGS.

Praline Meltaway Biscuits

⅓ cup butter, melted

⅓ cup brown sugar

⅓ cup chopped pecans

1 can (12 ounces) honey butter biscuits

Preheat oven to 425 degrees.

Mix butter, brown sugar, and pecans in a medium bowl. Divide mixture evenly among 10 muffin cups. Top each with a biscuit. Bake 11–13 minutes or until golden brown. Remove from oven and invert pan onto baking sheet. Leave pan over biscuits for at least 5 minutes. MAKES 10 SERVINGS.

Lemon Pull-Apart Coffee Cake

¼ **cup sugar**

⅓ **cup chopped walnuts**

¼ **cup golden raisins**

2 **tablespoons butter, melted**

1 **teaspoon lemon juice**

1 **can (7 ounces) buttermilk biscuits**

½ **cup confectioners' sugar**

1 **tablespoon lemon juice**

Preheat oven to 400 degrees.

In a large bowl, combine sugar, walnuts, raisins, butter, and lemon juice.

Cut each biscuit into fourths. Toss pieces into sugar mixture. Place into a lightly greased 9-inch round baking pan. Bake 20–25 minutes or until golden brown. Immediately invert onto a wire rack.

Combine confectioners' sugar and lemon juice and drizzle over cake. MAKES 8 SERVINGS.

Maple Breakfast Rolls

¼ cup butter, melted

1 cup brown sugar

½ cup chopped walnuts

⅓ cup maple syrup

1 package (8 ounces) cream cheese, softened

½ cup confectioners' sugar

2 cans (12 ounces each) biscuits

Preheat oven to 350 degrees.

In a medium bowl, combine butter, brown sugar, walnuts, and syrup. Spread into a greased 9 × 13-inch baking dish. In a mixing bowl, beat cream cheese and confectioners' sugar until smooth.

Flatten each biscuit into a 4-inch round. Spread a tablespoon of cream cheese down the center of each biscuit and fold over. Pinch to seal. Place, seam side down, on sugar mixture. Bake for 25–30 minutes or until golden brown. Immediately invert on serving plate. MAKES 10–15 SERVINGS.

Pineapple Biscuits

½ cup brown sugar

¼ cup butter, melted

1 can (8 ounces) crushed pineapple, drained

¾ teaspoon cinnamon

1 can (12 ounces) biscuits

Preheat oven to 425 degrees.

In a bowl, combine brown sugar, butter, pineapple, and cinnamon. Spoon into 10 greased muffin cups. Place a biscuit in each cup. Bake for 10–15 minutes or until golden brown. Let stand for 5 minutes. Invert on baking sheet. MAKES 10 SERVINGS.

Cinnamon Pull-Apart Bread

¾ **cup sugar**

2 **tablespoons cinnamon**

2 **cans (12 ounces each) biscuits**

½ **cup butter, melted, divided**

ICING:

4 **ounces cream cheese, softened**

½ **cup confectioners' sugar**

1 **tablespoon milk**

Preheat oven to 350 degrees.

Mix sugar and cinnamon in medium bowl. Cut each biscuit into fourths. Roll in cinnamon sugar. Place half of the biscuit pieces in greased Bundt pan. Drizzle with half of the butter. Top with remaining biscuit pieces, then drizzle with remaining butter. Sprinkle with remaining cinnamon sugar. Bake 30–35 minutes or until golden brown. Cool in pan 5 minutes. Invert onto serving plate.

Beat cream cheese and confectioners' sugar in small bowl with electric mixer on medium speed until well blended. Add milk and beat until well blended. Add additional milk until glaze is of desired consistency. Drizzle over warm bread. MAKES 10 SERVINGS.

Monkey Bread

½ cup sugar

1 teaspoon cinnamon

2 cans (12 ounces each) biscuits

1¼ cups brown sugar

½ cup butter or margarine

Preheat oven to 375 degrees.

Combine sugar and cinnamon in pie pan. Cut each biscuit into fourths and roll in cinnamon mixture. Place half of the biscuit pieces in a lightly greased Bundt pan.

In small saucepan, combine brown sugar and butter. Stir over medium heat until combined and butter is melted. Bring to a boil. Remove from heat and pour half of the mixture over biscuits in Bundt pan. Place remaining biscuit pieces in pan and top with remaining brown sugar mixture. Bake 30–35 minutes or until golden brown. Immediately invert on a serving plate and serve warm. MAKES 8–12 SERVINGS.

Breakfast

Breakfast Biscuit Sandwiches

1 can (16.3 ounces) buttermilk biscuits

4 eggs

4 tablespoons milk

¼ teaspoon salt

¼ teaspoon pepper

2 tablespoons grated sharp cheddar cheese

8 slices bacon, cooked

Preheat oven to 375 degrees.

Place biscuits on baking sheet and lightly grease 8 muffin cups.

In a small bowl, mix eggs, milk, salt, pepper, and cheese and then pour evenly into muffin cups. Place biscuits and eggs in oven. Bake for 15–17 minutes or until biscuits are golden brown and eggs are fully cooked.

Cut warm biscuits in half horizontally. Place eggs and bacon on bottom halves of biscuits. Cover with top halves of biscuits. MAKES 8 SERVINGS.

Cheddar Biscuit Quiche

  1 can (7 ounces) flaky biscuits
  2 cups grated cheddar cheese
  2 tablespoons flour
  3 eggs, slightly beaten
1¼ cups milk
  ¾ cup chopped ham
  ¼ cup diced tomato
  1 can (3 ounces) diced mild green chiles
  ½ teaspoon salt
  ¼ teaspoon pepper

Preheat oven to 350 degrees.

Line the bottom and the sides of a 9-inch pie pan with biscuits and press together to seal. Combine cheese and flour. Add eggs, milk, ham, tomato, chiles, salt, and pepper. Mix well and then pour into pan. Bake for 50–55 minutes. MAKES 8 SERVINGS.

Sausage Quiche

  1 pound breakfast sausage
  ¼ cup chopped onion
  ¼ cup chopped green bell pepper
 10 eggs
  1 cup grated cheddar cheese
  1 can (16.3 ounces) biscuits

Preheat oven to 375 degrees.

In a large frying pan, brown sausage with onion and bell pepper. Drain well. In a large bowl, beat eggs and then stir in cheese and sausage. Line the bottom and the sides of a lightly greased 9 × 13-inch baking dish with biscuits and press together to seal. Pour egg mixture into dish. Bake for 30–35 minutes or until eggs have set and crust is golden brown. MAKES 8 SERVINGS.

Herbed Biscuit Egg Bake

1   **can (7 ounces) biscuits**

1   **onion, chopped**

1   **tablespoon butter**

7   **eggs**

1   **teaspoon garlic powder**

½   **teaspoon dried tarragon**

½   **teaspoon dried thyme**

½   **teaspoon lemon pepper**

½   **teaspoon salt**

2   **cups chopped broccoli, steamed**

1   **cup grated cheddar cheese**

Preheat oven to 400 degrees.

Line the bottom and the sides of a lightly greased 8 × 8-inch baking pan with biscuits and press together to seal. In a frying pan, sauté onion in butter. Spread evenly on biscuits.

In a bowl, mix eggs and spices and then pour into crust. Add broccoli and sprinkle top with cheese. Bake for 35–40 minutes or until eggs are set and crust is golden brown. MAKES 4 SERVINGS.

Bacon Quiche Tarts

1 can (12 ounces) biscuits

1 package (8 ounces) cream cheese, softened

2 tablespoons milk

2 eggs

½ cup grated Swiss cheese

5 slices bacon, cooked and crumbled

1 tablespoon dried onion flakes

Preheat oven to 375 degrees.

Press each biscuit firmly in the bottom and up the sides of a lightly greased muffin cup.

In a medium bowl combine cream cheese, milk, and eggs; beat until smooth. Stir in cheese, bacon, and onion flakes and then spoon evenly into each muffin cup. Bake 20–25 minutes until eggs have set and the biscuits are golden brown. MAKES 10 SERVINGS.

COOKING TIP

If a recipe calls for muffin cups and there are empty cups after preparing the food (for instance, you have a 12-cup muffin tin and the recipe uses only 10 cups), be sure to fill the empty cups half full with water prior to baking. This will prevent uneven baking and damage to your muffin tin.

Scrambled Eggs Alfredo Bake

  2 **tablespoons butter**

  ¼ **cup chopped onion**

  ¼ **cup chopped green bell pepper**

  1 **jar (4.5 ounces) sliced mushrooms**

12 **eggs, beaten**

  ⅓ **cup cooked and crumbled bacon**

  ¾ **cup Alfredo sauce**

  1 **can (7 ounces) biscuits**

Preheat oven to 400 degrees.

Melt butter in a frying pan over medium heat. Sauté onion, bell pepper, and mushrooms, stirring occasionally, until vegetables are tender. Add eggs. Cook, stirring occasionally, until eggs are set; remove from heat. Gently stir in bacon and Alfredo sauce. Spread into a lightly greased 8 × 8-inch baking dish. Top with biscuits. Bake uncovered about 15 minutes until biscuits are golden brown. MAKES 6 SERVINGS.

Roasted Vegetable Strata

1 can (16.3 ounces) buttermilk biscuits

4 eggs

3 cups milk

2 tablespoons olive oil

1 teaspoon pepper

8 medium green onions, sliced

2 cups grated Monterey Jack cheese

5 small mushrooms, sliced

1 red bell pepper, diced

1 yellow bell pepper, diced

1 small zucchini, thinly sliced

Bake biscuits according to package directions. Then preheat oven to 450 degrees.

In large bowl, beat eggs, milk, oil, and pepper until blended. Break biscuits into random-sized pieces; spread in ungreased 9 × 13-inch glass baking dish. Pour egg mixture over biscuits. Sprinkle with onions and cheese. Cover; refrigerate at least 8 hours but no longer than 24 hours.

In a lightly greased 10 × 15-inch or 9 × 13-inch pan, stir together vegetables. Bake 15–20 minutes, stirring occasionally, until vegetables are tender. Cover and refrigerate.

When ready to bake, preheat oven to 350 degrees. Stir biscuit mixture in dish. Top with vegetables. Cover with foil and bake for 30 minutes; uncover and bake an additional 20–25 minutes or until top is golden brown and knife inserted in center comes out clean. Serve warm. MAKES 12–15 SERVINGS.

Breakfast Pockets

¼ cup chopped onion

1¼ cups grated hash browns

4 eggs, beaten

1½ tablespoons milk

¼ teaspoon salt

¼ teaspoon pepper

¼ teaspoon garlic salt

dash hot sauce

½ pound sausage or bacon, cooked, drained, and crumbled

1½ cups grated cheddar cheese

1 can (16.3 ounces) biscuits

Preheat oven to 350 degrees.

In a frying pan, combine onion, hash browns, eggs, milk, and seasonings. Cook, stirring regularly until eggs have set. Stir in meat. Sprinkle in cheese and mix.

Flatten biscuits into 6-inch rounds. Top each with about ⅓ cup egg mixture. Fold dough over and pinch edges to seal. Bake for 15–20 minutes or until golden brown. MAKES 8 SERVINGS.

Ham and Cheese Casserole

1 **can (16.3 ounces) biscuits**

3 **cups grated cheddar cheese**

2 **cups diced ham**

4 **tablespoons diced onion**

6 **eggs**

1½ **cups milk**

   dash salt

¼ **teaspoon pepper**

Preheat oven to 425 degrees.

Line the bottom of a lightly greased 9 × 13-inch baking dish with biscuits and press together to form a crust. Sprinkle cheese evenly across biscuits. Top with ham and sprinkle with onion.

Mix eggs, milk, salt, and pepper together. Pour over onion layer. Bake for 20–25 minutes or until knife inserted in center comes out clean. Let set a few minutes before serving. MAKES 8 SERVINGS.

Breakfast Sandwiches

1 **can (16.3 ounces) biscuits**

8 **sausage patties, cooked**

8 **slices American cheese**

Bake biscuits according to package directions. Brown sausage patties. Cut biscuits in half and place sausage patty on bottom half. Top with a slice of American cheese and replace top. MAKES 8 SERVINGS.

Ham and Egg Pizzas

3 red, green, or yellow bell peppers, cut into thin strips

1 onion, sliced

1½ teaspoons unsalted butter

2 cups diced ham

1 can (12 ounces) biscuits

3 cups grated Monterey Jack cheese

10 eggs

Preheat oven to 425 degrees.

In a large frying pan, sauté bell peppers and onion in butter. Stir in ham and remove from heat.

Flatten each biscuit into a 6-inch round. Divide the cheese among the biscuits and top it with the bell pepper mixture, making a well in the center. Crack and drop an egg carefully into the well of each shell. Bake the pizzas for 12–15 minutes, or until the egg yolks are set. MAKES 10 SERVINGS.

Sausage Biscuit Pinwheels

1 can (12 ounces) flaky biscuits

8 ounces ground sausage

2 tablespoons onion flakes

Flatten each biscuit into a 5-inch round. Place biscuits in two rows of five. Pinch edges together and roll out to form one large rectangle. Spread raw sausage evenly across dough and sprinkle onion flakes on top. Roll dough lengthwise to form one long log. Wrap in wax paper and refrigerate for at least 1 hour to firm dough.

Preheat oven to 350 degrees. Unwrap log and slice into 24 pinwheels. Place on a lightly greased baking sheet and bake for 20–25 minutes. MAKES 24 SERVINGS.

Bear Claws

4 ounces cream cheese, softened

¼ cup orange marmalade

1 can (12 ounces) flaky biscuits

¼ cup sliced almonds

1 tablespoon sugar

¼ cup orange juice

Preheat oven to 375 degrees.

Combine cream cheese and marmalade in a bowl. Blend well.

Cut biscuits in half horizontally. Flatten into 4-inch rounds. Spoon 1 table-spoon cream cheese mixture into the center of 10 biscuits. Moisten edges and place another biscuit on top. Press firmly around edges with a fork to seal. With a knife, cut five ¼-inch slits, 1 inch apart, around one side of the biscuit to resemble a bear claw.

In a small bowl, combine almonds and sugar. Brush top of each biscuit with orange juice. Sprinkle with almond mixture. Place biscuits on a baking sheet. Bake for 15–20 minutes or until golden brown. MAKES 10 SERVINGS.

Apple Coffee Cake

  2 apples, cored, peeled, and chopped, divided

  1 can (12 ounces) flaky biscuits

  1 tablespoon butter, softened

  ⅓ cup brown sugar

  ½ teaspoon cinnamon

  ⅓ cup light corn syrup

 1¼ teaspoons vanilla

  1 egg

  ½ cup chopped pecans

ICING:

  ⅓ cup confectioners' sugar

  ¼ teaspoon vanilla

  1 tablespoon milk

Preheat oven to 350 degrees.

Place two-thirds of apple pieces in a lightly greased 9-inch baking dish. Cut each biscuit into fourths. Arrange biscuit triangles in dish, resting on their circular edge with the points up. Top with remaining apples.

Combine butter, brown sugar, cinnamon, corn syrup, vanilla, and egg. Beat for 2–3 minutes or until sugar is partially dissolved. Stir in pecans and then spoon over biscuits. Bake for 35–45 minutes or until golden brown.

Combine confectioners' sugar, vanilla, and milk and then drizzle over warm cake. MAKES 8 SERVINGS.

Doughnuts

oil, for frying

1 can (12 ounces) honey butter biscuits

1 cup confectioners' sugar

Preheat oil to 350 degrees.

Flatten biscuits slightly. Punch a hole in the center of each biscuit. Place biscuit in fryer for 30 seconds on each side. Dip in confectioners' sugar. MAKES 10 SERVINGS.

Blueberry Monkey Bread

⅔ cup sugar

2 tablespoons cinnamon, divided

2 cans (16.3 ounces each) buttermilk biscuits

1¼ cups blueberries, divided

⅔ cup brown sugar

8 tablespoons butter

1 teaspoon vanilla

Preheat oven to 350 degrees. Thoroughly grease a Bundt pan. Mix sugar and 1 tablespoon cinnamon. Cut each biscuit into fourths. Roll each piece in sugar mixture. Place biscuits in a large bowl, add ¼ cup blueberries, and toss gently to evenly distribute berries. Put mixture in pan. In saucepan, combine brown sugar, butter, vanilla, remaining cinnamon, and the remaining blueberries. Bring to a boil and then reduce heat to low. Cook, stirring frequently, until sugar is dissolved and butter is melted. Pour over biscuits. Bake for 30–35 minutes or until done. Place serving plate, upside down, on pan and then invert; remove pan. MAKES 8–10 SERVINGS.

Lunch

Beefy Pepper Biscuits

  1 **can (16.3 ounces) biscuits**
  1 **can (10 ounces) French onion soup, condensed**
10 **ounces deli sliced beef, cut into strips**
  1 **large green bell pepper, chopped**
  ½ **teaspoon garlic pepper blend**
1⅓ **cups water, divided**
  ⅓ **cup flour**

Bake biscuits according to package directions.

In a 2-quart saucepan, mix soup, beef, bell pepper, garlic pepper, and 1 cup water. Heat to boiling over medium-high heat and then reduce to medium-low. In a small bowl, stir remaining water and flour until mixed; stir into beef mixture. Heat to boiling, stirring frequently until thickened. Serve warm over halved biscuits. MAKES 8 SERVINGS.

COOKING TIP

When flattening biscuits, it is easier to stretch the dough gradually around the edges, as with pizza dough, rather than to use a rolling pin.

Broccoli and Tuna on Biscuits

  1 can (16.3 ounces) biscuits

  2 cups frozen chopped broccoli

  2 cups milk

  ¼ cup Bisquick mix

  ¼ cup grated Parmesan cheese

  1 can (12 ounces) chunk tuna, drained

  ⅛ teaspoon pepper

Bake biscuits and cook broccoli according to package directions.

In a 2-quart saucepan, stir milk and Bisquick with a metal whisk until completely smooth. Cook over medium heat 9–11 minutes, stirring constantly, until sauce thickens. Gently stir in cheese, tuna, and pepper. Cook 1–3 minutes, stirring constantly until hot. Cut biscuits in half and cover the halves with tuna mixture and then top with broccoli. MAKES 8 SERVINGS.

Barbecue Pork Sandwiches

  2 cans (16.3 ounces each) biscuits

  2 containers (18 ounces each) refrigerated barbecue shredded pork

  2 cups frozen mixed vegetables, thawed and drained

  4 tablespoons maple syrup

Bake biscuits according to package directions.

Place pork in a microwavable bowl. Cover with microwavable plastic wrap, folding one edge back ¼ inch to vent steam. Microwave on high for 2 minutes; stir. Repeat if pork is not hot enough. Stir in vegetables and maple syrup. Cover and microwave on high for 1 minute. Cut biscuits in half and top each half with barbecue pork. MAKES 16 SERVINGS.

Cheddar Biscuits
with Ham Salad

½ cup grated sharp cheddar cheese

1 can (16.3 ounces) buttermilk biscuits

2 green onions, chopped

1 small celery stalk, cut into small pieces

1 jalapeño, seeded and quartered

½ pound sliced smoked ham, chopped

¼ cup mayonnaise

1 tablespoon Dijon mustard

  salt and pepper, to taste

Spread cheese evenly on a flat surface. Lightly press biscuit tops into cheese and place on a baking sheet, cheese side up. Bake according to package directions.

In a food processor, pulse onions, celery, and jalapeño until finely chopped. Add ham and pulse just until finely chopped. Pulse in mayonnaise and mustard; season lightly with salt and pepper. Cut biscuits in half; place salad between halves and serve. MAKES 8 SERVINGS.

Buttermilk Biscuits with Tomato Gravy

1 can (16.3 ounces) buttermilk biscuits

3 large tomatoes

½ cup butter or margarine

½ cup self-rising flour

2½ cups water

½ cup milk

salt and pepper, to taste

¼ cup grated mozzarella cheese

¼ cup grated cheddar cheese

Bake biscuits according to package directions.

Peel and dice tomatoes into a bowl, reserving the juice. In a saucepan, melt butter; add flour and stir until browned. Gradually add water and then stir in tomatoes and juice. Add milk, salt, and pepper; simmer for 15 minutes. Serve over halved biscuits. Top with cheeses. MAKES 8 SERVINGS.

Tomato and Kielbasa Sandwiches

1 can (16.3 ounces) biscuits

½ pound kielbasa, cut into ½-inch slices

1 pound plum tomatoes, cut into ½-inch slices

½ cup chopped onion

1 jalapeño, seeded and minced*

⅓ cup chopped fresh cilantro

1½ tablespoons lime juice

   salt, to taste

⅔ cup sour cream

2 teaspoons water

Bake biscuits according to package directions.

Brown kielbasa in a large frying pan over medium heat. Transfer to a bowl. In same frying pan, sauté tomatoes, onion, and jalapeño, stirring until the tomatoes are softened. Add tomato mixture to sausage and toss with cilantro, lime juice, and salt to taste.

Mix sour cream with water. Cut biscuits in half. Top each half with kielbasa mixture and sour cream. MAKES 16 SERVINGS.

*Reduce the amount of jalapeño for a less spicy sandwich.

Calzones

- ½ pound Italian pork sausage
- ⅓ cup chopped onion
- ¼ cup chopped red bell pepper
- 1 can (16.3 ounces) biscuits
- ½ cup grated mozzarella cheese
- 1½ cups marinara sauce, warmed

Preheat oven to 375 degrees.

In a medium frying pan, brown sausage with onion and bell pepper over medium heat. Drain and let cool.

Flatten each biscuit into a 6-inch diameter. Top each round with sausage mixture and cheese. Fold dough over filling and press edges firmly with a fork to seal. Bake on an ungreased baking sheet for 12–15 minutes or until golden brown. Serve with marinara sauce for dipping. MAKES 8 SERVINGS.

COOKING TIP

To reduce fat calories, choose reduced-fat biscuits and skim milk. Low-fat ingredients such as light soups, sour cream, and cream cheese can be substituted.

Tex-Mex Sandwiches

½ cup chopped roast beef

¼ cup taco sauce

¼ cup barbecue sauce

¼ cup sliced black olives

¼ cup sliced green olives

¼ cup sliced green onions

½ cup grated cheddar cheese

1 can (12 ounces) biscuits

½ cup sour cream

10 pimiento slices

Preheat oven to 350 degrees.

In a medium bowl, combine beef, taco sauce, barbecue sauce, olives, onions, and cheese.

Flatten each biscuit into a 5-inch round. Place 5 biscuits on an ungreased baking sheet and top with beef mixture. Brush edges of biscuits with water and then place another biscuit on top and press edges together with a fork. Make an indentation in the top of the biscuit, using a spoon. Bake for 14–22 minutes or until golden brown. Repeat indentation if necessary. Fill each indentation with a heaping teaspoon of sour cream. Garnish each with 2 pimiento slices. MAKES 5 SERVINGS.

Meatball Biscuits

- 1 can (12 ounces) flaky biscuits
- 10 frozen, fully cooked Italian-style meatballs, thawed and cut in half
- 2 sticks string cheese, each cut into 10 pieces
- 2 tablespoons grated Parmesan cheese
- 1 teaspoon Italian seasoning
- ½ teaspoon garlic powder
- 1 cup pizza sauce, warmed

Preheat oven to 375 degrees.

Cut each biscuit in half horizontally. Flatten each half into a 3-inch round. Place one meatball half and one string cheese piece in center of round. Wrap dough around meatball and press edges to seal. Place seam side down on an ungreased baking sheet. Once all balls have been placed on sheet, sprinkle evenly with Parmesan cheese, Italian seasoning, and garlic powder. Bake for 20–25 minutes or until golden brown and biscuits are no longer doughy in the center. Serve with pizza sauce for dipping. MAKES 20 SERVINGS.

Sammiches

- 1 can (12 ounces) biscuits
- 10 slices lunchmeat (turkey, ham, or beef)
- 10 slices American cheese
- 1 egg white

Preheat oven according to biscuit package directions.

Flatten each biscuit into a 5-inch round. Place a small amount of meat and a crumbled piece of cheese on each round. Fold over and seal. (Use a fork to press edges if dough doesn't stick.) Brush with egg white. Bake for 15 minutes or until golden. MAKES 10 SERVINGS.

Mini Pizza Bites

  1 can (16.3 ounces) biscuits

  1 can (8 ounces) tomato sauce

  1 cup grated sharp cheddar cheese

12 ounces ground beef, cooked and drained

  ½ cup minced green bell pepper

  ½ cup minced onion

  4 ounces sliced pepperoni

  ½ cup grated mozzarella cheese

Preheat oven to 425 degrees.

Cut each biscuit into 3 equal layers. Pinch up the edges of the circles to make a slight rim. Place on a greased baking sheet. Spread a little tomato sauce on each, then top with rest of ingredients. Bake for 10–15 minutes or until crust is brown and toppings are bubbling. MAKES 24 PIECES.

Hot Turkey Sandwiches

1 can (16.3 ounces) biscuits

1 cup turkey gravy

1 pound thinly sliced turkey

2 cups prepared stuffing

Prepare biscuits and turkey gravy according to package directions. Cut biscuits in half, then top lower half with turkey, stuffing, and gravy. Replace top half. Serve warm. MAKES 8 SERVINGS.

Bacon Tomato Biscuit Melts

1 can (16.3 ounces) biscuits
3 large tomatoes, sliced
16 strips bacon, cooked
2 cups grated mozzarella cheese

Bake biscuits according to package directions. Set oven temperature to broil.

Divide the biscuits in half. Top each half with 1 slice of tomato and 1 slice of bacon and sprinkle with cheese. Broil on top rack 1–2 minutes or until cheese begins to brown. MAKES 16 SMALL OPEN-FACED SANDWICHES.

Sesame Hot Dogs

8 hot dogs
8 slices American cheese
1 can (16.3 ounces) biscuits
2 tablespoons butter, melted
¼ cup sesame seeds

Preheat oven to 425 degrees.

Make a slit lengthwise in each hot dog. Fold a slice of cheese into fourths and place in the cut hot dog. Repeat for each hot dog. Flatten biscuits into 5-inch rounds. Wrap biscuits around each hot dog, brush with butter, and sprinkle with sesame seeds. Place on a lightly greased baking sheet and bake for 11–13 minutes. MAKES 8 SERVINGS.

Ham Biscuiwiches

    1 can (16.3 ounces) biscuits

   ¼ cup butter

    1 tablespoon finely grated onion

1½ tablespoons poppy seeds

    1 teaspoon Dijon mustard

    1 teaspoon Worcestershire sauce

    8 thin slices baked ham

    1 cup grated Swiss cheese

Bake biscuits according to package directions.

Beat butter, onion, poppy seeds, mustard, and Worcestershire sauce together. Split cooked biscuits in half and butter each side. Place on a lightly greased baking pan. Place a slice of ham on the bottom half and sprinkle with cheese. Replace tops and cover with aluminum foil. Return biscuits to oven and bake until cheese has melted, about 5 minutes. MAKES 8 SERVINGS.

Barbecups

    1 pound ground beef

   ½ cup barbecue sauce

   ¼ cup chopped onion

    2 tablespoons brown sugar

    1 can (12 ounces) biscuits

   ½ cup grated cheddar cheese

Preheat oven to 400 degrees. Grease 10 muffin cups.

Brown ground beef in large frying pan; drain. Stir in barbecue sauce, onion, and brown sugar. Cook for a minute longer, stirring frequently.

Flatten each biscuit into a 4-inch round. Place a biscuit in each muffin cup, firmly pressing into the bottom and up the sides. Spoon beef mixture into muffin cups. Sprinkle with cheese. Bake for 10–12 minutes or until edges of biscuits are golden brown. Allow to cool before serving. MAKES 10 SERVINGS.

Krautburgers

1 **gallon water**

1 **head cabbage**

4 **pounds ground beef**

4 **large onions, chopped**

1 **tablespoon salt**

2 **tablespoons pepper**

1 **tablespoon garlic powder**

2 **cans (16.3 ounces each) flaky biscuits**

Preheat oven to 375 degrees.

Fill a large pot with water and bring to a boil. Slice cabbage into thin strips. Place in water and boil until cabbage is limp, about 30 minutes. Drain.

In a frying pan, combine beef, onion, salt, pepper, and garlic powder. Cook over medium-high heat until meat is browned. Combine beef and cabbage and toss until evenly mixed.

Lightly grease two baking sheets. On a floured surface and with a floured rolling pin, roll biscuits until thin, about 7- to 8-inch squares. Place ½ cup mixture on each biscuit and pull up edges. Pinch dough to seal so no gaps are present and place pinched side down on baking sheet. Bake for 15–17 minutes or until golden brown. MAKES 16 SERVINGS.

Crab Shortcakes

1 can (10 ounces) biscuits

½ cup white wine

1 jar (16 ounces) Alfredo sauce

1 package (8 ounces) cream cheese

1 cup frozen baby peas

½ pound shrimp, shelled, deveined, and cooked

1 can (6 ounces) crabmeat, drained

½ cup grated cheddar cheese

¼ cup sliced green onions

Bake biscuits according to package directions.

In a large frying pan over high heat, cook wine for 3–5 minutes or until slightly reduced. Reduce heat to medium and add Alfredo sauce, cream cheese, peas, shrimp, and crabmeat; mix well. Simmer 8–10 minutes, stirring occasionally.

Cut biscuits in half and place bottom halves on individual serving plates. Spoon half of seafood mixture over biscuits. Cover with biscuit tops. Top with remaining seafood mixture. Sprinkle with cheese and onions. MAKES 5 SERVINGS.

Chicken Club Bake

5 boneless, skinless chicken breasts, uncooked

5 tablespoons bacon bits

2 medium tomatoes, sliced

1 cup mayonnaise

1 cup grated mozzarella cheese

2 teaspoons basil

1 can (10 ounces) biscuits

Preheat oven to 375 degrees.

Place chicken breasts in a baking dish. Layer bacon bits on top of chicken. Next layer tomatoes.

In a medium bowl, combine mayonnaise, cheese, and basil. Spread mixture over tomatoes. Place one biscuit on top of each chicken breast. Bake for 20 minutes or until biscuits are golden brown. MAKES 5 SERVINGS.

Dinner

Italian Casserole

1 pound ground beef

½ cup chopped onion

¾ cup water

¼ teaspoon pepper

1 can (8 ounces) tomato sauce

1 can (6 ounces) tomato paste

1 package (9 ounces) frozen mixed vegetables, thawed

2 cups grated mozzarella cheese, divided

1 can (12 ounces) buttermilk biscuits

1 tablespoon butter, melted

½ teaspoon oregano

¼ teaspoon basil

Preheat oven to 375 degrees.

In a large frying pan, brown beef and onion, and then drain. Stir in water, pepper, tomato sauce, and tomato paste. Simmer for 15 minutes, stirring occasionally. Remove from heat and stir in vegetables and 1½ cups cheese. Spoon mixture into a 9 × 13-inch baking dish.

Cut each biscuit in half horizontally. Place biscuits along outer edges of dish, overlapping slightly. Sprinkle remaining cheese in center. Brush biscuits with butter and sprinkle with oregano and basil. Bake for 22–27 minutes or until biscuits are golden brown. MAKES 6–8 SERVINGS.

Biscuits and Tuna

½ cup chopped onion

2 tablespoons butter

6 tablespoons flour

2 teaspoons granulated chicken bouillon

¼ teaspoon salt

¼ teaspoon dried thyme

⅛ teaspoon pepper

2 cups milk

1½ cups water

1 can (13 ounces) canned tuna, drained

1 cup frozen peas, thawed

1 cup sliced carrots

3 tablespoons parsley

1 can (12 ounces) biscuits

Preheat oven to 400 degrees.

Sauté onions in butter until tender. Stir in flour, bouillon, salt, thyme, and pepper. Add milk and water. Cook until thickened. Stir in tuna, vegetables, and parsley. Heat until bubbly. Pour into a 9 × 13-inch baking dish. Separate biscuits and place on top. Bake for 12–15 minutes. MAKES 6–8 SERVINGS.

Mexican Fiesta Bake

2   tablespoons butter, melted

1   can (16.3 ounces) buttermilk biscuits

1   can (10 ounces) buttermilk biscuits

1   jar (16 ounces) thick and chunky salsa

3   cups grated Monterey Jack cheese

½   cup chopped green bell pepper

⅓   cup sliced green onions

1   can (2.25 ounces) sliced black olives, drained

Preheat oven to 375 degrees.

Pour butter into a 9 × 13-inch baking dish and coat evenly.

Divide each biscuit into eight pieces, and then toss with salsa. Spoon evenly into baking dish. Sprinkle with cheese, bell pepper, onions, and olives. Bake for 35–45 minutes or until edges are golden brown and center is baked.

MAKES 6–8 SERVINGS.

Taco Casserole

1 can (12 ounces) buttermilk biscuits

1 jar (16 ounces) medium taco sauce

1½ cups grated sharp cheddar cheese, divided

1½ cups grated mozzarella cheese, divided

½ pound ground beef

¼ cup chopped green bell pepper

¼ cup chopped red bell pepper

1 can (4 ounces) mushrooms, drained

1 can (2.25 ounces) sliced black olives, drained

Preheat oven to 400 degrees.

Cut each biscuit into fourths. In a large bowl, toss biscuits in taco sauce. Place biscuits in a lightly greased 9 × 13-inch baking dish. Sprinkle with half the cheddar and mozzarella cheeses. Bake for 15–18 minutes or until bubbly and center is set.

In a large frying pan, brown ground beef with peppers and mushrooms and then drain. Sprinkle remaining cheeses and olives over biscuits and top with beef mixture. Bake an additional 5–7 minutes until mixture bubbles around edges. MAKES 6–8 SERVINGS.

Southwestern Bean Bake

1   can (15 ounces) kidney beans, drained and rinsed

1   can (15 ounces) great Northern beans, drained and rinsed

1   can (14.5 ounces) stewed tomatoes, with juices

½   cup salsa

¼   cup ketchup

1   can (12 ounces) buttermilk biscuits

Preheat oven to 375 degrees.

In a large saucepan, heat beans, tomatoes, salsa, and ketchup to boiling, stirring occasionally. Pour into a 9 × 13-inch baking dish.

Separate biscuits and place them evenly on top of bean mixture. Bake for 20–25 minutes or until biscuits are golden brown. MAKES 6–8 SERVINGS.

Turkey Pot Pie

1½   cups cooked turkey

2   cups frozen peas and carrots

1   medium onion, chopped

1   jar (12 ounces) turkey gravy

1   can (12 ounces) buttermilk biscuits

Preheat oven to 375 degrees.

In a saucepan, heat turkey, vegetables, onion, and gravy to boiling, stirring frequently. Pour into a 9 × 9-inch baking dish. Separate biscuits, and then place biscuits evenly across the top of mixture. Bake for 20–25 minutes or until biscuits are golden brown. MAKES 6–8 SERVINGS.

Chicken and Biscuit Casserole

  2 cups cooked and cubed chicken

10 ounces broccoli, steamed

  1 can (10.5 ounces) cream of chicken soup, condensed

  ¼ cup chopped onion

  ¼ cup sour cream

1½ teaspoons Worcestershire sauce

  ½ cup grated cheddar cheese

  1 can (7 ounces) flaky biscuits

Preheat oven to 375 degrees.

In a large bowl, combine chicken, broccoli, soup, onion, sour cream, and Worcestershire sauce. Pour into an 8 × 8-inch baking dish. Bake for 20–25 minutes or until bubbling.

Remove from oven and top with cheese. Arrange the biscuits across top of casserole and return to oven and bake an additional 25–30 minutes or until biscuits are golden brown. MAKES 4 SERVINGS.

Beef Pot Pie

½ pound roast beef, cubed

2 cups frozen mixed vegetables

1 medium onion, chopped

1 jar (12 ounces) beef gravy

1 can (12 ounces) buttermilk biscuits

Preheat oven to 375 degrees.

In a large saucepan, combine beef, vegetables, onion, and gravy. Bring to a boil over medium heat, stirring regularly. Pour into a 9 × 9-inch baking dish. Separate biscuits, and then place them evenly across top of mixture. Bake for 20–25 minutes or until biscuits are golden brown. MAKES 4–6 SERVINGS.

Turkey and Biscuits

¼ cup butter, melted

2 cups cooked and cubed turkey

½ cup flour

½ teaspoon basil

¼ teaspoon salt

¼ teaspoon pepper

1 cup chicken broth

⅔ cup milk

1 red bell pepper, cut into strips

1 can (4 ounces) mushrooms, drained

1 cup fresh spinach, cut into strips

1 can (12 ounces) buttermilk biscuits

Preheat oven to 400 degrees.

In a large bowl, combine butter, turkey, flour, basil, salt, pepper, broth, milk, bell pepper, and mushrooms. Pour into a greased 9 × 9-inch baking dish. Bake 20 minutes, stirring once after 10 minutes.

Remove casserole from oven and stir in spinach. Separate biscuits, and then place them evenly on top of turkey mixture. Return to oven and continue to bake for 15–20 minutes longer until biscuits are golden brown. MAKES 4–6 SERVINGS.

Pan Pizza

1 can (16.3 ounces) biscuits
1 can (14 ounces) pizza sauce
2 cups grated mozzarella cheese, divided
16 slices pepperoni

Preheat oven to 375 degrees.

Cut each biscuit into fourths. In a large bowl, combine biscuits, pizza sauce, and 1 cup cheese; toss to coat. Transfer mixture to an ungreased 9 × 9-inch baking dish. Top with pepperoni and the remaining cheese. Bake for 22–28 minutes or until golden brown and bubbly. MAKES 4–6 SERVINGS.

COOKING TIP

Different brands of biscuits have different weight measurements. Choose the size nearest to what is listed in the recipe ingredient list. If you only have one size of biscuit available, you can adjust most recipes. Jumbo biscuits can be split in half while still raw.

Louisiana Shrimp Casserole

 2 tablespoons butter

 1 teaspoon garlic, minced

 1 red bell pepper, cut into strips

 1 medium onion, sliced

 ¼ cup chopped celery

 2 tablespoons Bisquick mix

 1 can (14.5 ounces) diced tomatoes with juices

 ¼ teaspoon salt

 ¼ teaspoon Tabasco hot pepper sauce

 12 ounces large shrimp, peeled and deveined

 1 can (12 ounces) biscuits

Preheat oven to 400 degrees.

In a large frying pan over medium heat, melt butter and sauté garlic, bell pepper, onion, and celery until vegetables are tender. Stir Bisquick into mixture until blended. Stir in tomatoes, salt, pepper sauce, and shrimp. Reduce heat to medium low and cook about 7 minutes, stirring occasionally, until thick and bubbling. Pour mixture into an ungreased 9 × 9-inch baking dish.

Separate biscuits, and then place them evenly over shrimp mixture. Bake 20–30 minutes or until biscuits are golden brown. MAKES 4–6 SERVINGS.

Vegetable Casserole

1 medium onion, chopped

1 tablespoon butter

1 bag (16 ounces) frozen mixed vegetables

2 cups frozen chopped broccoli

1 jar (16 ounces) Alfredo sauce

1 can (12 ounces) biscuits

Preheat oven to 400 degrees.

In a large frying pan, sauté onion in butter until tender. Add vegetables, broccoli, and Alfredo sauce. Cook over medium heat 5–6 minutes, stirring occasionally, until mixture comes to a light boil. Spoon into an ungreased 9 × 9-inch baking dish.

Separate biscuits, and then place them on top of mixture. Bake for 20–25 minutes until biscuits are golden brown. MAKES 4–6 SERVINGS.

Turkey Salad with Biscuits

¼ cup mayonnaise

2 tablespoons Bisquick mix

2 cups cooked and cubed turkey

¼ cup grated cheddar cheese

2 celery stalks, sliced

2 green onions, sliced

1 can (7 ounces) buttermilk biscuits

Preheat oven to 425 degrees.

Combine mayonnaise and Bisquick and mix until well blended. Stir in turkey, cheese, celery, and onions. Separate biscuits and place around edges of a lightly greased 9 × 9-inch baking dish. Spoon turkey mixture into center. Bake for 18–20 minutes or until biscuits are golden brown and salad is hot. MAKES 4–6 SERVINGS.

Shrimp Newburg

1 can (16.3 ounces) flaky biscuits

2 cans (10.5 ounces each) cream of shrimp soup, condensed

½ cup milk

2 cups small cooked shrimp

¾ cup frozen peas

¼ cup sherry

1 cup grated sharp cheddar cheese, divided

Bake biscuits according to package directions.

In medium pan over medium heat, stir together soup and milk until smooth. Add shrimp and peas. Bring to simmer and cook slowly for 5 minutes. Stir in sherry and half of the cheese. Separate biscuits onto individual plates, sprinkle with remaining cheese, and spoon sauce over top. MAKES 8 SERVINGS.

COOKING TIP

Baking times may vary with different brands of biscuits. Refer to the package and adjust baking time accordingly. You should check the food near the end of the baking time to make sure it is cooking properly.

Beefy Cheese Bake

1½ **pounds ground beef**

½ **cup chopped onion**

1 **package (8 ounces) cream cheese, softened**

¼ **cup milk**

1 **can (10.5 ounces) cream of mushroom soup, condensed**

⅓ **cup sliced ripe olives (optional)**

¼ **cup ketchup**

½ **teaspoon salt**

¼ **teaspoon pepper**

1 **can (7 ounces) biscuits**

Preheat oven to 375 degrees.

Brown ground beef and onion in frying pan. In medium bowl, blend cream cheese and milk. Stir in soup, olives (if using), ketchup, salt, and pepper. Combine with meat mixture in 2-quart casserole. Bake 30 minutes.

Arrange biscuits on top and bake 15–18 additional minutes or until biscuits are browned. MAKES 6 SERVINGS.

Chicken with Biscuit Stuffing

4 boneless, skinless chicken breasts

1 can (10.5 ounces) cream of chicken soup, condensed

1 cup chopped celery

1 cup chopped onion

½ teaspoon salt

¼ teaspoon pepper

1 egg

1 can (7 ounces) biscuits

Preheat oven to 350 degrees.

Place chicken on bottom of a greased 9 × 13-inch baking pan.

In a large bowl, combine soup, celery, onion, salt, pepper, and egg. Mix until well blended. Cut each biscuit into 10 pieces and add to soup mixture, mixing well. Spoon evenly over chicken. Bake for 55–65 minutes. MAKES 4 SERVINGS.

Desserts

Mini Cherry Pies

½ cup flour

½ cup brown sugar

1 teaspoon cinnamon

½ cup butter, softened

1 can (16.3 ounces) flaky biscuits

1 can (21 ounces) cherry pie filling

1 cup whipped cream

Preheat oven to 375 degrees.

Combine flour, brown sugar, and cinnamon. Mix in butter until mixture is crumbly.

Cut each biscuit in half horizontally. Flatten into 5-inch rounds. Place into lightly greased muffin cups; press firmly into the bottom and up the sides. Fill cups evenly with pie filling. Top with sugar mixture. Bake 15–17 minutes or until biscuits are golden brown. Top with whipped cream. MAKES 8 SERVINGS.

Fruity Biscuits

1 can (14 ounces) fruit cocktail, with liquid

2 tablespoons flour

1¼ cups sugar, divided

1 can (16.3 ounces) biscuits

4 tablespoons butter, melted

2 teaspoons cinnamon

Preheat oven to 350 degrees.

In a saucepan, bring fruit cocktail to a boil, then pour into an ungreased 9 × 13-inch baking dish.

Combine flour and ¾ cup sugar and then sprinkle evenly over fruit. Separate biscuits and place on top of fruit. Drizzle butter over top. Combine remaining sugar and cinnamon and then sprinkle evenly across biscuits. Bake for 20 minutes. MAKES 10 SERVINGS.

Sweet and Tangy Apricot Biscuits

2 tablespoons sweetened powdered lemonade

2 tablespoons sugar

1 can (12 ounces) flaky biscuits

3 tablespoons butter, melted

½ cup miniature marshmallows

¼ cup apricot preserves

2 tablespoons chopped pecans

Preheat oven to 375 degrees. Grease a 9 × 9-inch baking pan.

Combine lemonade and sugar. Dip top of each biscuit in butter, then in sugar mixture. Place sugar side up in pan. Sprinkle remaining sugar over top. Make an indentation in each biscuit and fill with marshmallows. Combine preserves and nuts. Spoon over marshmallows. Bake for 17–20 minutes or until golden brown. MAKES 10 SERVINGS.

Crunchy Peanut Ring

½ **cup butter**

1 **cup chopped peanuts**

¾ **cup brown sugar**

¼ **cup maple syrup**

2 **cans (12 ounces each) honey butter biscuits**

Preheat oven to 350 degrees. Lightly grease a Bundt pan.

Melt butter in a saucepan. Stir in peanuts, brown sugar, and maple syrup. Pour ¼ cup sugar mixture into pan. Separate biscuits and then stand each biscuit on end, slightly overlapping, around the pan. Pour remaining sugar mixture over biscuits. Bake for 20–30 minutes or until golden brown. Let cool for 5 minutes and invert onto serving plate. MAKES 8–10 SERVINGS.

Chocolate Oatmeal Bars

1 **can (16.3 ounces) flaky biscuits**

1 **cup semisweet chocolate chips**

1 **can (14 ounces) sweetened condensed milk**

2 **cups oatmeal**

⅓ **cup brown sugar**

½ **cup butter, melted**

2 **teaspoons vanilla**

Preheat oven to 400 degrees.

Cut each biscuit in half horizontally. Place biscuits in ungreased 9 × 13-inch baking pan. Press over bottom and one inch up sides to form a crust. Sprinkle chocolate chips over dough. Pour condensed milk over chips. Combine remaining ingredients and spread evenly over top. Bake 15–20 minutes or until golden brown. Cool for 5 minutes and cut into bars. MAKES 3 DOZEN BARS.

Peach Pinwheels

½ cup sugar

2 teaspoons vanilla

1 tablespoon flour

1 can (14 ounces) peaches, drained

2 teaspoons lemon juice

½ cup brown sugar

2 tablespoons ginger

½ teaspoon cinnamon

1 can (16.3 ounces) honey butter biscuits

1 tablespoon butter, melted

3 tablespoons confectioners' sugar

Preheat oven to 375 degrees.

Blend sugar, vanilla, and flour. Add peaches and lemon juice and toss. Pour mixture into 10-inch cake pan. Bake until bubbling, about 30 minutes.

Mix brown sugar, ginger, and cinnamon. Cut each biscuit in half horizontally. Brush center and sides of biscuits with melted butter. Top bottom half with sugar mixture. Replace top. Slice each biscuit into 4 strips. Twist strips and form into pinwheels.

Once peach mixture is bubbling, place pinwheels on top and return to oven. Bake until biscuits are golden brown, about 15 minutes. Cool for 10 minutes. Dust with confectioners' sugar and serve. MAKES 10 SERVINGS.

Chantilly Cream Strawberry Shortcake

1 can (16.3 ounces) biscuits

4 pints strawberries, quartered

½ cup Grand Marnier

½ cup sugar

2 tablespoons lemon juice

1 cup heavy cream

2 tablespoons confectioners' sugar

Bake biscuits according to package directions.

In a mixing bowl, combine strawberries, Grand Marnier, sugar, and lemon juice. Stir gently. Let stand at room temperature until juices form.

In a chilled mixing bowl, whisk cream until it begins to thicken. Add confectioners' sugar and continue to whisk until peaks form.

Cut biscuits in half horizontally and place bottom halves in a bowl or on a plate. Spoon strawberries evenly among biscuits. Top with cream and biscuit top. Drizzle remaining juice from strawberries evenly among biscuits. MAKES 8 SERVINGS.

Apple Upside-Down Cake

3 tablespoons unsalted butter

½ cup brown sugar

1 pound apples, peeled, cored, and cut into thin wedges

1 can (12 ounces) honey butter biscuits

Preheat oven to 400 degrees.

Heat butter over moderate heat until foam disappears. Stir in brown sugar and remove from heat. Spread evenly along bottom of well-greased 9-inch pie pan. Place apples, slightly overlapping, evenly around pan. Top with biscuits. Bake for 15–20 minutes or until biscuits are golden. Cool about 3 minutes. Invert cake onto serving plate. MAKES 10 SERVINGS.

Orange Biscuits

  1 can (16.3 ounces) biscuits
  ¼ cup sugar
  1 teaspoon cinnamon
  1 cup orange juice, divided
  ½ cup sugar
  3 tablespoons butter, melted
  2 teaspoons orange zest

Preheat oven to 400 degrees.

Cut each biscuit into fourths. Combine ¼ cup sugar and cinnamon in a small bowl. Dip each biscuit piece in ½ cup orange juice and coat with sugar mixture. Place in a lightly greased 9-inch baking pan.

Combine ½ cup sugar, ½ cup orange juice, melted butter, and orange zest. Pour over biscuits. Bake 20–25 minutes. **MAKES 10 SERVINGS.**

Marmalade Biscuits

  1 cup orange marmalade
  4 tablespoons butter, softened
  1 can (12 ounces) honey butter biscuits

Preheat oven to 425 degrees.

Combine marmalade and butter, mixing well. Coat bottom of an 8-inch baking dish with mixture. Separate biscuits and place evenly in pan. Bake for 15–20 minutes or until biscuits are golden. Immediately invert onto a serving plate. **MAKES 10 SERVINGS.**

White Chocolate Berry Bread Pudding

1 can (12 ounces) honey butter biscuits

¾ cup grated white chocolate baking bars

⅔ cup sugar

3½ cups milk

1½ cups whipping cream

2 tablespoons butter, melted

1 tablespoon vanilla

4 eggs

1 cup raspberries, frozen

1 cup blueberries, frozen

SAUCE:

⅓ cup sugar

2 tablespoons Bisquick mix

1 cup raspberries, frozen

1 cup blueberries, frozen

½ cup water

Bake biscuits according to package directions. Break up biscuits into pieces; spread in a 9 × 13-inch baking dish. Sprinkle with white chocolate. In large bowl, beat sugar, milk, whipping cream, butter, vanilla, and eggs with electric mixer on low speed until blended. Pour over biscuits in baking dish. Cover and refrigerate at least 8 hours but no longer than 24 hours.

Preheat oven to 350 degrees. Stir berries into biscuit mixture. Bake uncovered about 1 hour or until golden brown and toothpick inserted in center comes out clean.

In a saucepan, combine sugar and Bisquick mix. Stir in berries and water. Cook over medium heat, stirring constantly, until mixture thickens and boils. Boil and stir 1 minute; remove from heat. Serve pudding warm, topped with sauce. Store in refrigerator. MAKES 10 SERVINGS.

Caramel Biscuit Bites

1 **can (16.3 ounces) biscuits**

1 **teaspoon sugar**

⅛ **teaspoon cinnamon**

2 **tablespoons caramel apple dip**

2 **teaspoons milk**

1 **teaspoon chopped pecans**

Bake biscuits according to package directions.

In a serving bowl, mix sugar and cinnamon. Cut each biscuit into 8 wedges; toss them in the sugar mixture.

In small microwavable bowl, mix caramel apple dip and milk. Microwave uncovered on high 15–30 seconds or until melted and hot. Evenly distribute biscuit pieces in eight dessert bowls. Stir caramel and drizzle over biscuit pieces. Sprinkle with pecans. MAKES 8 SERVINGS.

Sweet Potato Bread Pudding

    1 can (16.3 ounces) biscuits

    1 cup chopped pecans

    ½ cup raisins

    2½ cups milk

    2½ cups half-and-half

    1¼ cups mashed, baked sweet potatoes

    1 cup sugar

    ¼ cup butter, melted

    1 tablespoon vanilla

    ½ teaspoon cinnamon

    ½ teaspoon nutmeg

    4 eggs

SAUCE:

    2 cups confectioners' sugar

    1 cup butter, melted

    ½ cup orange juice

    2 teaspoons cornstarch

    4 egg yolks, beaten

Bake biscuits according to package directions. Break biscuits into random-sized pieces. Butter bottom and sides of a 9 × 13-inch baking pan. Spread biscuit pieces in pan. Sprinkle with pecans and raisins. In large bowl, beat all remaining pudding ingredients with electric mixer on low speed until blended. Pour over biscuits. Cover and refrigerate at least 2 hours but no longer than 8 hours.

Preheat oven to 350 degrees. Stir mixture in pan. Bake 1 hour or until top is golden and toothpick inserted in center comes out clean.

Meanwhile, in saucepan, heat all sauce ingredients over low heat 5–10 minutes, stirring constantly with wire whisk, until slightly thickened and temperature reaches 165 degrees for 15 seconds. Serve warm over pudding. Store covered in refrigerator. MAKES 10 SERVINGS.

Biscuit Cookies

1 can (16.3 ounces) biscuits

½ cup chocolate chips

½ cup brown sugar

2 teaspoons margarine

Preheat oven to 325 degrees.

Cut each biscuit in half horizontally. Flatten into 4-inch rounds. Cut into fourths or cut into shapes with a cookie cutter. Place on a lightly greased baking sheet.

Mix chocolate chips, sugar, and margarine in a microwavable bowl. Cook in microwave for about 2 minutes on high until chocolate has completely melted. Stir well. Spread chocolate mixture over biscuits. Bake for 8–10 minutes. MAKES APPROXIMATELY 32 COOKIES.

Doughnut Parfait

oil, for frying

1 can (7 ounces) biscuits

½ cup confectioners' sugar

2 cups cold milk

1 box (3.4 ounces) instant vanilla pudding mix

1 to 2 medium firm bananas, sliced

2 cups whipped cream

In a large frying pan or fryer, preheat oil to 350 degrees. Cut each biscuit into fourths. Place in oil for 30 seconds or until golden brown. Remove and toss in confectioners' sugar. Set aside to cool.

In a bowl, whisk milk and pudding for 2 minutes. Let stand for 2 minutes or until pudding has set. Place four doughnuts in each of four parfait glasses. Top with pudding, bananas, and whipped cream. Repeat layers. MAKES 4 SERVINGS.

Apple Turnovers

    1 can (16.3 ounces) biscuits
    1 can (14 ounces) apple pie filling
    1 tablespoon cinnamon
    4 tablespoons sugar

Preheat oven to 400 degrees.

Flatten each biscuit into a 6-inch round. Place 2 heaping tablespoons of pie filling on each biscuit. Moisten edges of dough with water. Fold over and press edges firmly with a fork to seal. Place on a lightly greased baking sheet.

Mix cinnamon and sugar and then sprinkle over top of biscuits. Bake for 15–20 minutes or until golden brown. **MAKES 8 SERVINGS.**

Fried Fruit Pies

    3 cups mixed dried fruit
    1 can (7 ounces) honey butter biscuits
       oil, for frying
       sugar

Place dried fruit in pot and cover with cold water. Bring to a boil, reduce heat, cook until tender, and sweeten to taste.

Flatten each biscuit into a 4-inch round. Evenly distribute fruit among biscuits, fold over, and press edges firmly with a fork to seal. Fry in hot oil for 30 seconds on each side. Sprinkle with sugar. **MAKES 10 SERVINGS.**

An asterisk (*) indicates that photos are shown in the insert pages.

Almonds
  Bear Claws, 263
  Creamy Basil and Almonds, 145
  Hot Turkey Salad, 34
Appetizers (with canned biscuits)
  Bruschetta, 239
  Cheese Balls, 235
  Cheese Crescents, 241
  Chicken and Dumplings, 235
  Cocktail Biscuits, 237
  Feta Biscuits, 242
  Jalapeño Puffers, 240
  Meatball Puffs, 234
  Pepperoni Bites, 241
  Potato Turnovers, 240
  Shrimp and Pork Pot Stickers, 236
  Spinach Artichoke Dip in Bread Bowls,
    233
  Tasty Flowers, 234
  Turkey Empanadas, 231
  Wrapped Smokies with Mustard Sauce,
    232
  Zucchini and Cheese Roll-Ups, 238
Appetizers (with canned soups)
  Baked Pepperoni Dip, 4
  Bean and Bacon Fondue, 8
  Beefy Bean Dip, 5
  Creamy Chicken Dip, 4
  New England Clam Dip, 8
  Pork Chili Dip, 5
  Salsa Nacho Cheese, 3
  Savory Pesto Cheesecake (var.), 7
  Savory Smoked Salmon Cheesecake
    (var.), 7
  Savory Sun-Dried Tomato Cheesecake, 7
  Sour Cream Meatballs, 3

  World's Easiest Cheese Fondue, 6
  Zesty Roast Beef Bites, 9
Appetizers (with meatballs)
  Asian Meatball Appetizers, 191
  Bacon-Wrapped Meatballs, 158
  Blue Cheese Buffalo Balls, 186
  Cheesy Meatballs, 192
  Cranberry Sauerkraut Meatballs, 185
  Crescent-Wrapped Meatballs, 161
  Crowd-Pleasing Meatballs, 183
  Easy Meatball Nachos, 163
  Feta Meatballs with Cucumber Yogurt
    Sauce, 189
  Ginger Ale Meatballs, 191
  Holiday Meatballs, 193
  Italian-Style Cocktail Meatballs, 185
  Magnificent Meatballs, 187
  Malaysian Meatballs, 161
  Maple Meatballs, 188
  Marinated Meatballs, 184
  Meatball Bruschetta, 158
  Meatball Jalapeño Poppers, 156
  Meatball Sliders, 157
  Mini Meatball Hamburgers, 155
  Parmesan Meatball Biscuits, 162
  Puff Pastry Meatball and Mushroom
    Pockets, 160
  Salsa Verde Meatballs, 192
  Saucy Meatballs, 187
  Sour Cream–Sauced Meatballs, 193
  Southwest Taco Salad, 162
  Spicy Jamaican Jerk Meatballs, 190
  Sports Day Meatballs, 186
  Sweet and Spicy Meatballs, 184
  Teriyaki Meatballs, 188
  Thai Pizza,* 159

Apples & applesauce
  Apple Coffee Cake, 264
  Apple Turnovers, 303
  Apple Upside-Down Cake, 297
  Caramel Apple Pull-Apart Biscuits, 249
  Chicken Curry Party Salad, 99
  Fall Cranberry Wrap, 181
Apricots
  Meatballs with Apricot Hoisin Sauce,* 214
  Sweet and Tangy Apricot Biscuits, 294
Artichokes
  Spinach Artichoke Dip in Bread Bowls, 233
Asian-style dishes
  Asian Meatball Appetizers, 191
  Broccoli Beef Stir-Fry, 44
  Chinese Beef Noodle Soup, 168
  Chop Suey, 134
  Malaysian Meatballs, 161
  Meatballs with Orange Peanut Sauce, 211
  Ravioli Meatball Stir-Fry, 203
  Sesame Stir-Fry, 208
  Shrimp and Pork Pot Stickers, 236
  Sizzling Rice Soup, 21
  Sweet and Sour Meatball Kabobs, 218
  Teriyaki Meatballs, 188
  Thai Pizza,* 159
Asparagus
  Creamy Baked Risotto Primavera, 19
  Creamy Pasta Primavera, 66
  Ham and Asparagus Rolls,* 77

B acon
  Bacon and Macaroni, 140
  Bacon and Tomato Mac, 142
  Bacon Quiche Tarts, 257
  Bacon Red Potato Chowder, 26
  Bacon Tomato Biscuit Melts, 275
  Bacon-Wrapped Meatballs, 158
  Baked Macaroni and Cheese, 112
  Breakfast Biscuit Sandwiches, 254
  Breakfast Pizzas, 72
  Bubble Ring, 244
  Decadent Spinach Casserole, 10
  Macaroni and Cheese with Mushrooms and Bacon, 123
  Savory Bacon Mac, 129
  Scrambled Eggs Alfredo Bake, 258

Bananas
  Doughnut Parfait, 302
Basil
  Creamy Basil and Almonds, 145
  Macaroni, Tomato, Corn, and Basil Salad, 104
Beans
  Bean Soup, 88
  Beef and Bean Burritos, 52
  Beefy Bean Dip, 5
  Corn Chip Casserole, 46
  Crowd-Pleasing Meatball Chili, 169
  Easy Meatball Nachos, 163
  Fiesta Mac, 143
  Hungarian Bean Soup, 93
  Meatball Minestrone, 164
  Quick Minestrone, 95
  Southwestern Bean Bake, 284
  Southwest Taco Salad, 162
  Spicy Mac and Cheese, 135
  Spicy Meatball Burritos, 226
  Taco Soup, 166
  Taco Stew, 28
  Tomato Basil Cannellini Salad, 102
  White Bean Salsa Chili, 170
  Winter Chili, 56
  World's Best Baked Beans, 16
Beans (green)
  Christmas Stew, 149
  Classic Green Bean Bake, 20
  Easy Italian Vegetable Soup, 87
  Midwest Veggie Casserole, 12
  Quick Minestrone, 95
  Tater Tot Gumbo Casserole, 47
  Tater Tot Kids' Casserole, 226
Beef. See also Beef (ground); Meatballs
  Beef Pot Pie, 285
  Beefy Pepper Biscuits, 266
  Broccoli Beef Stir-Fry, 44
  Chili Dogs, 150
  Corned Beef and Kraut, 124
  Creamy Tender Cube Steaks, 48
  Dried Beef Casserole, 126
  Effortless Beef and Mushrooms, 46
  Hot Dog Casserole, 128
  Sammiches, 273
  Sesame Hot Dogs,* 275
  Stadium Mac and Cheese, 138
  Taco Stew, 28

Beef *(cont.)*
    Tex-Mex Sandwiches, 272
    Wrapped-Up Pot Roast, 47
    Zesty Roast Beef Bites, 9
Beef (ground)
    Barbecups, 276
    Beef and Bean Burritos, 52
    Beefy Bean Dip, 5
    Beefy Cheese Bake, 291
    Beefy Macaroni and Cheese, 135
    Cheeseburger Pasta, 130
    Corn Chip Casserole, 46
    Debbie's Mushroom Burgers, 60
    Dr. Pepper Bake, 117
    Fajita Macaroni and Cheese, 118
    Family Favorite Meat Loaf, 69
    Goulash, 130
    Hamburger Vegetable Pie, 62
    Italian Casserole,* 280
    Italian-Style Macaroni and Beef, 128
    Krautburgers, 277
    Meat Loaf, 151
    Mexican Mac and Cheese, 137
    Mini Pizza Bites, 274
    Salsa Nacho Cheese, 3
    Sloppy Joes, 60
    Souper Tamale Pie, 43
    Spicy Hamburger Mac, 133
    Spicy Mac and Cheese, 135
    Taco Casserole, 283
    Taco Salad, 151
    Tater Tot Gumbo Casserole, 47
    Tex-Mex Macaroni and Cheese, 133
    Unstuffed Cabbage, 45
    Winter Chili, 56
Berries. *See also* Cranberry sauce;
    Raspberries; Strawberries
    Blueberry Monkey Bread,* 265
    White Chocolate Berry Bread Pudding,
      299
Biscuits. *See also* Canned biscuits
    Baked Potato Biscuits, 81
Blueberries
    Blueberry Monkey Bread,* 265
    White Chocolate Berry Bread Pudding,
      299
Blue cheese
    Meatballs in Blue Cheese Sauce, 197
    Paladin Blue Macaroni, 145

Bread pudding
    Main Dish Bread Pudding, 49
    Roasted Vegetable Strata, 259
    Sweet Potato Bread Pudding, 301
    White Chocolate Berry Bread Pudding,
      299
Breads. *See also* Tortillas
    Apple Coffee Cake, 264
    Baked Potato Biscuits, 81
    Blueberry Monkey Bread,* 265
    Bubble Ring, 244
    Caramel Apple Pull-Apart Biscuits, 249
    Cheese-Topped Biscuits, 245
    Cheesy Mexicali Cornbread, 79
    Cheesy Pull-Apart Bread, 244
    Cinnamon Biscuit Fans, 248
    Cinnamon Nut Biscuits, 247
    Cinnamon Pull-Apart Bread, 252
    Focaccia Bread, 243
    Garlic Bread, 246
    Herbed Biscuit Strips, 246
    Italian-Style Flatbread, 243
    Lemon Pull-Apart Coffee Cake, 250
    Maple Breakfast Rolls, 251
    Monkey Bread, 253
    No-Knead French Onion Bread, 82
    Pineapple Biscuits, 251
    Poppy-Onion Loaf, 245
    Praline Meltaway Biscuits, 249
    Savory Mushroom Muffins, 80
Breakfast & brunch
    Apple Coffee Cake, 264
    Bacon Quiche Tarts, 257
    Baked Brunch Enchiladas, 76
    Baked Hash Brown and Ham Casserole,
      73
    Bear Claws, 263
    Blueberry Monkey Bread,* 265
    Breakfast Biscuit Sandwiches, 254
    Breakfast Burritos, 220
    Breakfast Pizzas, 72
    Breakfast Pockets, 260
    Breakfast Sandwiches, 261
    Canadian Bacon and Egg English Muffins,
      70
    Caramel Apple Pull-Apart Biscuits, 249
    Cheddar Biscuit Quiche, 255
    Cheesy Egg and Sausage Casserole,
      74

Cinnamon Biscuit Fans, 248
Cinnamon Nut Biscuits, 247
Cinnamon Pull-Apart Bread, 252
Doughnuts, 265
Ham and Asparagus Rolls,* 77
Ham and Cheese Casserole, 261
Ham and Egg Pizzas,* 262
Herbed Biscuit Egg Bake, 256
Lemon Pull-Apart Coffee Cake, 250
Maple Breakfast Rolls, 251
Mix 'n' Match Quiche, 75
Monkey Bread, 253
Pineapple Biscuits, 251
Praline Meltaway Biscuits, 249
Roasted Vegetable Strata, 259
Sausage Biscuit Pinwheels, 262
Sausage Quiche, 255
Scrambled Eggs Alfredo Bake, 258
Spinach and Sausage Breakfast
    Casserole, 71
Broccoli
Broccoli and Tuna on Biscuits, 267
Broccoli and Turkey Macaroni, 141
Broccoli Beef Stir-Fry, 44
Cheesy Broccoli Meatballs, 206
Chicken and Biscuit Casserole, 285
Chicken and Broccoli Cups,* 33
Herbed Biscuit Egg Bake, 256
Vegetable Casserole, 289
Burgers
Debbie's Mushroom Burgers, 60
Meatball Sliders, 157
Mini Meatball Hamburgers, 155
Burritos
Beef and Bean Burritos, 52
Breakfast Burritos, 220
Spicy Meatball Burritos, 226

Cabbage & sauerkraut
Corned Beef and Kraut, 124
Cranberry Sauerkraut Meatballs, 185
Krautburgers, 277
Miracle Soup, 89
Unstuffed Cabbage, 45
Cakes
Apple Coffee Cake, 264
Apple Upside-Down Cake, 297
Chocolate Zucchini Cake, 84
Lemon Pull-Apart Coffee Cake, 250

Macaroni Cake, 148
Tomato Soup Cake,* 78
Canadian bacon
Canadian Bacon and Egg English Muffins,
    70
Canned biscuits (appetizers)
Bruschetta, 239
Cheese Balls, 235
Cheese Crescents, 241
Chicken and Dumplings, 235
Cocktail Biscuits, 237
Feta Biscuits, 242
Jalapeño Puffers, 240
Meatball Puffs, 234
Pepperoni Bites, 241
Potato Turnovers, 240
Shrimp and Pork Pot Stickers, 236
Spinach Artichoke Dip in Bread Bowls,
    233
Tasty Flowers, 234
Turkey Empanadas, 231
Wrapped Smokies with Mustard Sauce,
    232
Zucchini and Cheese Roll-Ups, 238
Canned biscuits (breads)
Apple Coffee Cake, 264
Blueberry Monkey Bread,* 265
Bubble Ring, 244
Caramel Apple Pull-Apart Biscuits, 249
Cheese-Topped Biscuits, 245
Cheesy Pull-Apart Bread, 244
Cinnamon Biscuit Fans, 248
Cinnamon Nut Biscuits, 247
Cinnamon Pull-Apart Bread, 252
Focaccia Bread, 243
Garlic Bread, 246
Herbed Biscuit Strips, 246
Italian-Style Flatbread, 243
Lemon Pull-Apart Coffee Cake, 250
Maple Breakfast Rolls, 251
Monkey Bread, 253
Pineapple Biscuits, 251
Poppy-Onion Loaf, 245
Praline Meltaway Biscuits, 249
Canned biscuits (breakfast)
Apple Coffee Cake, 264
Bacon Quiche Tarts, 257
Bear Claws, 263
Blueberry Monkey Bread,* 265

Canned biscuits (breakfast) *(cont.)*
    Breakfast Biscuit Sandwiches, 254
    Breakfast Pockets, 260
    Breakfast Sandwiches, 261
    Cheddar Biscuit Quiche, 255
    Doughnuts, 265
    Ham and Cheese Casserole, 261
    Ham and Egg Pizzas,* 262
    Herbed Biscuit Egg Bake, 256
    Roasted Vegetable Strata, 259
    Sausage Biscuit Pinwheels, 262
    Sausage Quiche, 255
    Scrambled Eggs Alfredo Bake, 258
Canned biscuits (desserts)
    Apple Turnovers, 303
    Apple Upside-Down Cake, 297
    Biscuit Cookies, 302
    Caramel Biscuit Bites, 300
    Chantilly Cream Strawberry Shortcake, 297
    Chocolate Oatmeal Bars, 295
    Crunchy Peanut Ring, 295
    Doughnut Parfait, 302
    Fried Fruit Pies, 303
    Fruity Biscuits, 294
    Marmalade Biscuits, 298
    Mini Cherry Pies, 293
    Orange Biscuits, 298
    Peach Pinwheels, 296
    Sweet and Tangy Apricot Biscuits, 294
    Sweet Potato Bread Pudding, 301
    White Chocolate Berry Bread Pudding, 299
Canned biscuits (dinner)
    Beef Pot Pie, 285
    Beefy Cheese Bake, 291
    Biscuits and Tuna, 281
    Chicken and Biscuit Casserole, 285
    Chicken with Biscuit Stuffing, 292
    Italian Casserole,* 280
    Louisiana Shrimp Casserole, 288
    Mexican Fiesta Bake, 282
    Pan Pizza, 287
    Shrimp Newburg, 290
    Southwestern Bean Bake, 284
    Taco Casserole, 283
    Turkey and Biscuits, 286
    Turkey Pot Pie, 284
    Turkey Salad with Biscuits, 289
    Vegetable Casserole, 289

Canned biscuits (lunch)
    Bacon Tomato Biscuit Melts, 275
    Barbecue Pork Sandwiches, 267
    Barbecups, 276
    Beefy Pepper Biscuits, 266
    Broccoli and Tuna on Biscuits, 267
    Buttermilk Biscuits with Tomato Gravy, 269
    Calzones, 271
    Cheddar Biscuits with Ham Salad, 268
    Chicken Club Bake, 279
    Crab Shortcakes, 278
    Ham Biscuiwiches, 276
    Hot Turkey Sandwiches, 274
    Krautburgers, 277
    Meatball Biscuits, 273
    Mini Pizza Bites, 274
    Sammiches, 273
    Sesame Hot Dogs,* 275
    Tex-Mex Sandwiches, 272
    Tomato and Kielbasa Sandwiches, 270
Canned soups (appetizers)
    Baked Pepperoni Dip, 4
    Bean and Bacon Fondue, 8
    Beefy Bean Dip, 5
    Creamy Chicken Dip, 4
    New England Clam Dip, 8
    Pork Chili Dip, 5
    Salsa Nacho Cheese, 3
    Savory Pesto Cheesecake (var.), 7
    Savory Smoked Salmon Cheesecake (var.), 7
    Savory Sun-Dried Tomato Cheesecake, 7
    Sour Cream Meatballs, 3
    World's Easiest Cheese Fondue, 6
    Zesty Roast Beef Bites, 9
Canned soups (baked goods)
    Baked Potato Biscuits, 81
    Cheesy Mexicali Cornbread, 79
    Chocolate Zucchini Cake, 84
    No-Knead French Onion Bread, 82
    Savory Mushroom Muffins, 80
    Sweet Potato Pies, 83
    Tomato Soup Cake,* 78
Canned soups (beef & pork)
    Beef and Bean Burritos, 52
    Broccoli Beef Stir-Fry, 44
    Corn Chip Casserole, 46
    Creamy Tender Cube Steaks, 48

Effortless Beef and Mushrooms, 46
Main Dish Bread Pudding, 49
Polynesian Pork and Rice,* 53
Pork Chops and Potatoes, 50
Pork Stew, 27
Saucy Pork Chops, 50
Shredded Barbecue Pork Sandwiches, 51
Slow-Cooked Potatoes and Sausage, 51
Souper Tamale Pie, 43
Taco Stew, 28
Tater Tot Gumbo Casserole, 47
Unstuffed Cabbage, 45
Wrapped-Up Pot Roast, 47
Canned soups (breakfast & brunch)
Baked Brunch Enchiladas, 76
Baked Hash Brown and Ham Casserole, 73
Breakfast Pizzas, 72
Canadian Bacon and Egg English Muffins, 70
Cheesy Egg and Sausage Casserole, 74
Ham and Asparagus Rolls,* 77
Mix 'n' Match Quiche, 75
Spinach and Sausage Breakfast Casserole, 71
Canned soups (family favorites)
Chile Relleno Casserole, 63
Classic Tuna Noodle Casserole, 58
Creamy Pasta Primavera, 66
Creamy Pesto Sauce, 55
Debbie's Mushroom Burgers, 60
Do-It-Yourself Quesadillas, 59
Easy Chicken Potpie, 61
Family Favorite Meat Loaf, 69
Florentine Lasagna Rolls, 67
Hamburger Vegetable Pie, 62
Harvest Veggie Stuffing Casserole, 64
Mushroom Roasted Garlic Sauce, 55
Never-Fail Veggie Soufflé, 65
Seafood Newburg Sauce, 55
Sloppy Joes, 60
Tangy Tomato Mustard Sauce, 54
Three Cheese Sauce, 54
Upside-Down Pizza Casserole, 57
Winter Chili, 56
Yummy Meatballs, 61
Canned soups (poultry & seafood)
Cajun Jambalaya, 41
Chicken and Broccoli Cups,* 33

Chicken Cordon Bleu Bake, 40
Chicken Curry in a Hurry, 36
Chicken Durango, 30
Chicken Fettuccine, 37
Chile Verde Chicken Enchiladas, 32
Company's Coming Chicken, 35
Cornbread Chicken, 40
Creamy Chicken Spaghetti, 39
Creamy Italian Chicken, 37
Dinner Stew in a Pumpkin, 22
Hot Turkey Salad, 34
Maryland Crab Cakes, 42
Parmesan Chicken and Rice Bake, 38
Seafood Gumbo Casserole, 41
Southwest Chicken Polenta Stacks, 31
Weeknight Bistro Chicken, 29
Canned soups (side dishes)
Caesar Veggie Bake, 17
Cheesy Baked Corn Pudding, 18
Cheesy Stuffed Mushroom, 68
Classic Green Bean Bake, 20
Creamy Baked Risotto Primavera, 19
Decadent Spinach Casserole, 10
Easy Cauliflower Casserole, 12
French Onion Mushroom Rice, 10
Grilled Potatoes, Mushrooms, and Onion, 13
Midwest Veggie Casserole, 12
Potluck Potatoes, 65
Souper Scalloped Potatoes, 15
Squash Cornbread Casserole, 11
Vegetable Custard Cups, 14
World's Best Baked Beans, 16
Canned soups (soups & stews)
Autumn Mushroom Soup, 25
Bacon Red Potato Chowder, 26
Cheesy Sausage Soup, 27
Chicken Enchilada Soup, 24
Creamy Corn Chowder, 25
Dinner Stew in a Pumpkin, 22
Easy Clam Chowder, 26
Effortless Beef and Mushrooms, 46
Oyster and Shrimp Soup, 28
Pork Stew, 27
Sizzling Rice Soup, 21
Taco Stew, 28
Wedding Soup, 23
Caramel
Caramel Biscuit Bites, 300

Carrots
    Biscuits and Tuna, 281
    Chicken Potpie, 116
    Christmas Stew, 149
    Hamburger Vegetable Pie, 62
    Harvest Veggie Stuffing Casserole, 64
    Hungarian Bean Soup, 93
    Pork Stew, 27
    Taco Stew, 28
    Turkey Pot Pie, 284
    Winter Stew, 169
Cauliflower
    Easy Cauliflower Casserole, 12
    Mock Mashed Potatoes, 148
Celery
    Catalina Salad, 107
    Goulash, 130
    Hot Turkey Salad, 34
    Quick Mac Salad, 106
    Sizzling Rice Soup, 21
Cheddar cheese
    Baked Brunch Enchiladas, 76
    Baked Hash Brown and Ham Casserole, 73
    Baked Macaroni and Cheese, 112
    Baked Potato Biscuits, 81
    Baked Tomato Macaroni, 118
    Bean and Bacon Fondue, 8
    Beef and Bean Burritos, 52
    Breakfast Pizzas, 72
    Breakfast Pockets, 260
    Cheddar Biscuit Quiche, 255
    Cheddar Biscuits with Ham Salad, 268
    Cheddar Mac Salad, 100
    Cheese Balls, 235
    Cheese Crescents, 241
    Cheese-Topped Biscuits, 245
    Cheesy Egg and Sausage Casserole, 74
    Cheesy Mexicali Cornbread, 79
    Cheesy Sausage Soup, 27
    Cheesy Triangles,* 149
    Chicken Casserole, 119
    Chicken Enchilada Soup, 24
    Coney Meatball Subs, 175
    Corn Chip Casserole, 46
    Creamy Chicken Spaghetti, 39
    Crispy Macaroni and Cheese, 115
    Curried Macaroni, 121

Dried Beef Casserole, 126
Easy Cauliflower Casserole, 12
Four Cheese Casserole, 113
Ham and Cheese Casserole, 261
Herbed Biscuit Egg Bake, 256
Jalapeño Puffers, 240
Kid-Friendly Taco Casserole, 228
Mac and Cheese Custard, 120
Mac and Cheese with Mustard and
    Worcestershire, 127
Macaroni and Cheese with Mushrooms
    and Bacon, 123
Mark's Mega Macaroni, 114
Midwest Veggie Casserole, 12
Mini Pizza Bites, 274
Mom's Mac and Cheese, 119
No-Knead French Onion Bread, 82
Pan-Fried Mac and Cheese, 152
Potato Turnovers, 240
Potluck Potatoes, 65
Salsa Macaroni and Cheese, 138
Sausage Quiche, 255
Shrimp Newburg, 290
Souper Scalloped Potatoes, 15
Souper Tamale Pie, 43
Southwest Taco Salad, 162
Taco Casserole, 283
Tavern Soup, 91
Wisconsin Mac, 136
Zucchini and Cheese Roll-Ups, 238
Cheese. *See also* Cheddar cheese; Cream
    cheese; Mac 'n' cheese; Monterey
    Jack cheese; Mozzarella cheese;
    Parmesan; Swiss cheese
    Beefy Bean Dip, 5
    Cavatini, 125
    Cheesy Baked Corn Pudding, 18
    Cheesy Meatballs, 192
    Cheesy Rice and Hamburger Soup, 171
    Creamy Mushroom Casserole, 126
    Crescent-Wrapped Meatballs, 161
    Do-It-Yourself Quesadillas, 59
    Easy Meatball Lasagna, 199
    Enchilada Casserole, 225
    Feta Biscuits, 242
    Feta Meatballs with Cucumber Yogurt
    Sauce, 189
    Florentine Lasagna Rolls, 67

Four Cheese Casserole, 113
Greek Chicken Pasta,* 131
Hash Brown Meatball Casserole, 227
Macaroni Cake, 148
Macaroni Chef Salad, 108
Macaroni Pie, 115
Main Dish Bread Pudding, 49
Meatball Fajita Quesadillas,* 223
Meatballs in Blue Cheese Sauce, 197
Mix 'n' Match Quiche, 75
Oaxaca Soup, 90
Paladin Blue Macaroni, 145
Pork Chili Dip, 5
Ricotta-Stuffed Shells and Meatballs,
    200
Salsa Balls, 152
Salsa Nacho Cheese, 3
Sammiches, 273
Southwest Chicken Polenta Stacks, 31
Spinach and Sausage Breakfast
    Casserole, 71
Three Cheese Sauce, 54
Cheesecakes
    Savory Pesto Cheesecake (var.), 7
    Savory Smoked Salmon Cheesecake
        (var.), 7
    Savory Sun-Dried Tomato Cheesecake, 7
Cherries
    Mini Cherry Pies, 293
Chicken
    Balsamic Chicken, 139
    Chicken and Biscuit Casserole, 285
    Chicken and Broccoli Cups,* 33
    Chicken and Dumplings, 235
    Chicken Casserole, 119
    Chicken Club Bake, 279
    Chicken Cordon Bleu Bake, 40
    Chicken Curry in a Hurry, 36
    Chicken Curry Party Salad, 99
    Chicken Durango, 30
    Chicken Enchilada Soup, 24
    Chicken Fettuccine, 37
    Chicken Macaroni Salad, 109
    Chicken Parmesan,* 147
    Chicken Potpie, 116
    Chicken Soup, 93
    Chicken Stuff, 134
    Chicken with Biscuit Stuffing, 292
    Chile Verde Chicken Enchiladas, 32

Company's Coming Chicken, 35
Cornbread Chicken, 40
Creamy Chicken Dip, 4
Creamy Chicken Spaghetti, 39
Creamy Italian Chicken, 37
Dinner Stew in a Pumpkin, 22
Easy Chicken Potpie, 61
Greek Chicken Pasta,* 131
Italian Chicken, 144
Parmesan Chicken and Rice Bake, 38
Salsa Verde, 139
Simple Ranch Salad, 97
Southwest Chicken Polenta Stacks, 31
Weeknight Bistro Chicken, 29
Chile peppers
    Beefy Macaroni and Cheese, 135
    Cheddar Biscuit Quiche, 255
    Cheesy Mexicali Cornbread, 79
    Chile Relleno Casserole, 63
    Chipotle Meatball Pasta, 195
    Four Cheese Casserole, 113
    Jalapeño Puffers, 240
    Lazarus Soup, 92
    Mac and Green Chiles, 142
    Meatball Jalapeño Poppers, 156
    Mexican Mac and Cheese, 137
    Oaxaca Soup, 90
    Southwest Crescent Pockets, 221
    Spicy Meatball Burritos, 226
Chili (canned)
    Chili Dogs, 150
    Chili Mac, 129
    Frito Pie, 144
    Pork Chili Dip, 5
Chili (recipes)
    Crowd-Pleasing Meatball Chili, 169
    White Bean Salsa Chili, 170
    Winter Chili, 56
Chocolate
    Biscuit Cookies, 302
    Chocolate Oatmeal Bars, 295
    Chocolate Zucchini Cake, 84
    White Chocolate Berry Bread Pudding,
        299
Chowder
    Bacon Red Potato Chowder, 26
    Creamy Corn Chowder, 25
    Easy Clam Chowder, 26
    Meatball Chowder, 167

Cinnamon
 Blueberry Monkey Bread,* 265
 Cinnamon Biscuit Fans, 248
 Cinnamon Nut Biscuits, 247
 Cinnamon Pull-Apart Bread, 252
 Monkey Bread, 253
Clams
 Easy Clam Chowder, 26
 New England Clam Dip, 8
Coconut milk
 Chicken Curry in a Hurry, 36
Coffee cakes
 Apple Coffee Cake, 264
 Lemon Pull-Apart Coffee Cake, 250
Colby & Colby Jack cheese
 Enchilada Casserole, 225
 Hash Brown Meatball Casserole, 227
 Macaroni Pie, 115
 Meatball Fajita Quesadillas,* 223
 Spinach and Sausage Breakfast
  Casserole, 71
Cookies & bars
 Biscuit Cookies, 302
 Chocolate Oatmeal Bars, 295
Corn
 Bacon Red Potato Chowder, 26
 Cheesy Baked Corn Pudding, 18
 Cheesy Mexicali Cornbread, 79
 Creamy Corn Chowder, 25
 Easy Italian Vegetable Soup, 87
 Fiesta Mac, 143
 Hot Dog Casserole, 128
 Macaroni, Tomato, Corn, and Basil Salad,
  104
 Meatball Chowder, 167
 Meatballs in Tomato and Corn Sauce,
  217
 Midwest Veggie Casserole, 12
 Souper Tamale Pie, 43
 Taco Soup, 166
 Taco Stew, 28
 Tex-Mex Macaroni and Cheese, 133
 White Bean Salsa Chili, 170
Corn chips
 Corn Chip Casserole, 46
 Frito Pie, 144
 Salsa Balls, 152
Cornmeal. See also Corn muffin mix
 Cheesy Baked Corn Pudding, 18

Cheesy Mexicali Cornbread, 79
 Souper Tamale Pie, 43
 Southwest Chicken Polenta Stacks, 31
Corn muffin mix
 Cornbread Chicken, 40
 Squash Cornbread Casserole, 11
Crabmeat
 Crab Shortcakes, 278
 Maryland Crab Cakes, 42
 Seafood Newburg Sauce, 55
 Seafood Pasta with Lemon Herb
  Dressing, 105
Cranberry sauce
 Cranberry Sauerkraut Meatballs, 185
 Fall Cranberry Wrap, 181
 Holiday Meatballs, 193
 Sweet and Spicy Meatballs, 184
Cream cheese
 Bacon Quiche Tarts, 257
 Baked Pepperoni Dip, 4
 Bear Claws, 263
 Beefy Cheese Bake, 291
 Caesar Veggie Bake, 17
 Cocktail Biscuits, 237
 Creamy Chicken Dip, 4
 Creamy Italian Chicken, 37
 Maple Breakfast Rolls, 251
 Meatball Jalapeño Poppers, 156
 New England Clam Dip, 8
 Roasted Pepper and Meatballs on Rye,
  177
 Savory Pesto Cheesecake (var.), 7
 Savory Smoked Salmon Cheesecake
  (var.), 7
 Savory Sun-Dried Tomato Cheesecake, 7
 Tasty Flowers, 234
 Zesty Roast Beef Bites, 9
Cucumbers
 Cucumber Dill Pasta Salad, 111
 Feta Meatballs with Cucumber Yogurt
  Sauce, 189
 Herbed Macaroni and Cucumber, 103
 Macaroni, Tomato, Corn, and Basil Salad,
  104
Curried dishes
 Chicken Curry in a Hurry, 36
 Chicken Curry Party Salad, 99
 Curried Macaroni, 121
 Meatballs in Curry Sauce, 208

Desserts. *See also* Cakes; Pies (dessert)
   Apple Turnovers, 303
   Biscuit Cookies, 302
   Caramel Apple Squares, 350
   Chantilly Cream Strawberry Shortcake, 297
   Chocolate Oatmeal Bars, 295
   Crunchy Peanut Ring, 295
   Doughnut Parfait, 302
   Fruity Biscuits, 294
   Marmalade Biscuits, 298
   Orange Biscuits, 298
   Peach Pinwheels, 296
   Sweet and Tangy Apricot Biscuits, 294
   Sweet Potato Bread Pudding, 301
   White Chocolate Berry Bread Pudding, 299
Dill
   Cucumber Dill Pasta Salad, 111
   Herbed Macaroni and Cucumber, 103
Dips
   Baked Pepperoni Dip, 4
   Bean and Bacon Fondue, 8
   Beefy Bean Dip, 5
   Creamy Chicken Dip, 4
   New England Clam Dip, 8
   Pork Chili Dip, 5
   Salsa Nacho Cheese, 3
   World's Easiest Cheese Fondue, 6
Doughnuts
   Doughnut Parfait, 302
   Doughnuts, 265
Dr. Pepper
   Dr. Pepper Bake, 117

Eggplant
   Eggplant Parmesan, 202
Eggs
   Baked Brunch Enchiladas, 76
   Breakfast Biscuit Sandwiches, 254
   Breakfast Burritos, 220
   Breakfast Pizzas, 72
   Canadian Bacon and Egg English Muffins, 70
   Cheesy Egg and Sausage Casserole, 74
   Classic Macaroni Salad, 100
   Denver Omelet, 150
   Egg Pasta Salad, 98
   Ham and Egg Pizzas,* 262

   Hot Turkey Salad, 34
   Macaroni Chef Salad, 108
   Never-Fail Veggie Soufflé, 65
   Scrambled Eggs Alfredo Bake, 258
Enchiladas
   Baked Brunch Enchiladas, 76
   Chile Verde Chicken Enchiladas, 32

Family favorites (with canned soups)
   Chile Relleno Casserole, 63
   Classic Tuna Noodle Casserole, 58
   Creamy Pasta Primavera, 66
   Creamy Pesto Sauce, 55
   Debbie's Mushroom Burgers, 60
   Do-It-Yourself Quesadillas, 59
   Easy Chicken Potpie, 61
   Family Favorite Meat Loaf, 69
   Florentine Lasagna Rolls, 67
   Hamburger Vegetable Pie, 62
   Harvest Veggie Stuffing Casserole, 64
   Mushroom Roasted Garlic Sauce, 55
   Never-Fail Veggie Soufflé, 65
   Seafood Newburg Sauce, 55
   Sloppy Joes, 60
   Tangy Tomato Mustard Sauce, 54
   Three Cheese Sauce, 54
   Upside-Down Pizza Casserole, 57
   Winter Chili, 56
   Yummy Meatballs, 61
Family favorites (with mac 'n' cheese)
   Baked Beefy Mac and Cheese, 224
   Cheesy Triangles,* 149
   Chicken Parmesan,* 147
   Chili Dogs, 150
   Christmas Stew, 149
   Denver Omelet, 150
   Fried Macaroni and Cheese, 146
   Macaroni Cake, 148
   Meat Loaf, 151
   Mock Mashed Potatoes, 148
   Pan-Fried Mac and Cheese, 152
   Pizza Mac, 147
   Salsa Balls, 152
   Taco Salad, 151
Family favorites (with meatballs)
   Baked Beefy Mac and Cheese, 224
   Breakfast Burritos, 220
   Caesar Meatball Kabobs,* 219
   Easy Meatball Pizza, 220

Family favorites (with meatballs) *(cont.)*
  Enchilada Casserole, 225
  Hash Brown Meatball Casserole, 227
  Instant Soft Taco, 222
  Kid-Friendly Taco Casserole, 228
  Meatball Fajita Quesadillas,* 223
  Meatball Pot Pie, 222
  Meatballs in Tomato and Corn Sauce,
    217
  Southwest Crescent Pockets, 221
  Spicy Meatball Burritos, 226
  Stuffing-Covered Meatball Casserole,
    224
  Sweet and Sour Meatball Kabobs, 218
  Tater Tot Kids' Casserole, 226
  Yummy Meatballs, 61
Feta cheese
  Feta Biscuits, 242
  Feta Meatballs with Cucumber Yogurt
    Sauce, 189
  Greek Chicken Pasta,* 131
Fish. *See also* Shellfish
  Biscuits and Tuna, 281
  Broccoli and Tuna on Biscuits, 267
  Catalina Salad, 107
  Classic Tuna Noodle Casserole, 58
  Savory Smoked Salmon Cheesecake
    (var.), 7
Fondue
  Bean and Bacon Fondue, 8
  World's Easiest Cheese Fondue, 6
Fruit. *See also* Fruit salads; *specific fruits*
  Fried Fruit Pies, 303
  Fruit Salad, 101
  Fruity Biscuits, 294

Garlic
  Garlic Bread, 246
  Garlicky Soup, 92
  Lazarus Soup, 92
Ginger ale
  Ginger Ale Meatballs, 191
Grains. *See* Cornmeal; Oats; Rice
Green beans
  Christmas Stew, 149
  Classic Green Bean Bake, 20
  Easy Italian Vegetable Soup, 87
  Midwest Veggie Casserole, 12
  Quick Minestrone, 95

Tater Tot Gumbo Casserole, 47
Tater Tot Kids' Casserole, 226
Greens. *See also* Spinach
  Chicken Macaroni Salad, 109
  Mediterranean Meatball Sandwiches,
    178
  Southwest Taco Salad, 162
  Taco Salad, 151

Ham
  Baked Brunch Enchiladas, 76
  Baked Hash Brown and Ham Casserole,
    73
  Cheddar Biscuit Quiche, 255
  Cheddar Biscuits with Ham Salad, 268
  Chicken Cordon Bleu Bake, 40
  Cocktail Biscuits, 237
  Creamy Corn Chowder, 25
  Ham and Asparagus Rolls,* 77
  Ham and Cheese Casserole, 261
  Ham and Egg Pizzas,* 262
  Ham Biscuiwiches, 276
  Macaroni Chef Salad, 108
  Macaroni Salad with Peas and Ham,
    96
  Mark's Mega Macaroni, 114
  Pork Chili Dip, 5
  Rachel's Macaroni, 140
  Sammiches, 273
  Seafood Gumbo Casserole, 41
Herbs. *See also* Basil; Dill
  Herbed Macaroni and Cucumber, 103
Hoisin sauce
  Malaysian Meatballs, 161
  Meatballs with Apricot Hoisin Sauce,*
    214
Hot dogs
  Chili Dogs, 150
  Hot Dog Casserole, 128
  Sesame Hot Dogs,* 275
  Stadium Mac and Cheese, 138

Italian-style dishes
  Bruschetta, 239
  Calzones, 271
  Cavatini, 125
  Chicken Parmesan,* 147
  Creamy Baked Risotto Primavera, 19
  Creamy Italian Chicken, 37

Creamy Pasta Primavera, 66
Easy Italian Vegetable Soup, 87
Eggplant Parmesan, 202
Florentine Lasagna Rolls, 67
Florentine Meatballs and Noodles, 196
Focaccia Bread, 243
Italian Casserole,* 280
Italian Chicken, 144
Italian Focaccia Meatball Sandwiches,
    179
Italian-Style Cocktail Meatballs, 185
Italian-Style Flatbread, 243
Italian-Style Macaroni and Beef, 128
Italian-Tossed Tortellini, 203
Meatball Bruschetta, 158
Meatball Fettuccine Alfredo, 194
Meatball Minestrone, 164
Pomodoro e Zucchina Minestra, 95
Quick Minestrone, 95
Wedding Soup, 23

Lettuce
Chicken Macaroni Salad, 109
Southwest Taco Salad, 162
Taco Salad, 151

Mac 'n' cheese (casseroles)
Baked Macaroni and Cheese, 112
Baked Tomato Macaroni, 118
Cavatini, 125
Chicken Casserole, 119
Chicken Potpie, 116
Corned Beef and Kraut, 124
Creamy Mushroom Casserole, 126
Crispy Macaroni and Cheese, 115
Curried Macaroni, 121
Dr. Pepper Bake, 117
Dried Beef Casserole, 126
Fajita Macaroni and Cheese, 118
Four Cheese Casserole, 113
Mac and Cheese Custard, 120
Mac and Cheese with Mustard and
    Worcestershire, 127
Macaroni and Cheese with Mushrooms
    and Bacon, 123
Macaroni Pie, 115
Mark's Mega Macaroni, 114
Mom's Mac and Cheese, 119
Potato Macaroni Gratin, 122

Mac 'n' cheese (family favorites)
Baked Beefy Mac and Cheese, 224
Cheesy Triangles,* 149
Chicken Parmesan,* 147
Chili Dogs, 150
Christmas Stew, 149
Denver Omelet, 150
Fried Macaroni and Cheese, 146
Macaroni Cake, 148
Meat Loaf, 151
Mock Mashed Potatoes, 148
Pan-Fried Mac and Cheese, 152
Pizza Mac, 147
Salsa Balls, 152
Taco Salad, 151
Mac 'n' cheese (salads)
Catalina Salad, 107
Cheddar Mac Salad, 100
Chicken Curry Party Salad, 99
Chicken Macaroni Salad, 109
Classic Macaroni Salad, 100
Confetti Salad, 99
Cucumber Dill Pasta Salad, 111
Egg Pasta Salad, 98
Fruit Salad, 101
Herbed Macaroni and Cucumber, 103
Macaroni, Tomato, Corn, and Basil Salad,
    104
Macaroni Chef Salad, 108
Macaroni Salad with Peas and Ham, 96
Mexican Salad, 97
Michelle's Special Salad, 110
Quick Mac Salad, 106
Seafood Pasta with Lemon Herb
    Dressing, 105
Shrimp and Macaroni Salad,* 106
Simple Ranch Salad, 97
Spinach and Tomato Salad, 98
Taco Salad, 151
Tomato Basil Cannellini Salad, 102
Mac 'n' cheese (saucepan)
Bacon and Macaroni, 140
Bacon and Tomato Mac, 142
Balsamic Chicken, 139
Broccoli and Turkey Macaroni, 141
Creamy Basil and Almonds, 145
Creamy Pesto, 145
Creamy Sage Macaroni, 143
Fiesta Mac, 143

Mac 'n' cheese (saucepan) *(cont.)*
    Frito Pie, 144
    Italian Chicken, 144
    Mac and Green Chiles, 142
    Paladin Blue Macaroni, 145
    Rachel's Macaroni, 140
    Salsa Macaroni and Cheese, 138
    Salsa Verde, 139
    Spiced-Up Macaroni, 141
    Stadium Mac and Cheese, 138
Mac 'n' cheese (skillet dishes)
    Beefy Macaroni and Cheese, 135
    Cheeseburger Pasta, 130
    Cheesy Pea Pasta, 132
    Chicken Stuff, 134
    Chili Mac, 129
    Chop Suey, 134
    Goulash, 130
    Greek Chicken Pasta,* 131
    Hot Dog Casserole, 128
    Italian-Style Macaroni and Beef, 128
    Mexican Mac and Cheese, 137
    Savory Bacon Mac, 129
    Spicy Hamburger Mac, 133
    Spicy Mac and Cheese, 135
    Tex-Mex Macaroni and Cheese, 133
    Wisconsin Mac, 136
Mac 'n' cheese (soups)
    Bean Soup, 88
    Chicken Soup, 93
    Easy Italian Vegetable Soup, 87
    Garlicky Soup, 92
    Hungarian Bean Soup, 93
    Lazarus Soup, 92
    Miracle Soup, 89
    Oaxaca Soup, 90
    Onion Soup, 94
    Pomodoro e Zucchina Minestra, 95
    Quick Minestrone, 95
    Tavern Soup, 91
    Tomato Soup, 87
    Vegetable Picante Soup, 94
Main dishes (with canned biscuits)
    Barbecups, 276
    Beef Pot Pie, 285
    Beefy Cheese Bake, 291
    Beefy Pepper Biscuits, 266
    Biscuits and Tuna, 281
    Broccoli and Tuna on Biscuits, 267

Buttermilk Biscuits with Tomato Gravy, 269
    Calzones, 271
    Chicken and Biscuit Casserole, 285
    Chicken Club Bake, 279
    Chicken with Biscuit Stuffing, 292
    Crab Shortcakes, 278
    Ham Biscuiwiches, 276
    Italian Casserole,* 280
    Krautburgers, 277
    Louisiana Shrimp Casserole, 288
    Meatball Biscuits, 273
    Mexican Fiesta Bake, 282
    Mini Pizza Bites, 274
    Pan Pizza, 287
    Sesame Hot Dogs,* 275
    Shrimp Newburg, 290
    Southwestern Bean Bake, 284
    Taco Casserole, 283
    Turkey and Biscuits, 286
    Turkey Pot Pie, 284
    Turkey Salad with Biscuits, 289
    Vegetable Casserole, 289
Main dishes (with canned soups)
    Beef and Bean Burritos, 52
    Broccoli Beef Stir-Fry, 44
    Cajun Jambalaya, 41
    Chicken and Broccoli Cups,* 33
    Chicken Cordon Bleu Bake, 40
    Chicken Curry in a Hurry, 36
    Chicken Durango, 30
    Chicken Fettuccine, 37
    Chile Relleno Casserole, 63
    Chile Verde Chicken Enchiladas, 32
    Classic Tuna Noodle Casserole, 58
    Company's Coming Chicken, 35
    Cornbread Chicken, 40
    Corn Chip Casserole, 46
    Creamy Chicken Spaghetti, 39
    Creamy Italian Chicken, 37
    Creamy Pasta Primavera, 66
    Creamy Tender Cube Steaks, 48
    Debbie's Mushroom Burgers, 60
    Do-It-Yourself Quesadillas, 59
    Easy Chicken Potpie, 61
    Effortless Beef and Mushrooms, 46
    Family Favorite Meat Loaf, 69
    Florentine Lasagna Rolls, 67
    Hamburger Vegetable Pie, 62

Harvest Veggie Stuffing Casserole, 64
Hot Turkey Salad, 34
Main Dish Bread Pudding, 49
Maryland Crab Cakes, 42
Never-Fail Veggie Soufflé, 65
Parmesan Chicken and Rice Bake, 38
Polynesian Pork and Rice,* 53
Pork Chops and Potatoes, 50
Saucy Pork Chops, 50
Seafood Gumbo Casserole, 41
Shredded Barbecue Pork Sandwiches,
    51
Sloppy Joes, 60
Slow-Cooked Potatoes and Sausage, 51
Souper Tamale Pie, 43
Southwest Chicken Polenta Stacks, 31
Tater Tot Gumbo Casserole, 47
Unstuffed Cabbage, 45
Upside-Down Pizza Casserole, 57
Weeknight Bistro Chicken, 29
Winter Chili, 56
Wrapped-Up Pot Roast, 47
Yummy Meatballs, 61
Main dishes (with mac 'n' cheese)
Baked Beefy Mac and Cheese, 224
Balsamic Chicken, 139
Beefy Macaroni and Cheese, 135
Broccoli and Turkey Macaroni, 141
Cheeseburger Pasta, 130
Chicken Casserole, 119
Chicken Parmesan,* 147
Chicken Potpie, 116
Chicken Stuff, 134
Chili Dogs, 150
Chili Mac, 129
Chop Suey, 134
Corned Beef and Kraut, 124
Denver Omelet, 150
Dr. Pepper Bake, 117
Dried Beef Casserole, 126
Fajita Macaroni and Cheese, 118
Fiesta Mac, 143
Goulash, 130
Greek Chicken Pasta,* 131
Hot Dog Casserole, 128
Italian Chicken, 144
Italian-Style Macaroni and Beef, 128
Mark's Mega Macaroni, 114
Meat Loaf, 151

Mexican Mac and Cheese, 137
Pizza Mac, 147
Rachel's Macaroni, 140
Salsa Verde, 139
Spicy Hamburger Mac, 133
Spicy Mac and Cheese, 135
Stadium Mac and Cheese, 138
Taco Salad, 151
Tex-Mex Macaroni and Cheese, 133
Main dishes (with meatballs)
Amazing Meatball Tortellini, 205
Baked Beefy Mac and Cheese, 224
Baked Ziti and Meatballs, 201
Breakfast Burritos, 220
Caesar Meatball Kabobs,* 219
Cajun Shrimp and Meatball Goulash, 212
Cheesy Broccoli Meatballs, 206
Chipotle Meatball Pasta, 195
Creamy French Onion Meatballs, 213
Creamy Meatball and Brown Rice
    Casserole, 210
Creamy Rice and Meatballs, 215
Easy Meatball Lasagna, 199
Easy Meatball Pizza, 220
Easy Rice and Meatballs, 207
Eggplant Parmesan, 202
Enchilada Casserole, 225
Enchilada Meatballs, 215
Hash Brown Meatball Casserole, 227
Instant Soft Taco, 222
Italian-Tossed Tortellini, 203
Kid-Friendly Taco Casserole, 228
Meatball Fajita Quesadillas,* 223
Meatball Fettuccine Alfredo, 194
Meatball Pot Pie, 222
Meatballs in Blue Cheese Sauce, 197
Meatballs in Curry Sauce, 208
Meatballs in Tomato and Corn Sauce,
    217
Meatball Stroganoff, 204
Meatballs with Apricot Hoisin Sauce,* 214
Meatballs with Orange Peanut Sauce, 211
Pesto Spaghetti and Meatballs, 200
Pineapple Meatballs and Rice, 211
Ravioli Meatball Stir-Fry, 203
Ricotta-Stuffed Shells and Meatballs, 200
Sesame Stir-Fry, 208
Slow-Cooked Tomato Soup Meatballs,
    198

Main dishes (with meatballs) *(cont.)*
   Southwest Crescent Pockets, 221
   Spicy Meatball Burritos, 226
   Stuffing-Covered Meatball Casserole, 224
   Sweet and Sour Meatball Kabobs, 218
   Swiss Mushroom Meatball Casserole, 209
   Taste of the Islands Meatballs, 216
   Tater Tot Kids' Casserole, 226
Maple syrup
   Maple Breakfast Rolls, 251
   Maple Meatballs, 188
Meat. *See also* Beef; Pork
   Mix 'n' Match Quiche, 75
Meatballs. *See also categories below*
   Meatball Biscuits, 273
   Meatball Puffs, 234
Meatballs (appetizers). *See also* Meatballs (dressed-up)
   Bacon-Wrapped Meatballs, 158
   Crescent-Wrapped Meatballs, 161
   Easy Meatball Nachos, 163
   Malaysian Meatballs, 161
   Meatball Bruschetta, 158
   Meatball Jalapeño Poppers, 156
   Meatball Sliders, 157
   Mini Meatball Hamburgers, 155
   Parmesan Meatball Biscuits, 162
   Puff Pastry Meatball and Mushroom Pockets, 160
   Sour Cream Meatballs, 3
   Southwest Taco Salad, 162
   Thai Pizza,* 159
Meatballs (dressed-up)
   Asian Meatball Appetizers, 191
   Blue Cheese Buffalo Balls, 186
   Cheesy Meatballs, 192
   Cranberry Sauerkraut Meatballs, 185
   Crowd-Pleasing Meatballs, 183
   Feta Meatballs with Cucumber Yogurt Sauce, 189
   Ginger Ale Meatballs, 191
   Holiday Meatballs, 193
   Italian-Style Cocktail Meatballs, 185
   Magnificent Meatballs, 187
   Maple Meatballs, 188
   Marinated Meatballs, 184
   Salsa Verde Meatballs, 192

   Saucy Meatballs, 187
   Sour Cream–Sauced Meatballs, 193
   Spicy Jamaican Jerk Meatballs, 190
   Sports Day Meatballs, 186
   Sweet and Spicy Meatballs, 184
   Teriyaki Meatballs, 188
Meatballs (family favorites)
   Baked Beefy Mac and Cheese, 224
   Breakfast Burritos, 220
   Caesar Meatball Kabobs,* 219
   Easy Meatball Pizza, 220
   Enchilada Casserole, 225
   Hash Brown Meatball Casserole, 227
   Instant Soft Taco, 222
   Kid-Friendly Taco Casserole, 228
   Meatball Fajita Quesadillas,* 223
   Meatball Pot Pie, 222
   Meatballs in Tomato and Corn Sauce, 217
   Southwest Crescent Pockets, 221
   Spicy Meatball Burritos, 226
   Stuffing-Covered Meatball Casserole, 224
   Sweet and Sour Meatball Kabobs, 218
   Tater Tot Kids' Casserole, 226
   Yummy Meatballs, 61
Meatballs (pasta dinners)
   Amazing Meatball Tortellini, 205
   Baked Ziti and Meatballs, 201
   Cheesy Broccoli Meatballs, 206
   Chipotle Meatball Pasta, 195
   Easy Meatball Lasagna, 199
   Eggplant Parmesan, 202
   Florentine Meatballs and Noodles, 196
   Italian-Tossed Tortellini, 203
   Meatball Fettuccine Alfredo, 194
   Meatballs in Blue Cheese Sauce, 197
   Meatball Stroganoff, 204
   Pesto Spaghetti and Meatballs, 200
   Ravioli Meatball Stir-Fry, 203
   Ricotta-Stuffed Shells and Meatballs, 200
   Slow-Cooked Tomato Soup Meatballs, 198
Meatballs (rice dinners)
   Cajun Shrimp and Meatball Goulash, 212
   Creamy French Onion Meatballs, 213
   Creamy Meatball and Brown Rice Casserole, 210
   Creamy Rice and Meatballs, 215
   Easy Rice and Meatballs, 207

Enchilada Meatballs, 215
Meatballs in Curry Sauce, 208
Meatballs with Apricot Hoisin Sauce,* 214
Meatballs with Orange Peanut Sauce, 211
Pineapple Meatballs and Rice, 211
Sesame Stir-Fry, 208
Swiss Mushroom Meatball Casserole,
    209
Taste of the Islands Meatballs, 216
Meatballs (sandwiches & wraps)
Coney Meatball Subs, 175
Easy Sloppy Joes, 182
Fall Cranberry Wrap, 181
Italian Focaccia Meatball Sandwiches,
    179
Mediterranean Meatball Sandwiches, 178
Open-Faced Meatball Sub, 180
Pesto Meatball Baguette Sandwiches,
    176
Philly Meatball Sub Sandwiches, 173
Piping Hot Buffalo Subs, 177
Roasted Pepper and Meatballs on Rye,
    177
Saucy Meatball Grinders, 174
Swedish Meatball Hero, 180
Yummy Stuffed Pitas, 181
Meatballs (soups, stews & chili)
Cheesy Rice and Hamburger Soup, 171
Chinese Beef Noodle Soup, 168
Crowd-Pleasing Meatball Chili, 169
Family Favorite Egg Noodle Soup, 166
Garden Veggie Soup with Bow Tie Pasta,
    172
Meatball Chowder, 167
Meatball Minestrone, 164
Meatball Zucchini Orzo Soup, 170
Southwestern Cilantro Rice Soup, 167
Taco Soup, 166
Tortellini Meatball Stew, 165
White Bean Salsa Chili, 170
Winter Stew, 169
Meat loaf
Family Favorite Meat Loaf, 69
Meat Loaf, 151
Monterey Jack cheese
Chile Relleno Casserole, 63
Chile Verde Chicken Enchiladas, 32
Four Cheese Casserole, 113
Ham and Egg Pizzas,* 262

Mark's Mega Macaroni, 114
Mexican Fiesta Bake, 282
Roasted Vegetable Strata, 259
Spicy Meatball Burritos, 226
Vegetable Custard Cups, 14
Mozzarella cheese
Bacon Tomato Biscuit Melts, 275
Baked Ziti and Meatballs, 201
Bruschetta, 239
Cavatini, 125
Cheese Crescents, 241
Cheesy Stuffed Mushroom, 68
Chicken Club Bake, 279
Chicken Parmesan,* 147
Corned Beef and Kraut, 124
Dr. Pepper Bake, 117
Easy Meatball Lasagna, 199
Easy Meatball Pizza, 220
Fried Macaroni and Cheese, 146
Italian Casserole,* 280
Italian Focaccia Meatball Sandwiches,
    179
Italian-Style Flatbread, 243
Mark's Mega Macaroni, 114
Meatball Bruschetta, 158
Meatball Puffs, 234
Open-Faced Meatball Sub, 180
Pan Pizza, 287
Pepperoni Bites, 241
Pesto Spaghetti and Meatballs, 200
Saucy Meatball Grinders, 174
Taco Casserole, 283
Three Cheese Sauce, 54
Upside-Down Pizza Casserole, 57
Muffins
Savory Mushroom Muffins, 80
Mushrooms
Autumn Mushroom Soup, 25
Caesar Meatball Kabobs,* 219
Cavatini, 125
Cheesy Stuffed Mushroom, 68
Chicken Casserole, 119
Chop Suey, 134
Classic Tuna Noodle Casserole, 58
Cocktail Biscuits, 237
Company's Coming Chicken, 35
Creamy Meatball and Brown Rice
    Casserole, 210
Creamy Mushroom Casserole, 126

Mushrooms (cont.)
   Debbie's Mushroom Burgers, 60
   Denver Omelet, 150
   Dinner Stew in a Pumpkin, 22
   Effortless Beef and Mushrooms, 46
   French Onion Mushroom Rice, 10
   Goulash, 130
   Grilled Potatoes, Mushrooms, and Onion,
      13
   Macaroni and Cheese with Mushrooms
      and Bacon, 123
   Meatball Stroganoff, 204
   Mushroom Roasted Garlic Sauce, 55
   Pizza Mac, 147
   Pork Stew, 27
   Puff Pastry Meatball and Mushroom
      Pockets, 160
   Savory Mushroom Muffins, 80
   Sweet and Sour Meatball Kabobs, 218
   Swiss Mushroom Meatball Casserole,
      209
Mustard
   Mac and Cheese with Mustard and
      Worcestershire, 127
   Tangy Tomato Mustard Sauce, 54

Nachos
   Easy Meatball Nachos, 163
Noodles
   Chinese Beef Noodle Soup, 168
   Classic Tuna Noodle Casserole, 58
   Family Favorite Egg Noodle Soup, 166
   Florentine Meatballs and Noodles, 196
   Saucy Pork Chops, 50
Nuts. See Almonds; Peanuts; Pecans;
   Walnuts

Oats
   Chocolate Oatmeal Bars, 295
   Peach Crisp, 347
Okra
   Cajun Jambalaya, 41
   Seafood Gumbo Casserole, 41
Olives
   Chicken Curry Party Salad, 99
   Dried Beef Casserole, 126
   Feta Biscuits, 242
   Greek Chicken Pasta,* 131
   Macaroni Chef Salad, 108

Mexican Salad, 97
Michelle's Special Salad, 110
Pizza Mac, 147
Simple Ranch Salad, 97
Tex-Mex Sandwiches, 272
Tomato Basil Cannellini Salad, 102
Omelets
   Denver Omelet, 150
Onions
   French Onion Mushroom Rice, 10
   Grilled Potatoes, Mushrooms, and Onion,
      13
   No-Knead French Onion Bread, 82
   Onion Soup, 94
   Potato Macaroni Gratin, 122
Onions (French fried)
   Classic Green Bean Bake, 20
   Crispy Macaroni and Cheese, 115
Orange marmalade
   Bear Claws, 263
   Marmalade Biscuits, 298
   Meatballs with Orange Peanut Sauce,
      211
Oranges
   Fruit Salad, 101
   Orange Biscuits, 298
   Taste of the Islands Meatballs, 216
Oysters
   Oyster and Shrimp Soup, 28

Parmesan
   Bubble Ring, 244
   Caesar Veggie Bake, 17
   Cheesy Pull-Apart Bread, 244
   Cheesy Stuffed Mushroom, 68
   Chicken and Broccoli Cups,* 33
   Chicken Fettuccine, 37
   Creamy Sage Macaroni, 143
   Florentine Lasagna Rolls, 67
   Ham and Asparagus Rolls,* 77
   Herbed Biscuit Strips, 246
   Parmesan Chicken and Rice Bake, 38
   Parmesan Meatball Biscuits, 162
   Three Cheese Sauce, 54
   Upside-Down Pizza Casserole, 57
Pasta. See also Mac 'n' cheese; Noodles
   Amazing Meatball Tortellini, 205
   Baked Ziti and Meatballs, 201
   Cheesy Broccoli Meatballs, 206

Chicken Fettuccine, 37
Chipotle Meatball Pasta, 195
Creamy Chicken Spaghetti, 39
Creamy Pasta Primavera, 66
Easy Meatball Lasagna, 199
Eggplant Parmesan, 202
Florentine Lasagna Rolls, 67
Florentine Meatballs and Noodles, 196
Garden Veggie Soup with Bow Tie Pasta,
    172
Italian-Tossed Tortellini, 203
Meatball Fettuccine Alfredo, 194
Meatballs in Blue Cheese Sauce, 197
Meatball Stroganoff, 204
Meatball Zucchini Orzo Soup, 170
Pesto Spaghetti and Meatballs, 200
Ravioli Meatball Stir-Fry, 203
Ricotta-Stuffed Shells and Meatballs, 200
Slow-Cooked Tomato Soup Meatballs,
    198
Tortellini Meatball Stew, 165
Peaches
Peach Pinwheels, 296
Peanut butter
Malaysian Meatballs, 161
Meatballs with Orange Peanut Sauce,
    211
Peanuts
Crunchy Peanut Ring, 295
Peas
Biscuits and Tuna, 281
Cajun Jambalaya, 41
Cheddar Mac Salad, 100
Cheesy Pea Pasta, 132
Chicken Curry in a Hurry, 36
Chicken Potpie, 116
Christmas Stew, 149
Classic Tuna Noodle Casserole, 58
Macaroni Salad with Peas and Ham, 96
Quick Minestrone, 95
Rachel's Macaroni, 140
Shrimp Newburg, 290
Sizzling Rice Soup, 21
Turkey Pot Pie, 284
Pecans
Apple Coffee Cake, 264
Cinnamon Nut Biscuits, 247
Praline Meltaway Biscuits, 249
Sweet Potato Bread Pudding, 301

Pepperoni
Baked Pepperoni Dip, 4
Cavatini, 125
Pan Pizza, 287
Pepperoni Bites, 241
Pizza Mac, 147
Upside-Down Pizza Casserole, 57
Peppers. See also Chile peppers
Balsamic Chicken, 139
Breakfast Pizzas, 72
Caesar Meatball Kabobs,* 219
Cajun Jambalaya, 41
Cheddar Mac Salad, 100
Chicken Curry Party Salad, 99
Chicken Durango, 30
Chop Suey, 134
Confetti Salad, 99
Creamy Pasta Primavera, 66
Denver Omelet, 150
Fiesta Mac, 143
Ham and Egg Pizzas,* 262
Italian-Tossed Tortellini, 203
Meatball Fajita Quesadillas,* 223
Meatballs with Apricot Hoisin Sauce,*
    214
Miracle Soup, 89
Philly Meatball Sub Sandwiches, 173
Pineapple Meatballs and Rice, 211
Polynesian Pork and Rice,* 53
Quick Mac Salad, 106
Roasted Pepper and Meatballs on Rye,
    177
Roasted Vegetable Strata, 259
Southwest Chicken Polenta Stacks, 31
Squash Cornbread Casserole, 11
Sweet and Sour Meatball Kabobs, 218
Taste of the Islands Meatballs, 216
Tex-Mex Macaroni and Cheese, 133
World's Best Baked Beans, 16
Yummy Meatballs, 61
Pesto
Bruschetta, 239
Creamy Pesto, 145
Creamy Pesto Sauce, 55
Focaccia Bread, 243
Pesto Meatball Baguette Sandwiches,
    176
Pesto Spaghetti and Meatballs, 200
Savory Pesto Cheesecake (var.), 7

Pies (dessert)
  Mini Cherry Pies, 293
  Sweet Potato Pies, 83
Pies (savory)
  Bacon Quiche Tarts, 257
  Beef Pot Pie, 285
  Cheddar Biscuit Quiche, 255
  Chicken Potpie, 116
  Easy Chicken Potpie, 61
  Hamburger Vegetable Pie, 62
  Meatball Pot Pie, 222
  Mix 'n' Match Quiche, 75
  Sausage Quiche, 255
  Turkey Pot Pie, 284
Pineapple
  Asian Meatball Appetizers, 191
  Fruit Salad, 101
  Pineapple Biscuits, 251
  Pineapple Meatballs and Rice, 211
  Polynesian Pork and Rice,* 53
  Sweet and Sour Meatball Kabobs, 218
  Taste of the Islands Meatballs, 216
  Teriyaki Meatballs, 188
  Thai Pizza,* 159
Pizza & calzones
  Breakfast Pizzas, 72
  Calzones, 271
  Easy Meatball Pizza, 220
  Ham and Egg Pizzas,* 262
  Mini Pizza Bites, 274
  Pan Pizza, 287
  Thai Pizza,* 159
Polenta
  Southwest Chicken Polenta Stacks, 31
Poppy seeds
  Poppy-Onion Loaf, 245
Pork. See also Bacon; Ham; Sausages
  Barbecue Pork Sandwiches, 267
  Canadian Bacon and Egg English Muffins, 70
  Polynesian Pork and Rice,* 53
  Pork Chops and Potatoes, 50
  Pork Stew, 27
  Saucy Pork Chops, 50
  Shredded Barbecue Pork Sandwiches, 51
  Shrimp and Pork Pot Stickers, 236
Potatoes
  Bacon Red Potato Chowder, 26

Baked Hash Brown and Ham Casserole, 73
Baked Potato Biscuits, 81
Breakfast Pockets, 260
Cheesy Egg and Sausage Casserole, 74
Dinner Stew in a Pumpkin, 22
Easy Clam Chowder, 26
Grilled Potatoes, Mushrooms, and Onion, 13
Hamburger Vegetable Pie, 62
Hash Brown Meatball Casserole, 227
Meatball Chowder, 167
Pork Chops and Potatoes, 50
Potato Macaroni Gratin, 122
Potato Turnovers, 240
Potluck Potatoes, 65
Slow-Cooked Potatoes and Sausage, 51
Souper Scalloped Potatoes, 15
Sweet Potato Bread Pudding, 301
Sweet Potato Pies, 83
Taco Stew, 28
Tater Tot Gumbo Casserole, 47
Tater Tot Kids' Casserole, 226
Winter Stew, 169
Pot pies
  Beef Pot Pie, 285
  Chicken Potpie, 116
  Easy Chicken Potpie, 61
  Meatball Pot Pie, 222
  Turkey Pot Pie, 284
Poultry. See Chicken; Turkey
Puddings. See also Bread pudding
  Cheesy Baked Corn Pudding, 18
Puff pastry
  Chicken and Broccoli Cups,* 33
  Puff Pastry Meatball and Mushroom Pockets, 160
Pumpkin
  Dinner Stew in a Pumpkin, 22

Quesadillas
  Do-It-Yourself Quesadillas, 59
  Meatball Fajita Quesadillas,* 223
Quiche
  Bacon Quiche Tarts, 257
  Cheddar Biscuit Quiche, 255
  Mix 'n' Match Quiche, 75
  Sausage Quiche, 255

Raspberries
White Chocolate Berry Bread Pudding, 299
Rice
Cajun Jambalaya, 41
Cajun Shrimp and Meatball Goulash, 212
Cheesy Rice and Hamburger Soup, 171
Cheesy Sausage Soup, 27
Creamy Baked Risotto Primavera, 19
Creamy French Onion Meatballs, 213
Creamy Meatball and Brown Rice Casserole, 210
Creamy Rice and Meatballs, 215
Easy Rice and Meatballs, 207
Enchilada Meatballs, 215
French Onion Mushroom Rice, 10
Ham and Asparagus Rolls,* 77
Meatballs in Curry Sauce, 208
Meatballs with Apricot Hoisin Sauce,* 214
Meatballs with Orange Peanut Sauce, 211
Parmesan Chicken and Rice Bake, 38
Pineapple Meatballs and Rice, 211
Seafood Gumbo Casserole, 41
Sesame Stir-Fry, 208
Sizzling Rice Soup, 21
Southwestern Cilantro Rice Soup, 167
Swiss Mushroom Meatball Casserole, 209
Taste of the Islands Meatballs, 216
Unstuffed Cabbage, 45
Weeknight Bistro Chicken, 29
Ricotta cheese
Cavatini, 125
Easy Meatball Lasagna, 199
Florentine Lasagna Rolls, 67
Macaroni Cake, 148
Ricotta-Stuffed Shells and Meatballs, 200

Salads (with mac 'n' cheese or meatballs)
Catalina Salad, 107
Cheddar Mac Salad, 100
Chicken Curry Party Salad, 99
Chicken Macaroni Salad, 109
Classic Macaroni Salad, 100
Confetti Salad, 99
Cucumber Dill Pasta Salad, 111
Egg Pasta Salad, 98
Fruit Salad, 101
Herbed Macaroni and Cucumber, 103

Macaroni, Tomato, Corn, and Basil Salad, 104
Macaroni Chef Salad, 108
Macaroni Salad with Peas and Ham, 96
Mexican Salad, 97
Michelle's Special Salad, 110
Quick Mac Salad, 106
Seafood Pasta with Lemon Herb Dressing, 105
Shrimp and Macaroni Salad,* 106
Simple Ranch Salad, 97
Southwest Taco Salad, 162
Spinach and Tomato Salad, 98
Taco Salad, 151
Tomato Basil Cannellini Salad, 102
Salmon
Savory Smoked Salmon Cheesecake (var.), 7
Salsa (jarred)
Bean and Bacon Fondue, 8
Beefy Bean Dip, 5
Enchilada Meatballs, 215
Fajita Macaroni and Cheese, 118
Magnificent Meatballs, 187
Mexican Fiesta Bake, 282
Mexican Mac and Cheese, 137
Mexican Salad, 97
Salsa Balls, 152
Salsa Macaroni and Cheese, 138
Salsa Nacho Cheese, 3
Salsa Verde Meatballs, 192
White Bean Salsa Chili, 170
Sandwiches & wraps. *See also* Burgers
Bacon Tomato Biscuit Melts, 275
Barbecue Pork Sandwiches, 267
Breakfast Biscuit Sandwiches, 254
Breakfast Sandwiches, 261
Cheddar Biscuits with Ham Salad, 268
Coney Meatball Subs, 175
Easy Sloppy Joes, 182
Fall Cranberry Wrap, 181
Hot Turkey Sandwiches, 274
Italian Focaccia Meatball Sandwiches, 179
Mediterranean Meatball Sandwiches, 178
Open-Faced Meatball Sub, 180
Pesto Meatball Baguette Sandwiches, 176

Sandwiches & wraps *(cont.)*
  Philly Meatball Sub Sandwiches, 173
  Piping Hot Buffalo Subs, 177
  Roasted Pepper and Meatballs on Rye,
    177
  Sammiches, 273
  Saucy Meatball Grinders, 174
  Shredded Barbecue Pork Sandwiches,
    51
  Sloppy Joes, 60
  Swedish Meatball Hero, 180
  Tex-Mex Sandwiches, 272
  Tomato and Kielbasa Sandwiches,
    270
  Yummy Stuffed Pitas, 181
Sauces
  Creamy Pesto Sauce, 55
  Mushroom Roasted Garlic Sauce, 55
  Seafood Newburg Sauce, 55
  Tangy Tomato Mustard Sauce, 54
  Three Cheese Sauce, 54
Sauerkraut
  Corned Beef and Kraut, 124
  Cranberry Sauerkraut Meatballs, 185
Sausages. *See also* Pepperoni
  Breakfast Pizzas, 72
  Breakfast Pockets, 260
  Breakfast Sandwiches, 261
  Cajun Jambalaya, 41
  Calzones, 271
  Cheesy Egg and Sausage Casserole,
    74
  Cheesy Sausage Soup, 27
  Chop Suey, 134
  Hungarian Bean Soup, 93
  Main Dish Bread Pudding, 49
  Sausage Biscuit Pinwheels, 262
  Sausage Quiche, 255
  Slow-Cooked Potatoes and Sausage,
    51
  Spinach and Sausage Breakfast
    Casserole, 71
  Tomato and Kielbasa Sandwiches, 270
  Upside-Down Pizza Casserole, 57
  Wrapped Smokies with Mustard Sauce,
    232
Seafood. *See* Fish; Shellfish
Sesame seeds
  Sesame Hot Dogs,* 275

Shellfish
  Cajun Jambalaya, 41
  Cajun Shrimp and Meatball Goulash, 212
  Catalina Salad, 107
  Crab Shortcakes, 278
  Easy Clam Chowder, 26
  Louisiana Shrimp Casserole, 288
  Maryland Crab Cakes, 42
  New England Clam Dip, 8
  Oyster and Shrimp Soup, 28
  Seafood Gumbo Casserole, 41
  Seafood Newburg Sauce, 55
  Seafood Pasta with Lemon Herb
    Dressing, 105
  Shrimp and Macaroni Salad,* 106
  Shrimp and Pork Pot Stickers, 236
  Shrimp Newburg, 290
  Sizzling Rice Soup, 21
Shrimp
  Cajun Jambalaya, 41
  Cajun Shrimp and Meatball Goulash,
    212
  Catalina Salad, 107
  Crab Shortcakes, 278
  Louisiana Shrimp Casserole, 288
  Oyster and Shrimp Soup, 28
  Seafood Gumbo Casserole, 41
  Seafood Newburg Sauce, 55
  Seafood Pasta with Lemon Herb
    Dressing, 105
  Shrimp and Macaroni Salad,* 106
  Shrimp and Pork Pot Stickers, 236
  Shrimp Newburg, 290
  Sizzling Rice Soup, 21
Side dishes (with canned soups)
  Caesar Veggie Bake, 17
  Cheesy Baked Corn Pudding, 18
  Cheesy Stuffed Mushroom, 68
  Classic Green Bean Bake, 20
  Creamy Baked Risotto Primavera, 19
  Decadent Spinach Casserole, 10
  Easy Cauliflower Casserole, 12
  French Onion Mushroom Rice, 10
  Grilled Potatoes, Mushrooms, and Onion,
    13
  Harvest Veggie Stuffing Casserole, 64
  Midwest Veggie Casserole, 12
  Never-Fail Veggie Soufflé, 65
  Potluck Potatoes, 65

Souper Scalloped Potatoes, 15
Squash Cornbread Casserole, 11
Vegetable Custard Cups, 14
World's Best Baked Beans, 16
Side dishes (with mac 'n' cheese)
Bacon and Macaroni, 140
Bacon and Tomato Mac, 142
Baked Macaroni and Cheese, 112
Baked Tomato Macaroni, 118
Cavatini, 125
Cheesy Pea Pasta, 132
Cheesy Triangles,* 149
Christmas Stew, 149
Creamy Basil and Almonds, 145
Creamy Mushroom Casserole, 126
Creamy Pesto, 145
Creamy Sage Macaroni, 143
Crispy Macaroni and Cheese, 115
Curried Macaroni, 121
Four Cheese Casserole, 113
Fried Macaroni and Cheese, 146
Frito Pie, 144
Mac and Cheese Custard, 120
Mac and Cheese with Mustard and
    Worcestershire, 127
Mac and Green Chiles, 142
Macaroni and Cheese with Mushrooms
    and Bacon, 123
Macaroni Pie, 115
Mock Mashed Potatoes, 148
Mom's Mac and Cheese, 119
Paladin Blue Macaroni, 145
Pan-Fried Mac and Cheese, 152
Potato Macaroni Gratin, 122
Salsa Balls, 152
Salsa Macaroni and Cheese, 138
Savory Bacon Mac, 129
Spiced-Up Macaroni, 141
Wisconsin Mac, 136
Sloppy joes
Easy Sloppy Joes, 182
Slow cooker dishes
Coney Meatball Subs, 175
Creamy French Onion Meatballs, 213
Crowd-Pleasing Meatballs, 183
Enchilada Meatballs, 215
Garden Veggie Soup with Bow Tie Pasta,
    172
Ginger Ale Meatballs, 191

Holiday Meatballs, 193
Magnificent Meatballs, 187
Meatball Stroganoff, 204
Pork Chili Dip, 5
Pork Stew, 27
Salsa Nacho Cheese, 3
Salsa Verde Meatballs, 192
Shredded Barbecue Pork Sandwiches,
    51
Slow-Cooked Potatoes and Sausage,
    51
Slow-Cooked Tomato Soup Meatballs,
    198
Sour Cream Meatballs, 3
Southwestern Cilantro Rice Soup, 167
Sports Day Meatballs, 186
Taste of the Islands Meatballs, 216
Teriyaki Meatballs, 188
Weeknight Bistro Chicken, 29
Winter Chili, 56
Winter Stew, 169
Soufflés
Never-Fail Veggie Soufflé, 65
Soups, canned. See Canned soups
Soups (with canned soups)
Autumn Mushroom Soup, 25
Bacon Red Potato Chowder, 26
Cheesy Sausage Soup, 27
Chicken Enchilada Soup, 24
Creamy Corn Chowder, 25
Easy Clam Chowder, 26
Oyster and Shrimp Soup, 28
Sizzling Rice Soup, 21
Wedding Soup, 23
Soups (with mac 'n' cheese)
Bean Soup, 88
Chicken Soup, 93
Easy Italian Vegetable Soup, 87
Garlicky Soup, 92
Hungarian Bean Soup, 93
Lazarus Soup, 92
Miracle Soup, 89
Oaxaca Soup, 90
Onion Soup, 94
Pomodoro e Zucchina Minestra, 95
Quick Minestrone, 95
Tavern Soup, 91
Tomato Soup, 87
Vegetable Picante Soup, 94

Soups (with meatballs)
    Cheesy Rice and Hamburger Soup, 171
    Chinese Beef Noodle Soup, 168
    Family Favorite Egg Noodle Soup, 166
    Garden Veggie Soup with Bow Tie Pasta, 172
    Meatball Chowder, 167
    Meatball Minestrone, 164
    Meatball Zucchini Orzo Soup, 170
    Southwestern Cilantro Rice Soup, 167
    Taco Soup, 166
Sour cream
    Sour Cream Meatballs, 3
    Sour Cream–Sauced Meatballs, 193
Southwestern-style dishes
    Baked Brunch Enchiladas, 76
    Bean and Bacon Fondue, 8
    Beef and Bean Burritos, 52
    Beefy Bean Dip, 5
    Breakfast Burritos, 220
    Cheesy Mexicali Cornbread, 79
    Chicken Enchilada Soup, 24
    Chile Relleno Casserole, 63
    Crowd-Pleasing Meatball Chili, 169
    Do-It-Yourself Quesadillas, 59
    Easy Meatball Nachos, 163
    Enchilada Casserole, 225
    Enchilada Meatballs, 215
    Fajita Macaroni and Cheese, 118
    Fiesta Mac, 143
    Instant Soft Taco, 222
    Kid-Friendly Taco Casserole, 228
    Meatball Fajita Quesadillas,* 223
    Mexican Fiesta Bake, 282
    Mexican Mac and Cheese, 137
    Mexican Salad, 97
    Oaxaca Soup, 90
    Pork Chili Dip, 5
    Salsa Macaroni and Cheese, 138
    Salsa Nacho Cheese, 3
    Salsa Verde, 139
    Salsa Verde Meatballs, 192
    Souper Tamale Pie, 43
    Southwest Chicken Polenta Stacks, 31
    Southwest Crescent Pockets, 221
    Southwestern Bean Bake, 284
    Southwestern Cilantro Rice Soup, 167
    Southwest Taco Salad, 162

Spicy Meatball Burritos, 226
Taco Casserole, 283
Taco Salad, 151
Taco Soup, 166
Taco Stew, 28
Tex-Mex Macaroni and Cheese, 133
Tex-Mex Sandwiches, 272
Turkey Empanadas, 231
White Bean Salsa Chili, 170
Winter Chili, 56
Spinach
    Cheesy Stuffed Mushroom, 68
    Creamy Pasta Primavera, 66
    Decadent Spinach Casserole, 10
    Florentine Lasagna Rolls, 67
    Florentine Meatballs and Noodles, 196
    Garlicky Soup, 92
    Meatball Minestrone, 164
    Spinach and Sausage Breakfast Casserole, 71
    Spinach and Tomato Salad, 98
    Spinach Artichoke Dip in Bread Bowls, 233
    Wedding Soup, 23
Squash & zucchini
    Bean Soup, 88
    Caesar Meatball Kabobs,* 219
    Chocolate Zucchini Cake, 84
    Dinner Stew in a Pumpkin, 22
    Harvest Veggie Stuffing Casserole, 64
    Meatball Zucchini Orzo Soup, 170
    Pomodoro e Zucchina Minestra, 95
    Roasted Vegetable Strata, 259
    Squash Cornbread Casserole, 11
    Zucchini and Cheese Roll-Ups, 238
Stews & chili
    Crowd-Pleasing Meatball Chili, 169
    Dinner Stew in a Pumpkin, 22
    Effortless Beef and Mushrooms, 46
    Pork Stew, 27
    Taco Stew, 28
    Tortellini Meatball Stew, 165
    White Bean Salsa Chili, 170
    Winter Chili, 56
    Winter Stew, 169
Strawberries
    Chantilly Cream Strawberry Shortcake, 297

Sweet potatoes
    Sweet Potato Bread Pudding, 301
    Sweet Potato Pies, 83
Swiss cheese
    Bacon and Macaroni, 140
    Chicken Cordon Bleu Bake, 40
    Ham and Asparagus Rolls,* 77
    Ham Biscuiwiches, 276
    Never-Fail Veggie Soufflé, 65
    Potato Macaroni Gratin, 122
    Swiss Mushroom Meatball Casserole, 209
    Weeknight Bistro Chicken, 29
    World's Easiest Cheese Fondue, 6

Tacos
    Instant Soft Taco, 222
Tarts & quiche
    Bacon Quiche Tarts, 257
    Cheddar Biscuit Quiche, 255
    Mix 'n' Match Quiche, 75
    Sausage Quiche, 255
Tomatoes
    Amazing Meatball Tortellini, 205
    Bacon and Tomato Mac, 142
    Bacon Tomato Biscuit Melts, 275
    Baked Tomato Macaroni, 118
    Bruschetta, 239
    Buttermilk Biscuits with Tomato Gravy, 269
    Cajun Shrimp and Meatball Goulash, 212
    Chili Mac, 129
    Chipotle Meatball Pasta, 195
    Confetti Salad, 99
    Corn Chip Casserole, 46
    Creamy Chicken Spaghetti, 39
    Crowd-Pleasing Meatball Chili, 169
    Do-It-Yourself Quesadillas, 59
    Easy Italian Vegetable Soup, 87
    Garlicky Soup, 92
    Greek Chicken Pasta,* 131
    Italian Chicken, 144
    Macaroni, Tomato, Corn, and Basil Salad, 104
    Meatball Sliders, 157
    Mom's Mac and Cheese, 119
    Oaxaca Soup, 90
    Pomodoro e Zucchina Minestra, 95

Quick Minestrone, 95
Savory Sun-Dried Tomato Cheesecake, 7
Southwestern Cilantro Rice Soup, 167
Spicy Hamburger Mac, 133
Spinach and Tomato Salad, 98
Stadium Mac and Cheese, 138
Tangy Tomato Mustard Sauce, 54
Tex-Mex Macaroni and Cheese, 133
Tomato and Kielbasa Sandwiches, 270
Tomato Basil Cannellini Salad, 102
Tomato Soup, 87
Vegetable Picante Soup, 94
Weeknight Bistro Chicken, 29
Tortillas
    Baked Brunch Enchiladas, 76
    Beef and Bean Burritos, 52
    Breakfast Burritos, 220
    Chicken Enchilada Soup, 24
    Chile Relleno Casserole, 63
    Chile Verde Chicken Enchiladas, 32
    Do-It-Yourself Quesadillas, 59
    Easy Meatball Nachos, 163
    Enchilada Casserole, 225
    Fall Cranberry Wrap, 181
    Instant Soft Taco, 222
    Kid-Friendly Taco Casserole, 228
    Meatball Fajita Quesadillas,* 223
    Spicy Meatball Burritos, 226
Tuna
    Biscuits and Tuna, 281
    Broccoli and Tuna on Biscuits, 267
    Catalina Salad, 107
    Classic Tuna Noodle Casserole, 58
Turkey
    Broccoli and Turkey Macaroni, 141
    Do-It-Yourself Quesadillas, 59
    Hot Turkey Salad, 34
    Hot Turkey Sandwiches, 274
    Sammiches, 273
    Turkey and Biscuits, 286
    Turkey Empanadas, 231
    Turkey Pot Pie, 284
    Turkey Salad with Biscuits, 289
    Wedding Soup, 23

Vegetables. *See also specific vegetables*
    Beef Pot Pie, 285
    Caesar Veggie Bake, 17

Vegetables (cont.)
  Chicken Macaroni Salad, 109
  Cornbread Chicken, 40
  Easy Chicken Potpie, 61
  Garden Veggie Soup with Bow Tie Pasta, 172
  Meatball Pot Pie, 222
  Mix 'n' Match Quiche, 75
  Never-Fail Veggie Soufflé, 65
  Ravioli Meatball Stir-Fry, 203
  Sesame Stir-Fry, 208
  Stuffing-Covered Meatball Casserole, 224
  Tortellini Meatball Stew, 165
  Vegetable Casserole, 289
  Vegetable Custard Cups, 14
  Vegetable Picante Soup, 94
Velveeta cheese
  Beefy Bean Dip, 5
  Creamy Mushroom Casserole, 126
  Pork Chili Dip, 5
  Salsa Nacho Cheese, 3

Walnuts
  Chocolate Zucchini Cake, 84
  Lemon Pull-Apart Coffee Cake, 250
  Maple Breakfast Rolls, 251
Water chestnuts
  Midwest Veggie Casserole, 12
  Shrimp and Pork Pot Stickers, 236
  Sizzling Rice Soup, 21

Yogurt
  Feta Meatballs with Cucumber Yogurt Sauce, 189
  Yummy Stuffed Pitas, 181

Zucchini
  Bean Soup, 88
  Chocolate Zucchini Cake, 84
  Harvest Veggie Stuffing Casserole, 64
  Meatball Zucchini Orzo Soup, 170
  Pomodoro e Zucchina Minestra, 95
  Roasted Vegetable Strata, 259
  Zucchini and Cheese Roll-Ups, 238